THE GREAT ESCAPE

THE GREAT ESCAPE

Health, Wealth, and the Origins of Inequality

ANGUS DEATON

Princeton University Press

Princeton and Oxford

Published by Princeton University Press,
41 William Street, Princeton, New Jersey 08540
In the United Kingdom: Princeton University Press, 6
Oxford Street, Woodstock, Oxfordshire OX20 1TW

press.princeton.edu

Jacket and endpaper art: Detail of *The Last Judgement,*
c. 1451 (oil on panel), Rogier van der Weyden
(1399–1464) / Musée de l'Hôtel-Dieu, Beaune, France.
© Paul Maeyaert / The Bridgeman Art Library.

Sixth printing, and first paperback printing, 2015
Paperback ISBN 978-0-691-16562-2
ISBN 978-0-691-15354-4
Library of Congress Control Number: 2013941754

British Library Cataloging-in-Publication Data
is available

This book has been composed in Hoefler Text
with Ultramagnetic display by Princeton Editorial
Associates Inc., Scottsdale, Arizona.

Printed on acid-free paper. ∞

Printed in the United States of America

20   19   18   17   16   15   14   13   12

In memory of Leslie Harold Deaton

Contents

Preface

THE GREAT ESCAPE is a movie about men escaping from a prisoner-of-war camp in World War II. The Great Escape of this book is the story of mankind's escaping from deprivation and early death, of how people have managed to make their lives better, and led the way for others to follow.

One of those lives was my father's. Leslie Harold Deaton was born in 1918 in a tough coal-mining village called Thurcroft in the South Yorkshire coalfield. His grandparents Alice and Thomas had given up agricultural labor in the hope of doing better in the new mine. Their eldest son, my grandfather Harold, fought in World War I, returned to the "pit," and eventually became a supervisor. For my father, it was difficult to become educated in Thurcroft between the wars because only a few children were allowed to go to high school. Leslie took odd jobs at the pit; like the other boys, his ambition was that, one day, he would get the chance to work at the face. He never made it; he was drafted into the army in 1939 and sent to France as part of the ill-fated British Expeditionary Force. After that debacle, he was sent to Scotland to be trained to be a commando; there he met my mother and was "fortunate" enough to be invalided out of the army with tuberculosis and sent to a sanitarium. Fortunate because the commando raid on Norway was a failure, and he would almost certainly have died. He was demobilized in 1942 and married my mother, Lily Wood, the daughter of a carpenter in the town of Galashiels in the south of Scotland.

Although deprived of a high school education in Yorkshire, Leslie had gone to night school to learn surveying skills that were useful in mining, and in 1942, with labor in short supply, those skills made him an attractive hire as an office boy in a firm of civil engineers in Edinburgh. He determined to become a civil engineer himself, and, starting from a base of almost nothing, he put in a decade of hard work and finally qualified. The courses were a great struggle, especially mathematics and physics; the night school he attended, now the Heriot-Watt University in Edinburgh, recently sent me his examination results, and struggle he certainly did. He took a job as a water supply engineer in the Borders of Scotland and bought the cottage where my mother's grandmother had lived, and where in earlier days Sir Walter Scott was said to have been an occasional visitor. For me, moving from Edinburgh—with its grime, soot, and miserable weather —to a country village—with its woods, hills, and trout streams and, in the summer of 1955, endless sunshine—was a great escape of its own.

In classic manner, my father then set about making sure that I could do better than he had done. Somehow, he managed to persuade my local schoolteachers to coach me outside class for the scholarship examination at a prestigious Edinburgh public (i.e., private) school, where I was one of the two kids in my year that got a free ride; the annual fees were more than my father's salary. I eventually went to Cambridge as a mathematics student and in time became an economics professor, first in Britain and then at Princeton. My sister went to university in Scotland and became a schoolteacher. Of my dozen cousins, we were the only ones to go to university and, of course, none of the previous generation had the chance to do so. Leslie's two grand-children live in the United States. My daughter is a partner in a suc-cessful firm of financial planners in Chicago and my son is a partner in a successful hedge fund in New York. Both received a rich and var-ied education at Princeton University—vastly superior in its depth, range of opportunities, and quality of teaching to my own dry and narrow experience as an undergraduate in Cambridge. Both of them have a standard of living beyond anything that Leslie could have imagined—though he lived long enough to see a good deal of it, and to be pleased by it. His great-grandchildren live in a world of wealth and opportunity that would have been a far-fetched fantasy in the Yorkshire coalfield.

My father's escape from Thurcroft is an example of what this book is about. He was not born into abject poverty, though it would seem so by today's standards, but he ended his life in comparative affluence. I do not have numbers for the Yorkshire mining villages, but for every thousand children born in England in 1918, more than a hundred did not live to see their fifth birthday, and the risks would likely have been higher in Thurcroft. Today, children in sub-Saharan Africa are more likely to survive to age 5 than were English children born in 1918. Leslie and his parents survived the great influenza pandemic of 1918–19, though his father died young, killed by a runaway wagon in the pit. My mother's father died young too, from an infection follow-ing an appendectomy. Yet Leslie, in spite of his youthful encounter with tuberculosis—the Captain of Death—lived into his 90th year. His great-grandchildren have a good chance of making it to 100.

Living standards are vastly higher today than a century ago, and more people escape death in childhood and live long enough to expe-rience that prosperity. Almost a century after my father was born, only five out of a thousand British children don't make it through the first five years, and even if the figure is a little higher in what is left of the Yorkshire coalfield—the Thurcroft pit closed in 1991—it is only a tiny fraction of what it was in 1918. The chance to be educated, so difficult for my father, is taken for granted. Even in my cohort, fewer than one in ten British kids went to college, while today the majority has some form of tertiary education.

My father's escape, and the future he built for his children and grandchildren, is not an unusual story. Yet it is far from universal. Very few of Leslie's cohort in Thurcroft ever obtained a professional qualification. My mother's sisters did not do so, nor did their spouses. Her brother and his family migrated to Australia in the 1960s when their ability to cobble together a bare living from multiple jobs collapsed with the closure of the railway line through the Scottish Borders. My children are financially successful and secure, but they (and we) are extraordinarily fortunate; the children of many well-educated and financially successful people are struggling to do as well as their parents did. For many of our friends, the future of their children and the education of their grandchildren is a constant source of worry.

This is the other side of the story. Even though my father and his family were living longer and prospering in a population that was living longer and prospering on average, not everyone was as motivated or dedicated as my father, nor was everyone as lucky. No one worked harder than my father, but his luck was important too—the luck not to be among those who died as children, the luck to be rescued from the pit by the war, the luck not to be on the wrong commando raid, the luck not to die from tuberculosis, and the luck to get a job in an easy labor market. Escapes leave people behind, and luck favors some and not others; it makes opportunities, but not everyone is equally equipped or determined to seize them. So the tale of progress is also the tale of inequality. This is especially true today, when the tide of prosperity in the United States is the opposite of equally spread. A few are doing incredibly well. Many are struggling. In the world as a whole, we see the same patterns of progress—of escapes for some, and of others left behind in awful poverty, deprivation, sickness, and death.

This book is about the endless dance between progress and inequality, about how progress creates inequality, and how inequality can sometimes be helpful—showing others the way, or providing incentives for catching up—and sometimes unhelpful—when those who have escaped protect their positions by destroying the escape routes behind them. This is a story that has been told many times, but I want to tell it in a new way.

It is easy to think of the escape from poverty as being about money—about having more and not having to live with the gnawing anxiety of not knowing whether there will be enough tomorrow, dreading that some emergency will come for which there will not be enough funds and which will sink you and your family. Money is indeed a central part of the story. But just as important, or even more so, are better health and the improved likelihood of living long enough to have the chance to prosper. Parents living with the constant fear and frequent reality that their children will die, or mothers giving birth to ten children so that five may survive to adulthood, reflect grisly deprivations that compound the worries about money that haunt many of the same people. Throughout history, and around the world today, the sickness and death of children, endless recurring morbidity for adults, and grinding poverty are partners that often visit the same families, and they do so over and over again.

Many books tell the story of wealth, and many others are about inequality. There are also many books that tell the story of health, and of how health and wealth go hand in hand, with inequalities in health mirroring inequalities in wealth. Here I tell both stories at once, taking the chance that professional demographers and historians will allow an economist to trespass into their lands. But the story of human wellbeing, of what makes life worth living, is not well served by looking at only a part of what is important. The Great Escape does not respect the boundaries of academic disciplines.

I have accumulated many intellectual debts throughout my life as an economist. Richard Stone was perhaps the most profound influence; from him I learned about measurement—how little we can say without it and how important it is to get it right. From Amartya Sen I learned how to think about what makes life worth living and about how we must study wellbeing as a whole, not just parts of it. The measurement of wellbeing is the heart of this book.

My friends, colleagues, and students have been extraordinarily generous in reading drafts of all or parts of this book. It is immeasurably better for their thoughtful and insightful reactions. I am especially grateful to those who disagree with me, yet who took the time not only to criticize and persuade but also to praise and agree when they could. I am grateful to Tony Atkinson, Adam Deaton, Jean Drèze, Bill Easterly, Jeff Hammer, John Hammock, David Johnston, Scott Kostyshak, Ilyana Kuziemko, David Lam, Branko Milanovic, Franco Peracchi, Thomas Pogge, Leandro Prados de las Escosura, Sam Preston, Max Roser, Sam Schulhofer-Wohl, Alessandro Tarozzi, Nicolas van de Walle, and Leif Wenar. My editor at Princeton University Press, Seth Ditchik, helped me to get started and provided help and good advice all along the way.

Princeton University has provided me with an unequaled academic environment for more than three decades. The National Institute of Aging and the National Bureau of Economic Research have helped fund my work on health and wellbeing, and the results from that research have influenced this book. I have frequently worked with the World Bank; the Bank is constantly faced with urgent, practical problems and has helped teach me which issues matter and which do not. In recent years, I have been a consultant to the Gallup Organization; they have pioneered the global investigation of wellbeing, and some of the information that they have collected appears in the early part of the book. I am grateful to all of them.

Last, and most, Anne Case read every word soon after it was written, and sometimes many times afterwards. She is responsible for innumerable improvements throughout, and without her endless encouragement and support this book would not exist.

What This Book Is About

LIFE IS BETTER NOW than at almost any time in history. More people are richer and fewer people live in dire poverty. Lives are longer and parents no longer routinely watch a quarter of their children die. Yet millions still experience the horrors of destitution and of premature death. The world is hugely unequal.

Inequality is often a *consequence* of progress. Not everyone gets rich at the same time, and not everyone gets immediate access to the latest life-saving measures, whether access to clean water, to vaccines, or to new drugs for preventing heart disease. Inequalities in turn affect progress. This can be good; Indian children see what education can do and go to school too. It can be bad if the winners try to stop others from following them, pulling up the ladders behind them. The newly rich may use their wealth to influence politicians to restrict public education or health care that they themselves do not need.

This book tells stories of how things got better, how and why progress happened, and the subsequent interplay of progress and inequality.

The Great Escape: The Movie

The Great Escape, a famous movie about prisoners of war in World War II, is based on the exploits of Roger Bushell (in the film, Roger Bartlett, played by Richard Attenborough), a South African in the Royal Air Force who was shot down behind German lines, and who repeatedly escaped and was repeatedly recaptured.[1] In his third attempt, as depicted in the film—the Great Escape—250 prisoners escaped with him through tunnels dug from Stalag Luft III. The movie tells the story of how the escape was planned; the ingenuity that went into constructing three tunnels, Tom, Dick, and Harry; and the improvisation and technical skills that went into making civilian clothes and forging papers, all under the eyes of the watchful guards. All but three of the POWs were eventually recaptured, and Bushell himself was executed on direct orders from Hitler. Yet the emphasis of the movie is not on the limited success of this particular escape, but on man's unquenchable desire for freedom, even under impossibly difficult circumstances.

In this book, when I speak of freedom, it is the freedom to live a good life and to do the things that make life worth living. The absence of freedom is poverty, deprivation, and poor health—long the lot of much of humanity, and still the fate of an outrageously high proportion of the world today. I will tell stories of repeated escapes from this kind of prison, how and why they came about, and what happened afterwards. It is a story of material and physiological progress, of people becoming richer and healthier, of escapes from poverty.

A phrase in my subtitle, "the origins of inequality," comes from thinking about the POWs who did not escape. All of the POWs could have stayed where they were, but instead a few escaped, some died, some were returned to the camp, and some never left. This is in the nature of most "great escapes": not everyone can make it, a fact that in no way makes the escape less desirable or less admirable. Yet when we think about the consequences of the escape, we need to think not just about those who were the heroes of the movie, but also about those who were left behind in Stalag Luft III and other camps. Why should we care about them? The movie certainly did not; they are not the heroes and are incidental to the story. There is no movie *The Great Left Behind*.

Yet we *should* think about them. After all, the number of POWs in German camps who did not escape was far greater than the few who did. Perhaps they were actually harmed by the escape, if they were punished or if their privileges were withdrawn. One can imagine that the guards made it even harder to escape than before. Did the escape of their fellow POWs inspire those still in the camps to escape too? They certainly could have learned from the escape techniques developed by the Great Escapees, and they might have been able to avoid their mistakes. Or were they discouraged by the difficulties or by the very limited success of the Great Escape itself? Or perhaps, jealous of the escapees and pessimistic about their own chances, they became unhappy and depressed, making camp conditions even worse.

As with all good movies, there are other interpretations. The success and exhilaration of the escape are all but extinguished by the end of the film; for most of the escapees, their freedom is only temporary. Humanity's escape from death and deprivation began around 250 years ago, and it goes on to this day. Yet there is nothing to say that it must continue forever, and many threats—climate change, political failures, epidemics, and wars—could bring it to an end. Indeed, there were many pre-modern escapes in which rising living standards were choked off by precisely such forces. We can and should celebrate the successes, but there is no basis for a thoughtless triumphalism.

Economic Growth and the Origins of Inequality

Many of the great episodes of human progress, including those that are usually described as being entirely good, have left behind them a legacy of inequality. The Industrial Revolution, beginning in Britain in the eighteenth and nineteenth centuries, initiated the economic growth that has been responsible for hundreds of millions of people escaping from material deprivation. The other side of the same Industrial Revolution is what historians call the "Great Divergence," when Britain, followed a little later by northwestern Europe and North America, pulled away from the rest of the world, creating the enormous gulf between the West and the rest that has not closed to this day.[2] Today's global inequality was, to a large extent, created by the success of modern economic growth.

We should not think that, prior to the Industrial Revolution, the rest of the world had always been backward and desperately poor. Decades before Columbus, China was advanced and rich enough to send a fleet of enormous ships under Admiral Zheng He—aircraft carriers relative to Columbus's rowboats—to explore the Indian Ocean.[3] Three hundred years before even that, the city of Kaifeng was a smoke-filled metropolis of a million souls whose belching mills would not have been out of place in Lancashire eight hundred years later. Printers produced millions of books that were cheap enough to be read by people of even modest means.[4] Yet those eras, in China and elsewhere, were not sustained, let alone taken as starting points for ever-increasing prosperity. In 1127, Kaifeng fell to an invasion of tribes from Manchuria who had been rashly employed to help it wage war; if you enlist dangerous allies, you had better make sure they are well paid.[5] Economic growth in Asia kept starting and kept being choked off, by rapacious rulers, by wars, or by both.[6] It is only in the last two hundred and fifty years that long-term and continuing economic growth in some parts of the world—but not in others—has led to persistent gaps between countries. Economic growth has been the engine of international income inequality.

The Industrial Revolution and the Great Divergence are among the more benign escapes in history. There are many occasions when progress in one country was at the *expense* of another. The Age of Empire in the sixteenth and seventeenth centuries, which preceded the Industrial Revolution and helped cause it, benefited many in England and Holland, the two countries that did best in the scramble. By 1750, laborers in London and Amsterdam had seen their incomes grow relative to laborers in Delhi, Beijing, Valencia, and Florence; English workers could even afford a few luxuries, such as sugar and tea.[7] Yet those who were conquered and plundered in Asia, Latin America, and the Caribbean were not only harmed at the time but in many cases saddled with economic and political institutions that condemned them to centuries of continuing poverty and inequality.[8]

Today's globalization, like earlier globalizations, has seen growing prosperity alongside growing inequality. Countries that were poor not long ago, like China, India, Korea, and Taiwan, have taken advantage of globalization and grown rapidly, much faster than have today's rich countries. At the same time, they have moved away from still poorer countries, many of them in Africa, creating new inequalities. As some escape, some are left behind. Globalization and new ways of doing things have led to continuing increases in prosperity in rich countries, though the rates of growth have been slower—not only than in the fast-growing poor countries, but also than they used to be in the rich countries themselves. As growth has slowed, gaps between people have widened *within* most countries. A lucky few have made fabulous fortunes and live in a style that would have impressed the greatest kings and emperors of centuries past. Yet the majority of people have seen less improvement in their material prosperity, and in some countries—the United States among them—people in the middle of the income distribution are no better off than were their parents. They remain, of course, many times better off than still earlier generations; it is not that the escape never happened. Yet many today have good reasons to worry whether their children and grandchildren will look back to the present not as a time of relative scarcity but as a long-lost golden age.

When inequality is the handmaiden of progress, we make a serious mistake if we look only at average progress or, worse still, at progress only among the successes. The Industrial Revolution used to be told as a story of what happened in the leading countries, ignoring the rest of the world—as if nothing was happening there, or as if nothing had *ever* happened there. This not only slighted the majority of mankind but also ignored the unwilling contributions of those who were harmed or, at best, just left behind. We cannot describe the "discovery" of the New World by looking only at its effects on the Old. Within countries, the average rate of progress, such as the rate of growth of national income, cannot tell us whether growth is widely shared—as it was in the United States for a quarter of a century after World War II—or is accruing to a small group of very wealthy people —as has been the case more recently.

I tell the story of material progress, but that story is one of *both* growth and inequality.

Not Just Income, but Health Too

Progress in health has been as impressive as progress in wealth. In the past century, life expectancy in the rich countries increased by thirty years, and it continues to increase today by two or three years every ten years. Children who would have died before their fifth birthdays now live into old age, and middle-aged adults who once would have died of heart disease now live to see their grandchildren grow up and go to college. Of all the things that make life worth living, extra years of life are surely among the most precious.

Here too progress has opened up inequalities. The knowledge that cigarette smoking kills has saved millions of lives in the past fifty years, yet it was educated, richer professionals who were the first to quit, opening up a health gap between rich and poor. That germs caused disease was new knowledge around 1900, and professionals and educated people were the first to put that knowledge into practice. We have known for the best part of a century how to use vaccines and antibiotics to stop children from dying, yet around two million children still die every year from vaccine-preventable disease. Rich people are treated in world-class modern medical facilities in São Paulo or Delhi while, a mile or two away, poor children are dying of malnutrition and easily preventable disease. The explanation for why progress should be so uneven differs from case to case; the reason why poor people are more likely to smoke is not the same as the reason why so many poor children are not vaccinated. These accounts are to come, but for now the point is simply that health progress creates gaps in health just as material progress creates gaps in living standards.

These "health inequalities" are one of the great injustices of the world today. When new inventions or new knowledge comes along, *someone* has to be the first to benefit, and the inequalities that come with waiting for a while are a reasonable price to pay. It would be absurd to wish that knowledge about the health effects of smoking had been suppressed so as to prevent new health inequalities. Yet poor people are still more likely to smoke, and the children who are dying today in Africa would not have died in France or the United States even sixty years ago. Why do these inequalities persist, and what can be done about them?

This book is mostly about two topics: material living standards and health. They are not the only things that matter for a good life, but they are important in and of themselves. Looking at health and income together allows us to avoid a mistake that is too common today, when knowledge is specialized and each specialty has its own parochial view of human wellbeing. Economists focus on income, public health scholars focus on mortality and morbidity, and demographers focus on births, deaths, and the size of populations. All of these factors contribute to wellbeing, but none of them *is* wellbeing. The statement is obvious enough, but the problems that arise from it are not so obvious.

Economists—my own tribe—think that people are better off if they have more money—which is fine as far as it goes. So if a few people get a lot more money and most people get little or nothing, but do not lose out, economists will usually argue that the world is a better place. And indeed there is enormous appeal to the idea that, as long as no one gets hurt, better off is better; it is called the Pareto criterion. Yet this idea is completely undermined if wellbeing is defined too narrowly; people have to be better off, or no worse off, in *wellbeing*, not just in material living standards. If those who get rich get favorable political treatment, or undermine the public health or public education systems, so that those who do less well lose out in politics, health, or education, then those who do less well may have gained money but they are *not* better off. One cannot assess society, or justice, using living standards alone. Yet economists routinely and incorrectly apply the Pareto argument to income, ignoring other aspects of wellbeing.

Of course, it is also a mistake to look at health, or at any one *component* of wellbeing, by itself. It is a good thing to improve health services, and to make sure that those who are in medical need are looked after. But we cannot set health priorities without attention to their cost. Nor should we use longevity as a measure of social progress; life in a longer-lived country is better, but not if the country is a totalitarian dictatorship.

Wellbeing cannot be judged by its average without looking at inequality, and wellbeing cannot be judged by one or more of its parts without looking at the whole. If this book were much longer, and its author knew much more, I would write about other aspects of wellbeing, including freedom, education, autonomy, dignity, and the ability to participate in society. But even thinking about health and income in the same book will free us from the mistakes that come from looking at one or the other alone.

How Does Progress Come About?

There is little doubt that our ancestors would have liked to have what we have now, could they have imagined our world. And there is no reason to think that parents ever become inured to watching their children die; if you doubt me (and it is only one account among many), read Janet Browne's description of the tortures suffered by Charles Darwin when his first two children died.[9] The desire to escape is always there. Yet the desire is not always fulfilled. New knowledge, new inventions, and new ways of doing things are the keys to progress. Sometimes inspiration comes from lone inventors who dream up something quite different from what has gone before. More often, new ways of doing things are by-products of something else; for example, reading spread when Protestants were required to read the Bible for themselves. More often still, the social and economic environment creates innovations in response to need. Wages were high in Britain after its success in the Age of Empire, and those high wages, together with plentiful coal, provided incentives for inventors and manufacturers to come up with the inventions that powered the

Industrial Revolution.[10] The British Enlightenment, with its relentless search for self-improvement, provided fertile intellectual soil in
which those inventions were more likely to come about.[11] The cholera
epidemics of the nineteenth century were an impetus for crucial
discoveries about the germ theory of disease. And the well-funded
medical research arising from the HIV/AIDS pandemic of today
uncovered the virus and developed medicines that, while not curing
the disease, greatly extend the lives of those who are infected. Yet
there are also cases in which inspiration never came, in which needs
and incentives failed to produce a magic solution, or even a mundane
one. Malaria has afflicted human beings for tens of thousands of
years, perhaps even for all of human history, and we still have no comprehensive way of preventing or treating it. Necessity may be the
mother of invention, but there is nothing that guarantees a successful
pregnancy.

Inequality also influences the process of invention, sometimes for
good and sometimes for ill. The sufferings of the deprived are a force
for finding new ways to close the gaps, if only because the fact that
some are not deprived demonstrates that the deprivation need not
exist. A good example is the discovery of oral rehydration therapy in
the refugee camps of Bangladesh in the 1970s; millions of children
suffering from diarrhea have been saved from dehydration and possible death by a cheap and easily made remedy. But it works the other
way too. Powerful interests have much to lose from new inventions
and new ways of doing things. Economists think of eras of innovation
as powering up waves of "creative destruction." New methods sweep
away old methods, destroying the lives and livelihoods of those who
were dependent on the old order. Globalization today has hurt many
such groups; importing cheaper goods from abroad is like a new way
of making them, and woe betide those who earned their livings making such goods at home. Some of those who would lose out, or who

fear that they might be hurt, are politically powerful and can outlaw or slow down the new ideas. The emperors of China, worried about threats to their power from merchants, banned oceangoing voyages in 1430, so that Admiral Zheng He's explorations were an end, not a beginning.[12] Similarly, Francis I, Emperor of Austria, banned railways because of their potential to bring about revolution and threaten his power.[13]

Why Does Inequality Matter?

Inequality can spur progress or it can inhibit progress. But does it matter in and of itself? There is no general agreement on this: the philosopher and economist Amartya Sen argues that even among the many who believe in some form of equality, there are very different views about *what* it is that ought to be made equal.[14] Some economists and philosophers argue that inequalities of income are unjust, unless they are necessary for some greater end. For example, if a government were to guarantee the same income for all of its citizens, people might decide to work a lot less so that even the very poorest might be worse off than in a world in which some inequality is allowed. Others emphasize equality of opportunity rather than equality of outcomes, though there are many versions of what equality of opportunity means. Yet others see fairness in terms of proportionality: what each person receives should be proportional to what he or she contributes.[15] On this view of fairness, it is easy to conclude that income *equality* is unfair if it involves redistributing income from rich to poor.

In this book, the arguments I emphasize are those about what inequality does, whether inequality helps or hurts, and whether it matters what kind of inequality we are talking about. Does society benefit from having very rich people when most are not rich? If not, does society benefit from the rules and institutions that allow some to get much richer than the rest? Or do the rich harm everyone else—for example by making it difficult for the nonrich to affect how society is run? Are inequalities in health like inequalities in income, or are they somehow different? Are they always unjust, or can they sometimes serve a higher good?

A Road Map

The aim of the book is to provide an account of wealth and health around the world, focusing on today but also looking back to see how we got to where we are. Chapter 1 is an introductory overview. It gives a snapshot of the world from outer space: a map of where life is good and of where it is not good. It documents a world in which there has been great progress in reducing poverty and lowering the chances of death, but also a world of difference—of huge inequalities in living standards, in life chances, and in wellbeing.

The three chapters of Part I are about health. They look at how the past has shaped our health today, why the hundreds of thousands of years that people spent as hunter-gatherers are relevant for understanding health today, and why the mortality revolution that began in the eighteenth century set patterns that are echoed in contemporary health advances. The move to agriculture, seven to ten thousand years ago, made it possible to grow more food, but it also brought new diseases and new inequalities as hierarchic states replaced egalitarian bands of hunter-gatherers. In England of the eighteenth century, globalization brought new medicines and new treatments that saved many lives—but mostly the lives of those who could afford them. While the new methods eventually lowered death rates for everyone, it was the aristocracy whose life chances first pulled away from those of the common people. By the end of the nineteenth century, the development and acceptance of the germ theory of disease had set the stage for another explosion of progress as well as for the opening up of another great chasm—this time between the life chances of those who were born in rich countries and the chances of those who were not.

I tell the story of the fight to save the lives of children in the world that was left behind. This is a story of progress, mostly after World War II—a catch-up that would begin to close the chasm that had begun to open in the eighteenth century. It is a story with many great successes, in which antibiotics, pest control, vaccinations, and clean water saved millions of children, and in which life expectancy sometimes increased at (the apparently impossible rate of) several years each year. The chasm in life expectancy between the poor and rich worlds was narrowed, but not closed. There were also terrible setbacks, including a catastrophic man-made famine in China between 1958 and 1961, and the recent HIV/AIDS epidemic that, for several African countries, wiped out three decades of progress against mortality. Even without those disasters, much remains undone; many countries do not have adequate systems for routine health care, many children still die just because they were born in the "wrong" country, and there remain places—most notably but not only in India—where half of the children are seriously malnourished.

One of the (good) reasons why the mortality gap between rich and poor has not closed more rapidly is because mortality has been falling in rich countries too, but in a very different way, benefiting children less and adults more. The final installment of the health story is about mortality decline in rich countries, about how and why the gap in life expectancy between men and women has been closing, about the (huge) role played by cigarette smoking, and about why the fight against heart disease has been so much more successful than the fight against cancer. Once again we see progress coupled with growing health inequalities, just as happened in Britain in the late eighteenth century.

The two chapters of Part II are about material living standards. I start with the United States; although America is indeed exceptional and is often extreme, for example in its degree of income inequality, the forces at work apply to other rich countries too. Economic growth brought new prosperity to Americans after World War II, but growth had been slowing, decade by decade, even before the Great Recession. Postwar growth brought marked reductions in poverty, especially among African-Americans and the elderly, and there was little expansion in inequality. Until the early 1970s, the United States was the very model of a modern major economy. Since then, the story has been one of less growth and greater inequality, the latter driven especially by runaway growth in incomes at the very top of the distribution. As always, there is a good side to this inequality: rewards to education, to innovation, and to creativity are higher than they have ever been. But the United States is also a good example of the dark side, of the political and economic threats to wellbeing that come from plutocracy.

I also look at living standards in the world as a whole. Here is the story of perhaps the greatest escape in all of human history, and certainly the most rapid one: the reduction in global poverty since 1980. Much of it was driven by the performance of the two largest countries in the world, China and India, where recent economic growth has transformed the lives of more than a billion people. That global poverty should have fallen goes against the almost universally accepted doomsday predictions of the 1960s, that the population explosion would doom the world to deprivation and disaster. The world has done much better than the pessimists predicted. Yet a billion or so people *still* live in terrible destitution; while many have escaped, many have been left behind.

Part III consists of a single chapter, an epilogue in which I stop telling stories and argue for what ought to be done—and more importantly for what ought not to be done. I believe that we—meaning those of us who are fortunate enough to have been born in the "right" countries—have a moral obligation to help reduce poverty and ill health in the world. Those who have escaped—or at least have escaped through the struggles of their predecessors—must help those who are still imprisoned. For many people, that moral duty is fulfilled by foreign aid, through the efforts of national governments (most of whom have official aid agencies), through international organizations like the World Bank or the World Health Organization, or through the thousands of nongovernmental aid organizations that operate nationally and internationally. While some of this aid has clearly done good—and I think the case for assistance to fight disease such as HIV/AIDS or smallpox is strong—I have come to believe that most external aid is doing more harm than good. If it is undermining countries' chance to grow—as I believe it is—there is no argument for continuing it on the grounds that "we must do something." The something that we should do is to stop.

The Postscript is a coda that returns to the main themes. It asks whether we can expect the real Great Escape—unlike the movie *The Great Escape*—to have a happy ending.

Measuring Progress, Measuring Inequality

Whenever it is possible to do so, I support my arguments with data, and almost always with graphs. Progress cannot be coherently discussed without definitions and supporting evidence. Indeed, enlightened government is impossible without the collection of data. States have been counting their populations for thousands of years—the Roman census that sent Mary and Joseph to Bethlehem, Joseph's city of birth, is a famous example. The U.S. Constitution mandates that there be a census of the population every ten years; without it, a fair democracy is not possible. Even earlier, in 1639, the colonists in present-day Massachusetts mandated a complete count of births and deaths; without such vital statistics, public health policy is blind.

Not the least of the health problems faced by the poor countries of the world today is the lack of good information on the numbers of people who die, let alone on what causes their deaths. There is no lack of invented and interpolated numbers from international agencies, but it is not always widely understood that these are not an adequate basis for policy or for thinking about or assessing external aid. The need to do something tends to trump the need to understand what needs to be done. And without data, anyone who does anything is free to claim success. As I go along, I will try to explain the basis for my numbers, where they come from and how credible (or incredible) they are. I will also try to make the case that the missing data are a scandal that is not being adequately addressed.

Unless we understand how the numbers are put together, and what they mean, we run the risk of seeing problems where there are none, of missing urgent and addressable needs, of being outraged by fantasies while overlooking real horrors, and of recommending policies that are fundamentally misconceived.

National Happiness and National Income

Much of this book is about material wellbeing, typically measured by income, the amount of money that people have to spend or to save. Money must always be adjusted by the costs of what people buy, but, that done, it is a reasonable indicator of people's ability to buy the things on which material wellbeing depends. Yet many argue that too much attention is given to income. A good life certainly means more than money, but the argument often goes further, to claim that money does nothing to make people's lives better, at least once basic needs have been met.

Some evidence for this argument comes from happiness surveys that show, it is claimed, that money does little or nothing to make people happy except for those in poverty. If this is correct, and if happiness is the right way to measure wellbeing, then much of my argument would be undercut. So it is good to start out by considering how happiness relates to money. The discussion will also give me the chance to introduce and explain a way of drawing graphs that I will use throughout the book.

Surveys often ask people how their lives are going, for example by reporting how satisfied they are with their lives in general. These data are often referred to as measures of "happiness," though it is easy to think of examples in which unhappy people believe that their lives are going well, or vice versa. Indeed, as we shall see, it is a bad mistake to confuse life satisfaction and happiness; the former is an overall judgment about life that comes from consideration, while the latter is an emotion, a mood, or a feeling, which is part of experiencing life.[16]

The Gallup Organization asks people around the world to rate their lives by imagining a "ladder of life" with eleven steps; the bottom step, 0, is "the worst possible life for you" while 10 is "the best possible life for you." Each respondent is asked to indicate "on which step of the ladder would you say you personally feel you stand at this time?" We can use these data to see how countries do relative to one another and, in particular, whether higher-income countries do better on this measure.

Figure 1 shows the average life evaluation for each country against its national income per head, or more precisely gross domestic product (GDP) per head; it shows the averages for the years 2007 through 2009. Income is measured in U.S. dollars that have been adjusted for

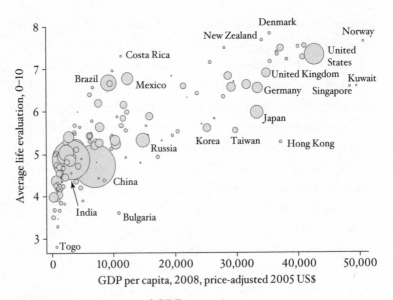

FIGURE 1 Life evaluation and GDP per capita.

differences in price levels between countries; in Chapter 6, I will explain where these numbers come from as well as the considerable reservations that should be attached to them. The circles in the figure have areas proportional to the populations of each country; the two big countries on the left are China and India, and the big country at the top right is the United States. I have marked a few other countries that are particularly interesting.

We can see at once that the people who live in the really poor countries on the left of the figure are generally very dissatisfied with their lives; not only are they poor in income, but they also rate their lives poorly. At the other end of the world, in the United States and the other rich countries, people have high incomes and evaluate their lives highly. The worst country is Togo—one of the poorest countries in the world, where people have very little freedom of any kind—while the best is Denmark—a rich, free country. The Scandinavian countries regularly outrank the United States in these comparisons, but the average life evaluation in the United States is still among the best in the world. There are lots of exceptions to the rule of income. East Asian countries and former communist countries tend to have low life evaluations—Bulgaria is the most extreme example—while countries in Latin America tend to do relatively well. Income is certainly not the only thing that matters in people's evaluations of their lives.

If we look at the bottom left of the picture, where the poor countries are, we see that life evaluation rises with national income quite rapidly. After we pass China and India, traveling from bottom left to top right, the rise in life evaluation with income is a bit less steep, and once we get to Brazil and Mexico the life evaluation scores are close to seven out of ten, only a point or so less than those for the really rich countries at the top right. Income matters more among the very poor than among the very rich. Indeed, it is very tempting to look at the picture and conclude that once GDP per capita reaches around $10,000 a year, more money does nothing to improve people's lives, and many have made this claim.[17] Yet this claim is false.

To explain why money matters even among the rich countries, we need to redraw Figure 1 in a somewhat different form. When we think about money, we think in dollar terms, but we also think in percentage terms. On the rare occasions when my Princeton colleagues discuss their salaries with one another, they are likely to report that one got a 3 percent increase, while another got 1 percent. Indeed, the dean is more likely to signal his pleasure or displeasure through the size of the percentage increase than through the size of the increase in dollars. While a 1 percent increase means more dollars to someone who earns $200,000 a year than a 2 percent increase means to someone earning $50,000 a year, the latter will (correctly) feel that she has done better in the past year. Percentage changes become the basic unit in these sorts of calculations; 10 percent is the same no matter what the baseline income is.

We can do just this for the data in Figure 1, though the differences between countries are so huge that it makes sense to think, not in terms of percentages, but in terms of the number of times income is quadrupled. Think of $250 a year as the base; only Zimbabwe and the Democratic Republic of the Congo (DRC) are at or below $250. Countries such as Uganda, Tanzania, and Kenya are near $1,000, four times the base; China and India are another fourfold increase over Tanzania and Kenya, near the marker for sixteen times the base. Mexico and Brazil are four times China and India, and the world's richest countries have incomes that are four times larger still; they are 256 times richer than the world's poorest countries. (In Chapter 6 I shall explain why these numbers should only be taken as rough guides.) Instead of using the dollar value of incomes to compare with life evaluations, we can use this scheme of fourfold comparison, marking off units as 4 times, 16 times, 64 times, and 256 times the base, and this is what is done in Figure 2.

Figure 2 contains *exactly the same data* as Figure 1, but income is now plotted on this 1, 4, 16, 64, and 256 scale. I have, however, marked these five points by their original dollar amounts, $250 through $64,000 so that the link with income itself is clear. Moving along the horizontal axis from one tick to the next always represents a fourfold increase in income. More generally, equal distances from left to right represent equal percentage increases in income, not equal dollar amounts, as in Figure 1. A scale with this property is known as a *logarithmic* (or log) scale, and we will see it again.

Although the only change is in the labeling of the horizontal axis, Figure 2 looks completely different from Figure 1. The flattening among the rich countries has vanished, and the countries now lie

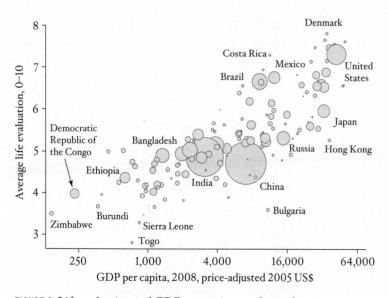

FIGURE 2 Life evaluation and GDP per capita on a log scale.

more or less along a straight line. What this says is that equal *percentage* differences in income produce equal absolute shifts in life evaluation. On average, if we move from one country to another whose per capita income is four times as high, the life evaluation score will move by about one point on a zero to ten scale, and this is true whether we are moving between poor countries or rich ones. And just to remove any misunderstanding: yes, there are lots of exceptions, and lots of countries are higher or lower than we might expect them to be given their national incomes. It is not always true that all rich countries have higher life evaluations than all the countries that are poorer; China and India are two notable examples. But on average over all the countries, rich or poor, a fourfold difference in incomes comes with a one-point increase in the evaluation of life.

Is Figure 1 right, or is Figure 2 right? Both are, just as it is true that the professor who got a 2 percent raise on $50,000 got a raise of

$1,000 while the professor who got a 1 percent raise on $200,000 got $2,000. The same percentage increase involves more money if we move from India to the United States than if we move from the DRC to India, even though both involve a fourfold shift. Figure 1 tells us that the same *absolute* increase in dollars means less to the life satisfaction of a rich person than to a poor person, while Figure 2 tells us that the same *percentage* increase makes for the same increase in life satisfaction.

Life evaluation scores capture important aspects of life beyond income, and this has led to arguments that we should downplay the importance of income. This is fine if the implication is to consider other aspects of wellbeing, like health or education or the ability to participate in society. It is not fine if the implication is that income is not worth anything, or that income adds nothing to life for those of us who live in countries richer than Mexico. It is even less fine if the argument is that we should focus on life evaluations and ignore everything else. Life evaluation measures are far from perfect. People are not always sure what the questions mean, or how they are expected to answer, and international comparisons can be compromised by national differences in reporting styles. In many places, "mustn't grumble" or "not so bad" is about as good as anyone would ever claim, but people in other cultures are more exuberant about their feelings and less reticent about their successes. So Figure 2 is important because it shows that focusing on income is not seriously misleading. Richer countries have higher life evaluations, even among the world's richest countries.

I shall return to measures of happiness and life satisfaction in the next chapter, but my main purpose there is to look more widely at the wellbeing of the world today—at those who have made the Great Escape, and then some, as well as those who are still waiting.

ONE

The Wellbeing of the World

THE GREATEST ESCAPE in human history is the escape from poverty and death. For thousands of years, those who were lucky enough to escape death in childhood faced years of grinding poverty. Building on the Enlightenment, the Industrial Revolution, and the germ theory of disease, living standards have increased by many times, life spans have more than doubled, and people live fuller and better lives than ever before. The process is still going on. My father lived twice as long as either of my grandfathers; his real income as a civil engineer was many times the income of his father, who was a coal miner; and my education and income as a professor greatly exceed his education and his income. Mortality rates of children and of adults continue to fall throughout the world. But the escape is far from complete. A billion people suffer living standards, schooling, and life spans that are little better than those of their (or our) forebears. The Great Escape has made a world of difference to those of us who are richer, healthier, taller, bigger, and better educated than our grandparents and their grandparents. It has also made a world of difference in another, less positive sense: because much of the world's population was left behind, the world is immeasurably more unequal than it was three hundred years ago.

This book tells the story of the Great Escape, of the benefits to mankind that it brought, and how it was responsible for today's unequal world. It also explains what we need to do—or not to do—to help those who are still trapped in deprivation.

I use the term *wellbeing* to refer to all of the things that are good for a person, that make for a good life. Wellbeing includes material wellbeing, such as income and wealth; physical and psychological wellbeing, represented by health and happiness; and education and the ability to participate in civil society through democracy and the rule of law. Much of this book will focus on two of these components, health and wealth; in this overview I also say something about happiness.

I start with an overview of wellbeing in the world as it is today, and how it has changed over the last thirty to fifty years. I present the basic facts with only minimal explanation; in later chapters I shall explore individual topics in more detail, ask how we got here, and where and how we should be going next.

Health and Wealth

Health is the obvious starting point for an enquiry into wellbeing. You need a life to have a *good* life, and poor health and disability among the living can severely limit the capability to enjoy an otherwise good life. So I begin with life itself.

A girl born in the United States today can expect to live for more than 80 years. This official estimate is in fact very conservative because it ignores any future reductions in mortality that might take place during her life; given past progress, it is implausible that progress will suddenly stop. Of course, it is hard to project future health improvements, but a reasonable guess would be that a white, middle-class girl born in affluent America today has a 50-50 chance of making it to 100.[1] This is a remarkable change from the situation of her great-grandmother, born in 1910, say, who had a life expectancy at birth of 54 years. Of all the girls born in the United States in 1910, 20 percent died before their fifth birthday, and only two out of every five thousand lived to celebrate their hundredth birthday. Even for her grandmother, born in 1940, life expectancy at birth was 66, and thirty-eight out of every thousand girls born in 1940 did not make it to their first birthday.

These historical differences pale in comparison with the differences between countries today. There are many places in the world whose health today is worse than it was in the United States in 1910. A quarter of all children born in Sierra Leone (or Angola or Swaziland or the Democratic Republic of the Congo or Afghanistan) will not live to see their fifth birthday, and life expectancy at birth is only a little above 40. Women typically bear between five and seven children, and most mothers will suffer through the death of at least one of their children. In these countries, one out of every thousand births leads to the death of the mother, a risk that accumulates to one in a hundred for women who have ten children. Bad though these numbers are, they are much *better* than those a few decades ago: even in the worst places, where nothing else seems to go right, the chances of dying have been falling. In some of the countries with the worst outcomes, such as Swaziland, if children make it past age 5, they run the risk of HIV/AIDS, which has greatly increased the risk of dying in the young adult years—a time of life when very few usually die. But such horrors are not universal in tropical countries, or even in all poor countries. There are many countries, including at least one tropical country (Singapore), where a newborn has survival chances as good as or better than those in the United States. Even in China and India (which in 2005 contained between them more than a third of the world's people and almost half of the world's poorest people), new-borns today can expect to live for 64 years (India) and 73 years (China.)

Later in this chapter, I say more about where these numbers come from, but it is worth emphasizing now that the poorer the country, the worse its health statistics tend to be. Even so, we have good information about the deaths of children—the fractions who die before age 1 or age 5—but much worse information about adult deaths—including maternal mortality rates, or how long a 15-year-old can expect to live.

Health is not just a matter of being alive, and living a long time, but of living in good health. Good health has many dimensions and is harder to measure than the mere fact of whether or not someone is alive, but here too there is evidence of improvement over time as well as of differences between rich and poor countries. People in rich countries report less pain and less disability than people in poor countries. Disability has been falling over time in rich countries. IQ scores are rising over time. In most of the world, people are getting taller. Those who do not get enough to eat as children, or who live through childhood diseases, often do not grow as tall as their genes would have allowed under ideal conditions. Being shorter than they ought to have been may indicate early life misfortunes that compromise brain development and further restrict their opportunities in adult life. Europeans and Americans are taller than Africans, on average, and much taller than Chinese or Indians. Grown children are taller than their parents, and taller still than their grandparents. Global improvements in health and income, as well as global inequalities, can even be seen in people's bodies.

Differences in health are often mirrored by differences in material living standards or in poverty. Americans are much richer than they were in 1910 or in 1945, and the countries with the lowest life expectancies today have incomes that are a(n almost incredibly) tiny fraction of American incomes today. The (grotesquely misnamed) Democratic Republic of the Congo (DRC, and known as Zaire under the rule of Joseph Mobutu from 1965 to 1997) has a per capita national income that is about three-quarters of 1 percent of the per capita national income of the United States. More than half the population of the DRC lives on less than a dollar per person per day; the fractions for Sierra Leone and Swaziland are similar. Some of the worst places are not even documented because they are currently engulfed in conflict; Afghanistan is one example.

According to the U.S. Census Bureau, 14 percent of the American population was poor in 2009, but the poverty line in the United States is much higher, around $15 a day. It is hard to imagine living in the United States on a dollar per person per day (although one calculation suggests that $1.25 is possible if we exclude the cost of housing, health, and education),[2] yet this, or something close to it, is typical of what the very poorest people in the world survive on.

The link between life expectancy and poverty, although real enough, is far from exact. In China and India, with life expectancies of 73 and 64 years, respectively, many people live on less than a dollar a day—about a quarter of the population in India and a seventh of the rural population in China. And although the Chinese economy will soon overtake the U.S. economy in total size, per capita incomes in China are only around 20 percent of American incomes; on average five Chinese share the income of one American. There are other, even poorer countries that do well in life expectancy. Bangladesh and Nepal, with life expectancies in the mid-60s, are examples; Vietnam is only a little better off but in 2005 had a life expectancy of 74.

There are also some rich countries that do much worse than their incomes warrant. A notable example is the United States, whose life expectancy is one of the lowest among the richest countries. Another case of a different kind is Equatorial Guinea, which in 2005 had a per capita income that was bloated by oil revenues, but a life expectancy of less than 50 years. Equatorial Guinea, once a Spanish colony in West Africa, is ruled by President Teodoro Obiang Nguema Mbasogo, who has a good claim to the highly contested title of Africa's worst dictator and whose family is the beneficiary of most of the country's revenue from exporting oil.

High life expectancy, good health, the absence of poverty, democracy, and the rule of law are among the features that we would include were we to design an ideal country. They allow people to live good lives and to pursue what is important to them. Yet, without asking people, we don't know *exactly* what they care about, how they might trade off health and income, or even the extent to which these things matter to them at all. People are sometimes capable of adapting to what might seem intolerable conditions, and perhaps they can extract some modicum of happiness or even live a good life in places where mortality and poverty are common—as it were, prospering in the valley of the shadow of death. Poor people may report that they are living good lives in the most difficult conditions, and rich people, who seem to have everything, may feel that their lives are deeply unsatisfactory.

In such cases, we might still choose to measure their wellbeing in terms of the opportunities that people have to lead a good life, rather than what they themselves make of their lives. That a poor man is happy and adaptable does not detract from his poverty any more than the misery or greed of a billionaire detracts from his wealth. A focus on what Amartya Sen calls "capabilities" leads to an examination of freedom from deprivation in terms of the possibilities that are opened up by objective circumstances, rather than what people make of, or feel about, those circumstances.[3] Yet feeling that one's life is going well is good in and of itself, and it is better to be happy than to be sad.

Those feelings contribute to a good life, and it is important to ask people about them, even if they are not given any special priority in the assessment of wellbeing. This is a different position from that proposed by some utilitarians, such as the economist Richard Layard,[4] who argue that self-assessed happiness is the only thing that is important, that good circumstances are good only insofar as they promote happiness, and that bad circumstances are not bad if people are happy in spite of them. Even so, as we saw from Figures 1 and 2 in the Introduction, it turns out that people are not at all content with their lives in countries where life is nasty, brutish, and short, and that the inhabitants of the rich, long-lived countries are generally well aware of their good fortune.

Life Expectancy and Income in the World

To look at the general patterns—as well as to pick out the exceptions, which are often of great interest—we need to look at the world as a whole, mapping patterns of health, wealth, and happiness. One of the most useful ways of doing this was pioneered by the demographer Samuel Preston in 1975.[5] Preston's picture, updated to 2010, is redrawn in Figure 1; it shows life expectancy and income around the world.

The horizontal axis shows GDP per capita of each country while the vertical axis shows life expectancy at birth for men and women taken together. Each country is shown as a circle, and the areas of the circles are proportional to population size. The huge circles in the middle of the plot are China and India, while the considerably smaller but still large circle at the top right is the United States. The curve that runs from bottom left to top right illustrates the general relation between life expectancy and national income, rising rapidly among the low-income countries and then flattening out among the rich, long-lived countries.

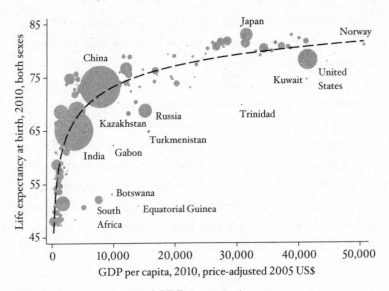

FIGURE 1 Life expectancy and GDP per capita in 2010.

GDP per capita is a measure of average income originating in each country and is measured here in a common unit across countries. The unit, the 2005 international dollar, is constructed so that, at least in principle, a dollar is worth the same in all countries and we are comparing like with like; an international dollar in Brazil or Tanzania buys the same as a dollar in the United States. GDP includes incomes that are not directly received by people or families, such as government tax receipts and the profits of firms and banks, as well as incomes that belong to foreigners. Generally only a fraction, albeit a substantial fraction, of GDP is available to households for their own purchases. Other components of GDP benefit households directly (government expenditures on education, for example), or indirectly (investment for the future). GDP, which is gross *domestic* product, is different from GNP, gross *national* product. GNP includes, and GDP excludes, income owned by residents but generated abroad, and GNP excludes, and GDP includes, incomes generated domestically but owned by foreigners. The difference is usually small, but it is very important for some countries. Luxembourg, where many earners live in Belgium, France, or Germany, is an example of a country where GNP is much smaller than GDP. Another is the tiny Chinese peninsula of Macau, now the world's largest gambling casino. These two countries, which would appear beyond the right-hand boundary of the graph, are excluded, along with Qatar and the United Arab Emirates, oil-rich states that, along with Luxembourg and Macau, had the world's highest levels of GDP per head in 2010. GNP is a better measure of national income, but the data are more consistently available for GDP, which is why I use it here and in many places throughout the book.

An important feature of the graph is the "hinge point" near China where the curve begins to flatten. The hinge point marks the *epidemiological transition*. For countries to the left of the transition, infectious diseases are important causes of deaths, and many of the deaths are among children, so that in the poorest countries, about half of all deaths are of children under the age of 5. After the transition, as we move to the richer countries, child deaths become quite uncommon, and most deaths are of old people, who die not from infectious disease but from *chronic* diseases, the most important of which are heart disease (or more broadly, cardiovascular disease, including stroke) and cancer. Chronic diseases are becoming increasingly common causes of death in poor countries, too, but few people in rich countries die of infectious disease, except for small numbers of the elderly who die from pneumonia. One way in which the transition is sometimes summarized is to say that diseases move out of the bowels and chests of infants into the arteries of the elderly.

That life expectancy and incomes are positively related is important for thinking about the worldwide distribution of wellbeing.

Health and wealth are two of the most important components of wellbeing, and the graph shows that they generally (although not inevitably) go together. People who suffer deprivation in terms of material living standards—such as much of the population of sub-Saharan Africa—are generally also the people who suffer deprivation in terms of health; they get to live for fewer years, and they live with the misery of seeing many of their children die. At the other end of the curve, among the rich of the world, few parents ever experience the death of a child, and they get to enjoy their high standard of living for almost twice as many years as those in the poorest countries. Looking at the world in terms of health and income together forces us to see that the divisions are compounded, and that the dispersion of wellbeing is wider than it appears if we look only at health or at income. One crude and sometimes useful (although ethically unattractive) trick is to combine life expectancy and income by multiplying the two to give a measure of lifetime income. This is a poor measure of wellbeing (an extra year of life is valued by the income of the recipient, so a year of the life of a rich person is worth more than a year of the life of a poor person), but it illustrates the effects on the gaps between countries. In the DRC, for example, per capita income is estimated to be about three-quarters of 1 percent of that of the United States, and life expectancy is less than two-thirds of that of the United States, so that average lifetime income in the United States is more than two hundred times the average lifetime income in the DRC.

What the figure does *not* establish is that it is higher income that *causes* better health, or that it is poverty that causes what are often called the "diseases of poverty." Nor does the graph rule it out, and indeed income *must* be important in some ways and at some times—an idea that will be explored extensively in the rest of this book. Income is important in places where improving health requires better nutrition—for which people need money—or cleaner water and better sanitation—for which governments need money. Among the rich countries, it is less obvious how money can tackle cancer or heart disease—though research and development are certainly expensive—so that we have the beginnings of a simple account of the flattening of the curve as countries pass through the epidemiological transition. It is also possible that there is some upper limit to human life expectancy—perhaps surprisingly, the idea is hotly contested—so that, when life expectancy is as high as it is Japan, or even the United States, it gets harder and harder push it up further.

It is sometimes claimed that there is *no* relation between income and life expectancy among the better-off countries of the world.[6] As was the case for the graphs of life evaluation versus GDP in the Introduction, it is useful to redraw Figure 1 using a log scale for income. Figure 2, which uses exactly the same data as Figure 1, gives a very different impression. To a first approximation, the slope of the line is the same on the right as on the left of the picture, although the relationship at the top is a little flatter—largely driven by the poor performance of the United States—and among the very richest countries the lack of a relationship is still apparent. But for much of the world, proportional increases in income are associated with the same increase in years of life, just as they are associated with the same increase in life satisfaction, as we saw in the Introduction. Of course, because the rich countries have much higher incomes, the same proportional increase in a rich country involves a much larger absolute increase than in a poor country, so that, as in Figure 1, the same amount of money comes with fewer additional years of life among the rich than among the poor. But even among the rich countries, higher incomes still come with more years of life. However, as Figure 2 shows, the ranking of countries by life expectancy is far from identical to the ranking by income.

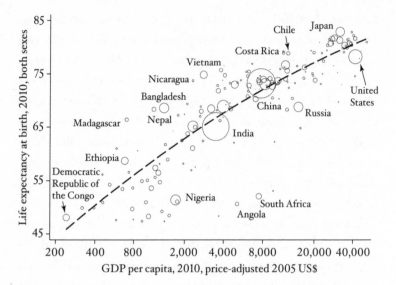

FIGURE 2 Life expectancy and GDP per capita in 2010 on a log scale.

The stories of the countries off the curve are as important as the stories of those that are on it. Among the countries that do much worse than might be expected given their levels of income, some have been affected by wars. Others—including Botswana and Swaziland (as well as other African countries not highlighted)—are suffering from the HIV/AIDS epidemic, which in several countries has taken back all or most of the gains in life expectancy achieved since World War II. For those countries, the disease has shifted them down and away from the curve. I have already discussed Equatorial Guinea, which is the most egregious of all. But the same factor—extreme inequality of income—is also partly responsible for South Africa's position, which has been below the curve for many years, long before the advent of HIV/AIDS. South Africa can be thought of—even after the demise of apartheid—as a small, rich country embedded in a much larger, poor country. Indeed, if we were to draw a line joining

Nigeria to the United States in Figure 1, and then move 10 percent of the way from Nigeria to the United States—10 percent being the share of the white population in South Africa—we come close to South Africa's position on the graph.

Russia is another of the large poor performers. It is a country where life expectancy decreased rapidly after the fall of communism, possibly in response to the chaos and disruption of the transition; consistent with this story, excess alcohol consumption was one of the precipitating factors, especially among men. What happened in Russia remains disputed, if only because mortality among men was increasing well before the change in political system.[7] Whatever the truth, Russia and the countries of the former Soviet Union are places where both health and life evaluation are worse than might be expected given their incomes. They are also places where the transition from one economic system to another brought difficulties in the measurement of income, which may well be overstated in the figures. The transition in Russia, although inevitable in some form and probably beneficial in the long run, brought enormous costs in lost incomes and lost years of life. It does not rank with some of the other catastrophes of the postwar world—the AIDS epidemic or the Great Chinese Famine—but there was still enormous suffering and loss of wellbeing.

The United States is a poor performer relative to its income. Yet the United States spends a larger share of its national income on health care than any other country, so it provides a good illustration of the fact that there is no tight relation between income and health, and even less between health and expenditures on health care. Chile and Costa Rica have as good life expectancy as the United States, at about a quarter of per capita income and about 12 percent of per capita health expenditures. I shall return to U.S. health and health-care financing in Chapters 2 and 5.

Other countries do much better than might be expected from their incomes. Figure 2, with the log scale, shows these more clearly than does Figure 1. Nepal, Bangladesh, Vietnam, China, Costa Rica, Chile, and Japan are important countries whose life expectancy is high relative to where we might expect it to be from the international curve. The poorest of these countries do well by managing to have unusually low infant (aged less than 1 year) and child (aged less than 5 years) mortality rates, while those at the top, especially Japan, have unusually low mortality among the middle-aged and elderly. I shall explore these exceptions in more detail later in the book, but the main point is that there is nothing predestined about the curve; poor countries can do better than would be expected given their resources, and rich countries can do worse. There are ways of ensuring good health at low incomes and ways of spending large sums of money to no purpose. War, epidemic disease, and extreme inequality also make health worse at any income level, although at least the first two are much more likely to occur among poor countries than rich countries.

Onward and Upward, with Catastrophic Interruptions

Figures 1 and 2 give a snapshot of the world in 2010. But the curve linking life expectancy and income has not stayed still. Figure 3 plots the data and two curves, one repeating the 2010 curve and one for 1960. Countries in 1960 are shown with lighter shading to distinguish them from countries in 2010. The areas of the circles are once again proportional to population, but within each year separately, so population change cannot be determined by comparing the size of the circle for a given country in 1960 with the size of the circle for that country in 2010.

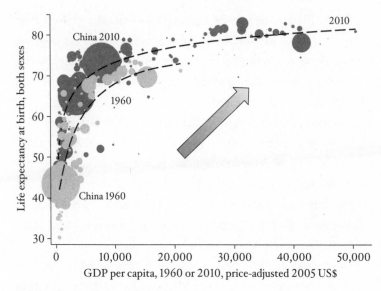

FIGURE 3 Longer lives, richer lives.

Almost all of the darker circles are above and to the right of the lighter circles; since 1960, nearly all countries have become richer and their residents longer lived. This is perhaps the most important fact about wellbeing in the world since World War II: that things are getting better, that both the health and income parts of wellbeing have improved over time. The economist and historian Robert Fogel, covering a longer span of history, has written about what he calls the escape from hunger and premature death.[8] That Great Escape has continued apace throughout the world since World War II. Although a few countries have not escaped, and many more are only partway there, we should note and celebrate the successes. Many millions of people have escaped from a world of sickness and material deprivation. Amartya Sen writes of development as freedom,[9] and Figure 3 shows that the world is freer in 2010 than it was in 1960. And if we were to fill in the diagram with the (much less complete) information for 1930 or 1900, we would see that the expansion of freedom has been going on for a long time, starting around 250 years ago, gathering momentum, and involving more and more countries in the past half-century.

In spite of overall progress, there have been catastrophes. One of the worst in human history was China's "Great Leap Forward" in 1958–61, when deeply misguided industrialization and food-procurement policies led to the deaths of around thirty-five million people from starvation and prevented the births of perhaps forty million more. Weather conditions were not unusual in these years; the famine was entirely man-made.

Mao Zedong and his fellow leaders were determined to show the superiority of communism, to quickly overtake production levels in Russia and in Britain, and to establish Mao's leadership of the communist world. Outlandish production targets were set to match the food needs of rapidly industrializing cities and to earn foreign exchange through exports of food. Under the totalitarian system maintained by the Communist Party of China, rural communes competed to exaggerate their output, further inflating the already un-attainable procurement quotas and leaving nothing for people to eat. At the same time, the Party caused chaos in the countryside by order-ing that all private land be turned into communes, confiscating pri-vate property and even private cooking utensils, and making people eat in communal kitchens. Given the enormous increases in produc-tion that were confidently expected, peasant labor was diverted to public works projects and rural steel-making plants, most of which achieved nothing. Draconian restrictions on travel and communica-tion prevented word from getting out, and the penalties for dissent were clear; three-quarters of a million people had been executed in

1950–51. (In any case, in these early years of the revolution, the Party was widely trusted.)

When Mao learned of the disasters (though probably not of their full scale), he doubled down on the policies, purging the messengers, labeling them "right-deviationists," and blaming peasants for secretly hoarding food. To do otherwise and admit the error of the Great Leap Forward would have imperiled Mao's own leadership position, and he was prepared to sacrifice tens of millions of his countrymen to prevent that happening. If Mao had reversed course when the extent of the mass starvation first became clear to the leadership, the famine would have lasted one year, not three, and in any case there was more than enough grain in government stores to prevent everyone from starving.[10]

According to several accounts, life expectancy in China, which was nearly 50 in 1958, fell to below 30 in 1960; five years later, once Mao had stopped killing people, it had risen to nearly 55.[11] Nearly a third of those born during the Great Leap Forward did not survive it. We sometimes have a hard time identifying the benefits of policies, or even convincing ourselves that policy makes a difference. Yet the catastrophic effects of bad policies can be all too obvious, as the Great Leap Forward shows. Even in the absence of war or epidemic disease, bad policy within a totalitarian political system caused the deaths of tens of millions of people. Of course, bad policies happen all the time without causing millions to die. The problem in China was that the policy took so long to be reversed because of the totalitarian system and the lack of any mechanism to make Mao change course. The political system in China today is not so different from the system that Mao created; what is different is the flow of information. In spite of continuing state control, it is hard to believe that such a famine could happen today without the Chinese leadership, and the rest of the world, finding out very quickly. Whether the rest of the world would be able help any more today than it could then is far from clear.

The HIV/AIDS epidemic has been another great disaster. As we have already seen, it has raised mortality and dramatically decreased life expectancy in many countries in sub-Saharan Africa. The position of South Africa provides a graphic illustration. In Figures 1 and 2, we see South Africa far below the curve. If we go back to 1960, long before HIV/AIDS had any effect on mortality, it was in a very similar position—not because of disease, but because of the extreme inequality between its white and black populations. If we were to run these curves as a movie and watch them change, decade by decade, we would see South Africa moving upwards, closer and closer to the curve as apartheid crumbled and racial differences in health narrowed. Or at least that was what happened up to 1990. After that, with increasing deaths from AIDS, the country tumbled back to its original position, falling back to where we see it in Figure 1.

In the past few years, antiretroviral drugs have begun to stanch the loss of life in Africa. The epidemic itself is another reminder that escapes can be temporary, and that great epidemics of infectious disease—HIV/AIDS now, cholera in the nineteenth century, and the Black Death in medieval times—are not safely confined to the past. Much attention, in both the scientific and the popular press, has been paid to current threats from "emerging" infectious diseases, particularly those, like HIV/AIDS, that crossed from animal reservoirs to humans. There are many such "zoonotic" diseases, some spectacularly and quickly lethal. Yet this is a lethality that makes it almost impossible for them to turn into large-scale epidemics; killing victims is good for neither the victims nor the bugs. HIV/AIDS, which is not easily transmitted and which kills very slowly, poses a much greater danger, and the pandemic that it caused should discourage us from believing that such diseases can be safely ignored in the future.

Turning away from catastrophes, we can see from Figure 3 not only that countries are getting richer and healthier, but that the curve linking life expectancy and income is itself moving up over time. The 2010 curve is above the 1960 curve, and if we were to go back through time, we would see that the 1960 curve is above the 1930 curve, which is above the 1900 curve, and so on. This upward movement was noted by Preston, who concluded that some systematic factor *other than income* must be responsible. If income were the most important thing —with other factors, like epidemic disease or country health policies, more or less without any pattern—then countries would move up or down (mostly up) the curve. But while countries did indeed move up the curve, that is not all that happened. Even with no change in income, life expectancy improved over time, and did so the world over, at low and high income levels. Preston attributed this upward movement of the curve to improvements in scientific and medical knowledge, or at least to the greater practical implementation of existing scientific and medical knowledge. He thought of movements *along the curve* as the contribution of improved living standards to health, and movements *of the curve itself* as the contribution of new practical knowledge.[12] This division of the credit for increases in well-being between income and knowledge will occupy us throughout the book. I shall argue that it is knowledge that is the key, and that income—although important both in and of itself and as a component of wellbeing, and often as a facilitator of other aspects of wellbeing— is not the ultimate cause of wellbeing.

Global Poverty and Global Inequality

Material living standards are improving in most countries of the world. Yet there is nothing in logic that guarantees an automatic link between growth and reductions in global poverty; it might be that the poorest countries in the world are not growing at all—as was true in much of Africa in the 1980s and early 1990s—or it might be that, where there is growth, it has benefited only the already well-to-do within each country. Those who believe that globalization and economic growth are benefiting only the rich often make one or both of these arguments. Certainly, as we have already seen, there are almost unimaginable differences in average material living standards between countries, and the gaps between rich and poor within each country are hardly less wide. Are these inequalities getting wider with general economic progress? Is everyone benefiting or is it only the already rich who made the Great Escape, leaving the less fortunate behind?

One way to answer the question is to see whether initially poor countries have grown faster than initially rich countries, something that must happen if the gaps between them are to narrow. If it is progress in science and practical knowledge that makes economic growth possible, then we might expect country living standards to move closer to one another, at least if the knowledge and techniques can easily be transferred from one country to another.

Start with Figure 4, which shows a more or less random scatter of dots. Each point in the figure is a country and shows its average per capita growth rate on the vertical axis against its initial GDP per person on the horizontal axis. The dark circles take 1960 as the starting point and look at growth from 1960 to 2010, while the lighter circles start from 1970 and show growth from 1970 to 2010. The lack of any patterns in the dots means that the poor countries did not grow faster than the rich countries, so that there was no catch-up, and no reduction in the inequality between countries. Nor did the rich countries grow faster than the poor countries. Overall, cross-country inequality did not change by very much. Nearly all of the growth rates are positive and lie above the broken line that indicates zero growth.

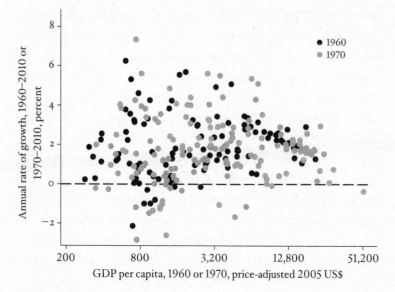

FIGURE 4 Growth, country by country.

There has been lots of growth in the world over the past half-century; only four countries had lower per capita incomes in 2010 than in 1960, and only fourteen had lower incomes than in 1970. As always, we should remember that some of the worst-performing countries (e.g., those at war) are excluded because there are no data for them, or because they did not exist in the earlier years. (The two worst performers in Figure 4 are the DRC and Liberia, both of which suffered wars.)

There is a different and more positive way of looking at exactly the same data. Figure 5, which was first drawn in this way by economist Stanley Fischer, is identical to Figure 4, but each country is now plotted with a circle whose area is proportional to its population in the starting year.[13] Looked at in this way, we get an immediate visual impression of a strong *negative* relation, with poorer countries growing faster. But we already know that the poorer countries did *not* grow more rapidly! The difference in perception comes from blowing up the dots for the biggest countries. The two largest countries in the world, China and India, have grown very rapidly over the past half-century. And because there are so many people in both, their growth has brought the average incomes of more than two billion people from the bottom of the world income distribution—where they began—to somewhere much closer to the middle—where they are now. If each person in each country had the average income of the whole country, Figure 5 would show that the living standards of all the people in the world have drawn closer together, although there has been no narrowing of the average living standards of countries. Of course, it is not at all true that everyone shares the same income in each country; not only is there income inequality within countries but, as we shall see in Chapter 6, income inequality is widening in many (but not all) countries. Once within-country income inequality is taken into account, what is happening to income inequality over all the citizens of the world is much less clear, though a good case can be made that it is decreasing.

The rapid growth of China and India has not only enabled hundreds of millions of the world's citizens to make the Great Escape but made the world a more equal place. If we care about *people,* rather than *countries,* the optimistic picture in Figure 5, not the pessimistic picture in Figure 4, is the correct one.

The story of global poverty is also much affected by what has been happening in China and India. The World Bank regularly calculates the total number of people in the world who live in households whose daily income is less than a dollar a person. The latest version of these numbers up to 2008, as calculated by the World Bank, is shown in Figure 6.[14] The total number of dollar-a-day poor people in the world fell by three-quarters of a billion between 1981 and 2008 in spite of an increase in the total population of poor countries of about two bil-

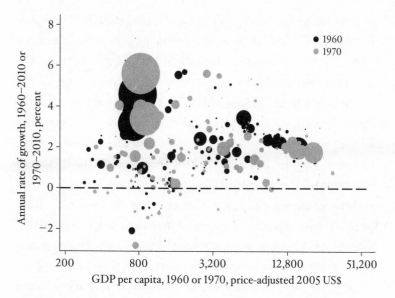

FIGURE 5 Growth weighted by country population.

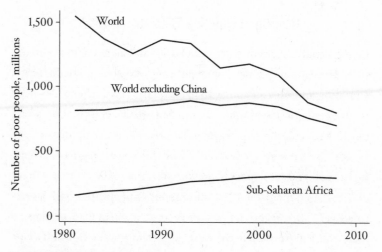

FIGURE 6 World poverty is falling.

lion. As a result the fraction of the world's population that lives below a dollar a day has fallen from more than 40 percent to 14 percent. Although the poverty rate has fallen in other regions of the world, the fall in absolute numbers of poor has been driven in large part by the rapid growth of China, so that, at least until the past ten years, the absolute number of non-Chinese poor has continued to increase. (As we shall see in Chapter 6, there is a case to be made that Indian statistics are missing an increasing share of what people actually have, so that these numbers would understate how much progress India has made in reducing poverty.) For Africa south of the Sahara, the Bank calculates that 37 percent of the population lived on less than a dollar a day in 2008, down from a peak of 49 percent in 1993; African economies have been growing in recent years, albeit from low levels. As always, African data should be treated with a good deal of caution. So in global poverty, too, there is general progress—not everywhere and not at all times, but a quarter-century of global growth has done much to reduce global poverty.

How Do People See Their Own Lives?

Living a good life needs more than health and money, and the escape from deprivation that development brings should also involve better education and a better ability to participate in civic affairs. My main focus here is on health and income, but the general picture is very much the same: there has been great progress in recent decades, although much remains to be done. More children are regularly attending school, and more people are literate. And while there are many dictators, and many hundreds of millions of people live with (sometimes very severe) restrictions on their civic participation, there is more political freedom in the world now than was the case half a century ago. Life is getting better for most of the world, at least in terms of the opportunities that these circumstances allow.[15] Yet it is always possible that people do not see their lives in terms of these measures, and that they are more prized by development experts or academic commentators than by the people who are experiencing them. Or people may value different things that are not included in our lists. So there is a good deal to be said for asking people how *they* think their lives are going.

One way to do this is to use self-reported measures of wellbeing, like those described in Figures 1 and 2 of the Introduction. Economists, psychologists, and philosophers have recently become interested in these measures, and a number of national statistical offices are moving toward the routine collection of such data.[16] These measures, which are often loosely referred to as measures of happiness, have many attractions: they come directly from the people whose wellbeing we are trying to assess, they measure actual achieved outcomes, and they might possibly include the effects of factors that are important for wellbeing, but which we do not know about, or which we know about but cannot measure.

Yet many writers, both economists and philosophers, have reservations about the validity and usefulness of self-reported measures of wellbeing. We do not always know what people are thinking when they answer these questions, and there are doubts about whether the questions are interpreted the same way by different people or by different nations. Translation of questions is sometimes difficult even when a direct translation exists; Americans use "happy" more freely and more frequently than the French use "heureux," and East Asians seem especially reluctant to say that they are happy.[17] In the United States, the pursuit of happiness is one of the unalienable rights enumerated in the Declaration of Independence, yet in the Calvinist Scottish village in which I grew up, such a pursuit would have been seen as indicating a serious weakness of character.

Of greater concern still is adaptation; people living in desperate circumstances can come to believe that this is the best that life can offer and report that they are happy. Others, who live in the lap of luxury, have become so used to wealth that they can become dissatisfied over the absence of trivial luxuries.[18] A full and happy life can sometimes involve pain and loss; the philosopher Martha Nussbaum writes about the "happy warrior" going into battle, expecting to meet nothing but pain and possible death, who nevertheless feels that he is leading a good and worthy life.[19] These reservations do not mean that we should ignore what people say about their lives, only that we should be alert to the potential problems and not turn off our skepticism.

If people always adapt so as to be satisfied with what they have, the average answer should not vary much across countries; most of the rich countries of the world have been rich for a long time, and most of the poor countries have been poor for a long time, so that people have had plenty of time to get used to their circumstances. But the figures in the Introduction show that this is not what happens.

The life evaluation score for Denmark (perennially the best performer in these comparisons) is 7.97 (on a "ladder" scale with "steps" marked from 0 to 10), followed by the other Nordic countries— Finland 7.67, Norway 7.63, and Sweden 7.51—with the United States only a little behind them at 7.28. Togo (a long-standing dictatorship) is 2.81, Sierra Leone (after years of civil war) is 3.00, and Zimbabwe (yet another long-standing dictatorship) is 3.17. Burundi at 3.56, Benin at 3.67, and Afghanistan at 3.72 come next on the roll of misery. The philosophical doubts about these measures are real enough, but when it comes to assessing deprivation and identifying the countries where people do or do not flourish, the life evaluation measures are in close accord with measures of income, health, or political freedom. The rich, developed, and democratic countries of Europe, America, and the European offshoots are better places to live than the poorest countries of sub-Saharan Africa, Asia, and Latin America, and we get the same result from direct questions about how life is going as we do from looking at income or longevity.

It would be good to look at answers to the life evaluation question over the past half-century, to go back and compare what has happened since 1960, just as I did for the relationship between income and health. But Gallup's World Poll began only in 2006, and although there are scattered data for a few countries from earlier years, we know little about the reliability of these numbers, or even how the respondents were selected. So we currently cannot say whether or not the growth in the world over the past half-century has brought an increase in life evaluation.

Even so, that the residents of richer countries systematically value their lives more highly than those of poorer countries creates a strong presumption that growth is good for the way that people feel about their lives. The most obvious difference between Denmark and the United States on the one hand, and Sierra Leone, Togo, and Zimbabwe on the other, is that one group is rich and the other poor; that difference is the result of 250 years of growth in the rich countries versus none in the poor countries. There are also enormous differences in life expectancy, as we have already seen, but life expectancy too has increased along with economic growth in the past half-century. So it would be strange indeed if the average life evaluation in China, Germany, Japan, or the United States in 2008 would not be higher than those countries' average life evaluations in 1960. But this seemingly uncontroversial conclusion has been mired in debate.

In 1974, the economist and historian Richard Easterlin, a pioneer in measuring self-reported wellbeing, argued that economic growth in Japan had not made people's lives better by their own reports, and in subsequent work he extended the finding to a number of countries, including the United States.[20] His claim, then and now, is that economic growth does not improve the human lot. Easterlin is unusual among economists in arguing that growth is worthless in and of itself. (He does not question the health and other benefits that have come with—although not necessarily *because* of—economic growth.) His position resonates with many psychologists, religious leaders, and others who deny the materialist basis of wellbeing, except perhaps among the most deprived. The economists Betsey Stevenson and Justin Wolfers have challenged these beliefs and argue that, with properly comparable data, economic growth within countries improves life evaluation in exactly the way that we would expect from the differences in life evaluation between rich and poor countries.[21]

The effects of economic growth on a country's life evaluation are much harder to see than are the effects of differences between rich and poor countries. Even fifty years of economic growth does not move a country very far compared with international differences that are the result of *centuries* of differences in growth rates. If a country were to maintain a constant rate of growth of 2 percent a year for half a century (about the average in Figure 4), its per capita national income would be 2.7 times larger at the end of the period. This is a substantial increase, but it is about the same as the difference between India and Thailand today. Given that countries do not lie exactly on the line linking life evaluation and income, it would not be surprising if such periods of economic growth were accompanied by increases in life evaluation that are small, hard to detect, or even perverse. Indeed, as Figure 1 in the Introduction shows, China, whose per capita income in 2008 was twice that of India's, has a substantially lower life evaluation score.

Just as there are countries whose health is better or worse than can be expected from looking at their incomes, there are countries whose residents rate their lives more or less highly than can be expected from their incomes. We have already seen that the Scandinavian countries are wellbeing superstars, but they are also very rich countries, and their life evaluation scores are not much higher than would be predicted from their national incomes. Another frequent finding is that Latin American countries often do very well. Several of the East Asian countries do relatively badly, including China, Hong Kong, Japan, and Korea. We do not know whether these continental differences come from genuine differences in some objective aspect of wellbeing, from national differences in disposition, or from national differences in the way people respond to the ladder question. One frequent finding is an exceptionally low level of wellbeing for Russia, the countries of the former Soviet Union, and the countries of Eastern Europe that were once part of the communist bloc. It is the elderly who are particularly unhappy with their lives in these Eastern European and former Soviet countries.[22] Young people there have opportunities that were not available to previous generations, including the chance to travel, to study abroad, and to find a place for their talents in the global economy. At the same time, their grandparents have seen the collapse of the world that they knew and that gave meaning to their lives, and in some cases have also experienced disruptions to their pensions and health-care systems.

Emotional Wellbeing

Life evaluation measures are often described as measures of happiness, even though, as in the ladder question, there may be no mention of happiness in the question. There is now good evidence that life evaluation measures, which ask people to think about how their lives are going, pick up different aspects of experience and give different results from questions about feelings or experienced emotions. It is possible to be unhappy or worried, or to feel stress, even at times when you think your life is generally going well. Indeed, sadness, pain, and stress might be inevitable during some of the experiences one must go through in order to build a good life. Army boot camp, graduate studies in economics, medical school, or dealing with the death of a parent are examples of unpleasant experiences that are nevertheless an essential part of life; young people go on dates that sometimes result in dreadful experiences, yet they are a necessary part of emotional learning. These emotional experiences and others are important contributors to current wellbeing in their own right. Yet feeling happy is better than feeling sad, and stress, worry, and anger reduce wellbeing at the time they are being experienced, even if they sometimes have payoffs in the future.

Just as we can ask people to evaluate their own lives, we can also ask them about their emotional experiences. The Gallup World Poll, in addition to its life evaluation question, asks people about the emotions and feelings that they experienced the day before the survey, asking about worry, stress, sadness, depression, happiness, anger, and pain. It turns out that national average responses to these questions are quite different from national averages of life evaluation.

The global map of happiness is shown in Figure 7, which plots national income against the fraction of the population who report that they experienced happiness during a lot of the day yesterday. This map is quite different from the map of life evaluation; most notably, there is a much weaker relationship with national income. Although it is true that some of the very poorest countries—such as Burkina Faso, Burundi, Madagascar, and Togo—report very little happiness, there is little systematic difference in happiness between rich and poor in countries other than the very poorest. Denmark, where people think that their lives are going extremely well, is not so good a place for experiencing happiness. Nor is Italy, and indeed a

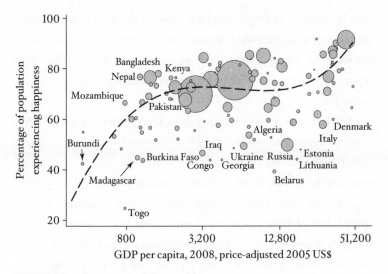

FIGURE 7 Happiness around the world.

larger fraction of Bangladeshis, Kenyans, Nepalese, and Pakistanis experience a great deal of happiness than do Danes or Italians.

The limited relationship between income and experienced happiness holds true within the United States too. Poverty generates misery, but beyond a certain point (about $70,000 a year), additional money does nothing to improve happiness, even though those with more money report that they have better lives.[23] For happiness money matters only up to a point. This is useful to know, if only because the experience of happiness is a positive one that makes life better. But it makes happiness a poor measure of overall wellbeing, because there are many places in the world where people manage to find happiness even in the midst of poor health and material poverty; life evaluation measures are much better measures of overall wellbeing. The cases of Denmark and Italy are good examples.

The happiness map shows that the United States, where being happy is something of a civic responsibility, is third from the top, bettered only by Ireland and New Zealand. Russia and its former satellites are among the unhappiest countries in the world. Yet most people in the world are happy; nearly three-quarters of the world's population report that they experienced happiness during a lot of the day yesterday.

Other measures of emotional experience provide different pictures yet again. In 2008, 19 percent of the world's population experienced anger during a lot of the day before the survey, 30 percent experienced stress, 30 percent experienced worry, and 23 percent experienced pain. There is more pain in poorer countries, though there is lots of variation at any given income level. But the national averages of worry, stress, and anger are not at all related to national income, although they too vary a great deal from one country to another. For example, three-quarters of Filipinos report a great deal of stress, followed by the citizens of Hong Kong, Lebanon, Syria, and the United States, where 44 percent report that they experienced stress during a lot of the previous day. National income seems to do little to relieve these negative emotions.

Life evaluation and happiness (or other emotions) paint different pictures of the world. Which is correct? This is a sensible question only if we expect such measures to yield a single measure of overall wellbeing, something that is a goal of much of the happiness literature. But this is not the right way to think about wellbeing. It is good to be happy, it is not good to be worried or to be angry, and it is good to think that your life is going well. But these feelings are not the same thing, and all are consistent with good or bad outcomes in other aspects of wellbeing, such as income and physical and mental health. There is no magic question that provides a touchstone for judging wellbeing. Even if people carried a personal "hedonimeter," which, like a wristwatch, would register happiness at every moment, there is no reason to suppose that the reading on the hedonimeter would be useful for assessing the goodness in their lives. Human well-being has many different aspects, often related but not the same, and if we are to measure the wellbeing of the world, we must recognize and do justice to that richness.

The historian Keith Thomas writes about changes in the ways that people sought personal fulfillment in England, and how, by the eighteenth century, the pursuit of wealth came to be seen as a legitimate and ethical route to happiness.[24] Adam Smith's *Wealth of Nations* crystallized the long-evolving idea that the pursuit of wealth not only was a respectable activity for individuals but also brought benefits to society as a whole. Smith's metaphor of the "invisible hand" has become part of our understanding of how capitalism works. Yet, as Thomas notes, Smith was skeptical about the personal benefits of wealth. Indeed, in his *Theory of Moral Sentiments,* Smith described the idea that wealth would make as happy as a deception, albeit a useful one "which rouses and keeps in perpetual motion the industry of mankind." He was also skeptical about the extent of inequality, arguing that the rich, by employing others "in the gratification of their own vain and insatiable demands," brought about an approximately equal distribution of the "necessaries of life." As for the rich man, his great possessions "keep off the summer shower, not the winter storm, but leave him always as much, and sometimes more exposed than before, to anxiety, to fear, and to sorrow; to diseases, to danger, and to death."[25]

Smith wrote as the Great Divergence was about to begin, and in an age in which infectious disease threatened poor and rich alike. As we shall see in the next chapter, life expectancy was no higher for English aristocrats than for the common people. Even today, as we have just seen, the emotional lives of the poor are not very different from those of the rich, though they are much less satisfied with their lives; riches are no protection against anxiety, fear, and sorrow, and they are not required to experience the happiness and enjoyment of everyday life. But the world has changed in the past 250 years. There is no reasonable interpretation of the evidence in which even the "necessaries of life" are equally distributed around the world, nor is it likely that they were so in Britain in Smith's day. And riches today provide powerful protection against the dangers of disease and of death. As the world as a whole has become richer and has learned more, especially over the past sixty years, these protections have been extended to more and more of its population.

Income and health have improved almost everywhere since World War II. There is not a single country in the world where infant or child mortality today is not lower than it was in 1950.[26] Economic growth has propelled millions of people out of awful destitution, particularly in China and in India. Yet there have been terrible reversals. The Chinese famine, the HIV/AIDS pandemic, the collapse of longevity in the former Soviet Union, and scores of wars, massacres, and famines remind us that the curses of disease, war, and bad politics are not monsters safely confined to history. It would be rash indeed to suppose otherwise: as in the movie, the Great Escape might not bring permanent freedom but only a temporary reprieve from the evil, darkness, and disorder that surround us.

PART I   LIFE AND DEATH

TWO

From Prehistory to 1945

THE WORLD IS A HEALTHIER PLACE now than at almost any time in the past. People live longer, they are taller and stronger, and their children are less likely to be sick or to die. Better health makes life better in and of itself, and it allows us to do more with our lives, to work more effectively, to earn more, to spend more time learning, and to enjoy more and better time with our families and friends. Health is not a single quantity like temperature; someone might have terrific eyesight but poor physical stamina, or might live for many years but have serious recurrent depression or migraines. The seriousness of any given limitation depends on what a person does or would like to do. My lousy throwing arm was an occasional embarrassment in high school, but it is not a problem for a professor. Health has many dimensions, and it is hard to boil it down to a single convenient number. However, one aspect of health is easy to measure and is of overriding importance: the simple fact of being alive or dead. Knowing this is of limited use for an individual—one would certainly expect more from one's physician than the diagnosis "well, you are alive"—but measures of life and death are invaluable for thinking about the health of groups of people, either whole populations or subgroups, such as men and women, blacks and whites, or children and the elderly.

One familiar measure of life and death is how long a newborn baby can expect to live. This is known as life expectancy at birth, or often simply life expectancy. Provided life is worth living, having more years to live is good, and it is usually true (but not inevitably so) that populations in which people live longer are also populations in which people are healthier while they are alive. We saw in Chapter 1 how life expectancy varies around the world, how it is longer in richer countries, and how it has been generally increasing over time. In this chapter, we look in more detail at the how and why of life expectancy and how the world got to where it is now. This book is not a history of health, nor a history of life expectancy,[1] but there is much to be learned from looking at the past, and we will not have much chance of a better future if we do not try to understand it.

To establish where we are now, and to introduce some of the ideas that we shall need, I start with the past century or so of mortality and life expectancy in the United States. I then retreat back—way back— to see what life was like at its very beginnings, and then fast-forward to about 1945. The end of World War II is a convenient resting point because, after 1945, there are much better data, and because the story line changes.

Basic Notions of Life and Death, Illustrated by the United States

Life expectancy in the United States increased from 47.3 years in 1900 to 77.9 years in 2006. Figure 1 plots the numbers separately for men and women; women typically live longer than men, and they did so throughout the twentieth century. Both men and women had large increases in life span: 28.8 years for men and 31.9 years for women.

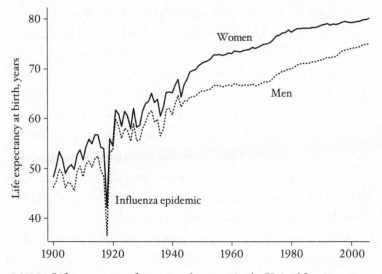

FIGURE 1 Life expectancy for men and women in the United States.

The rate of increase was faster in the first half of the century but continues on today; in the past quarter-century, the life span of men has increased by one year every five years, and the life span of women, by one year every ten years. The first thing to take away from the figure, as is the case for much of this book, is that things are getting better, and hugely so. To have increased life spans by thirty years over a little more than a century is an extraordinary achievement, a Great Escape indeed. Having registered that big fact, we can note some of the secondary features of the figure. Why are men and women so different, not only in the years of life they can expect, but also in the rates at which their life expectancies are improving? Why does the first half-century look so different from the period after World War II?

An immediate feature of the figure is the large dip in life expectancy during the influenza epidemic at the end of World War I. Life expectancy in 1918 was 11.8 years lower than life expectancy in 1917 and then rose again by 15.6 years in 1919, and life expectancy was back on its trend immediately after the epidemic. In the world as a whole, more than fifty million people may have died in the epidemic, more than half a million of them in the United States. Yet the way that life expectancy is defined tends to exaggerate the epidemic's effect on the life chances of a newborn child. In hindsight, we know that the flu epidemic would last only one year, so that if the baby made it through its first year of life, there would be no further threat from the epidemic. But when demographers calculate life expectancy in 1918, they assume that the epidemic will be permanent, and in 1919, they forget that it ever existed. This may seem like an odd way to assess life chances, but, in fact, it is hard to see how to do better.

When we are presented with a newborn child today and asked to calculate how long we think he or she will live, we need to know about the risks of dying in the years ahead, something that we do not know. Demographers work around that problem by using information on the risks at the time of birth, and they calculate how long the baby would be expected to live if the risks of dying at each age were exactly the same as they are today. In the case of an epidemic like the 1918–19 influenza epidemic, the mortality risk at every age was suddenly increased in 1918, so when life expectancy at birth is calculated for that year, the assumption is that the baby will face the age-specific risks of the epidemic in every year of life. This would make sense if the epidemic were to last forever, or at least for the lifetime of the child, but if the epidemic lasts only a year or two, the sharp drop in life expectancy overstates the real risks over the child's life. We can do better than this, but only with hindsight, once we wait until everyone in the child's birth cohort has died—which will be a wait of more than a century—or if we make forecasts. But forecasts have difficulties of their own—for example, no one in 1917 would have predicted the influenza epidemic at all.

Standard life expectancy measures—the ones that do not wait until everyone is dead and that do not make forecasts—are called "period" measures, meaning that they are calculated on the assumption that the mortality risks of the period are fixed forever. Not only can this be an issue for episodes like the influenza epidemic but it is also a problem for thinking about life expectancy today. When we look at Figure 1 and think about the future, it is hard not to think that life expectancy will continue to increase and mortality rates will continue to fall. Which means that life expectancy today, which is a little over 80 for a girl child born in the United States, is likely to underestimate the expectation of life for today's newborn, who might reasonably expect—if progress continues—to live to be a centenarian.

The influenza epidemic is only one of the reasons why the graphs in Figure 1 are so much more variable before 1950 than after 1950. While there was nothing comparable to that disaster, there were many smaller waves of disease that were large enough to show up in the life expectancy of the population. Infectious diseases that do not concern us much today were still threats in the United States in 1900, when the leading causes of death were, in order of importance, influenza, tuberculosis, and diarrhea. Tuberculosis remained in the top three until 1923, and in the top ten until 1953. Infectious diseases, including pneumonia, diarrheal disease, and measles, brought early death to many children. At the beginning of the century the deaths of children from these infectious diseases were relatively more important than they are today, when most deaths are among the elderly, and from chronic diseases like cancer and heart disease, not from infections. This change is the same epidemiological transition that we saw in Chapter 1 when we compared rich and poor countries today, and which took place over time in today's rich countries.

The "aging of death," from children to the elderly, makes life expectancy less sensitive to year-to-year fluctuations in deaths which, with the reduction in infectious disease, are themselves less pronounced today than in the past. Saving the lives of children has a bigger effect on life expectancy than saving the lives of the elderly. A newborn who might have died but does not has the chance to live many more years, which is not the case when a 70-year-old is pulled through a life-threatening crisis. This is also one of the reasons why the rate of increase in life expectancy has slowed down in recent years; mortality among children is now so low that progress can only really take place among older adults, among whom reductions in mortality rates have smaller effects on life expectancy.

Just because life expectancy is more sensitive to early-life than to late-life mortality, it does not follow that it is more important or more worthwhile to save the life of a child than to save the life of an adult. That is an ethical judgment that depends on many factors. On the one hand, saving a child saves many more potential years of life, while on the other, the death of a newborn does not entail the end of the many projects, interests, relationships, and friendships that are part of an adult life. Along these lines, the economist Victor Fuchs has suggested that the value of a life might be judged by the number of people who come to the funeral, a not entirely serious proposal that neatly captures the idea of down-weighting the very young as well as the very old. But such matters cannot be settled by the mechanical choice of a particular measure of health, such as life expectancy. Life expectancy is a useful measure, and it captures much that is important about population health. However, if we choose it as a measure of wellbeing, and set it as one of society's targets, we are buying into an ethical judgment that more heavily weights mortality at younger ages. Such judgments need to be explicitly defended, not simply adopted without thought.

The choice of life expectancy can sometimes be downright mis-leading. Figure 1 shows that life expectancy rose much more rapidly in the first half of the twentieth century than in the second half. This happened because infant and child mortality was high in 1900, and because reductions in mortality among the young have much larger effects on life expectancy than the reductions in mortality among the middle-aged and elderly that were so important at the end of the century. If we think of life expectancy as *the* measure of population health, or even as a good measure of general social progress, we can easily convince ourselves that the United States did better before 1950 than after 1950. It is certainly possible to argue that case, but focusing on life expectancy prioritizes mortality decline among the young over mortality decline among the old, and that is an ethical choice that needs to be argued, not just taken for granted. The same issue appears when we compare mortality decline in poor countries—mostly among children—with mortality decline in rich countries—mostly among the elderly. If we use life expectancy, poor countries are catching up in health and welfare, but such a catch-up is not a *fact* about health or even about mortality in general but an *assumption,* that life expectancy is the best indicator of health and social progress. I shall return to these issues in Chapter 4.

Figure 1 shows that the difference in life expectancy between American men and women, although always in favor of women, is dif-ferent today than it was in the past. The difference in life spans was two to three years at the beginning of the twentieth century and rose in fits and starts until the late 1970s, after which it fell again, in the early years of the twenty-first century, to about five years. The differ-ences in mortality rates between males and females are far from fully understood. Women face lower risks of death than men throughout the world, and throughout life; men are at higher risk even before they are born. The exception is maternal mortality, a risk from which men are exempt, and the reduction in maternal mortality in twentieth-century America is one reason why women's life expectancy has risen faster than men's.

A much more important reason is changing patterns of smoking. Smoking causes death both through heart disease—relatively quickly—and through lung cancer—with about a thirty-year wait between exposure and death. The slowdown in the rate of improvement in life expectancy among men in the 1950s and 1960s owes much to the earlier rise in their cigarette smoking. Men started smoking much earlier than women—among whom smoking was socially disapproved for many years, an injustice that did wonders for women's health!—but men also quit much sooner. The slowdown in life expectancy growth for women happens right at the end of the graph, two or three decades after the corresponding slowdown for men. In recent years, American women have also sharply reduced their smoking, and the rates of lung cancer for women have begun to turn down, as did those for men many years ago. For the rich countries of the world in the second half of the twentieth century, smoking is one of the most important determinants of mortality and of life expectancy.

The inequality in mortality between men and women is far from the only inequality between groups in the United States. In 2006, life expectancy at birth for African-American men was six years less than life expectancy for white men; for women, the difference was in the same direction, but smaller: 4.1 years. And like the differences between men and women, these differences have not remained constant over time. The Centers for Disease Control and Prevention estimate that, at the beginning of the twentieth century, there was a more than fifteen-year gap in life expectancy between whites and what were then known as nonwhites, a broader category than African-Americans.

Inequalities in life expectancy echo other inequalities between black and white in America—in income, in wealth, in education, and for much of the century, even in the opportunity to vote or to run for office. This consistent pattern of inequality in so many dimensions means that the gaps in wellbeing are even starker than the gaps in any one dimension, such as mortality or income. Any study of inequities between blacks and whites in the United States has to look at the whole picture at once, not just at health or only at wealth. Inequalities in mortality between ethnic and racial groups are not well understood, although unequal provision of health care is certainly important. The reduction of gaps in life expectancy and in child mortality is part of the general reduction in racial differences over the century, and a reduction in one inequality tends to contribute to reductions in others. That such differences defy simple explanations is shown by the mortality rates of Hispanics in the United States, whose life expectancy in 2006 was two and a half years *longer* than the life expectancy of non-Hispanic whites. The Great Escape from premature death in the United States has come to both men and women, and to all racial and ethnic groups, but the different groups started from different places, and made their escapes at different rates, so that patterns of inequalities have also changed over time.

Although the United States spends almost twice as much on health care as any other country, its citizens are not the longest lived. British and American life expectancies were very similar until the 1950s. There then followed a twenty-year period of British advantage which was lost in the 1980s, but then opened up again in the late 1990s and the early years of the new century. A gap of less than half a year in 1991 had grown to a gap of one and a half years by 2006. The gap between the United States and Sweden is much larger, more than three years in favor of the Swedes. Although the Swedish advantage has grown in the past few years, it goes back as long as we have records. In Chapter 4, I shall return to the gaps in life expectancy between the rich countries and try to explain what might be causing them. As is the case between groups within the United States, the experience of escape has been different for different countries. As we shall see, these differences are dwarfed by the differences between rich and poor countries.

To understand more about life expectancy, we need to dig deeper and look at mortality at different ages. Figure 2 shows how mortality rates vary with age for a selection of countries and years: Sweden in 1751 (Swedish data go back further than in any other country), the United States in 1933 and in 2000, and the Netherlands, also in 2000.[2] (The graph for Sweden in 2000 is close to that for the Netherlands, but a little lower at young and high ages.) These graphs show mortality rates for each age up to age 80—the number of people older than 80 thins out to the point where the graphs are unreliable. Mortality

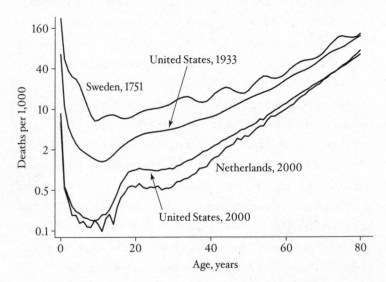

FIGURE 2 Mortality rates by age, selected countries and periods.

rates are shown as deaths per thousand people who are alive at that age. So, for example, the top curve shows that in Sweden in 1751, more than 160 out of every thousand newborns did not make it to their first birthday, while at age 30, only ten out of every thousand 30-year-olds did not survive to become 31. The logarithmic scale is useful here too, and I have used it for the vertical axis, so that the (fourfold) move from 0.5 to 2 shows up as the same size as the (fourfold) move from 10 to 40. The lowest mortality rates in the graph, for 10-year-olds today, are a thousand times lower than the mortality rates for newborns in Sweden in 1751, or only a tenth of the rates for 10-year-olds in the United States in 1933.

Mortality curves have a characteristic shape, reminiscent of the Nike "swoosh": starting high at low ages, falling sharply to reach a low point in the early teens, and then rising steadily with age. The risk of death is at its greatest early in life and then again in old age. A vivid illustration comes from a sign in the washroom of a maternity hospital that I visited, urging patrons to wash their hands thoroughly because "the first few days of life are critical." Beneath this was scrawled, "not as critical as the last few days." The joke mostly pokes fun at the medical profession's use of the word *critical,* but it neatly highlights the fact that we are in most danger of dying very early and very late in life.

Whether young life or old life is the more dangerous has changed over the years. In Sweden in 1751—well before the modern mortality decline—it was riskier to be a newborn than to be an 80-year-old. Today, when the chance of dying in the first year of life is less than 1 percent, it is more than six times riskier to be an 80-year-old. In the eighteenth century and for thousands of years before that, many people died as children; in Sweden in 1751, about a third of children died before their fifth birthday. Today, in Sweden and in other rich countries, almost everyone lives to die when they are old; indeed the Swedish infant mortality rate today is only around three per thousand.

The changing balance between young and old mortality means that, in a country where many children die, almost no one will actually live the number of years that national life expectancy says they should. We usually think of an average as a sort of "representative" or typical figure, but one of the peculiarities of the average number of years lived is that this is incorrect. In Sweden in the late eighteenth century, life expectancy was in the low to mid-30s, from which one might easily, but wrongly, conclude that few people lived to be old, and that few children ever got to know their grandparents. But this was not true; if you were lucky enough to get past the dangers of childhood, then you had a good chance of making it into old age—not as good as would be the case today, but enough to ensure that you had a fair chance of knowing your grandchildren. An extreme case would be one in which half of newborns die at birth and the other half live to be 50. Life expectancy at birth is 25, but no one dies at 25, and remaining life expectancy at first birthday is 49 years, 24 years longer than life expectancy at birth! A less extreme but real example comes from England in the middle of the nineteenth century, where life expectancy at 15 (sometimes called "adult" life expectancy) was higher than life expectancy at birth; I will come back to this later. More generally, keeping the mortality "swoosh" in mind is the key to understanding changes in life chances over time as well as the differences between rich and poor countries.

The mortality "swooshes" in Figure 2 show steady progress over time, with the "swooshes" for later dates always beneath those for earlier dates. We do not have data for the United States or the Netherlands in the eighteenth century, but we can suppose that the picture was roughly similar to that for Sweden. Life in 1933 and in 2000 was much less risky, with very large percentage reductions in mortality compared with earlier years, especially at younger ages, but not excluding the elderly, who did particularly well between 1933 and 2000. The comparison of the Netherlands and the United States in 2000 shows, once again, that the United States does badly compared with other rich countries; mortality rates in the United States in 2000 were higher than mortality rates in the Netherlands at all ages up to age 73. This pattern between the United States and the Netherlands carries over to comparisons between the United States and other rich countries. For those who live long enough, mortality rates are extraordinarily low in the United States, perhaps because of the willingness of the American medical system to use every means available to save lives, even among those with only a few years left to live.

The bottom two curves, for the United States and the Netherlands in 2000, show a temporary peak in mortality around age 20. Between ages 15 and 34, the leading causes of death are not disease—except briefly during the AIDS epidemic and before the advent of anti-retroviral drugs—but accidents, homicide, and suicide. The mortality curves for earlier periods show that these dangerous and sometimes deadly behaviors by young people—particularly young men—are much more pronounced now than seventy years ago, and they do not appear at all in Sweden in the eighteenth century.

Where do the numbers in the figures come from? How do we know about mortality rates? In the wealthy countries of the Organisation for Economic Co-operation and Development (OECD) today, all births and deaths are registered with the government as they occur. Babies have birth certificates, and when people die, doctors or hospitals issue death certificates listing their particulars, including age, sex, and cause of death. This is known as the "vital registration system," *vital* in this context meaning to do with life and death. In order to make sure that birth and death records are correct, the vital registration system needs to be *complete*, meaning that every birth and every death must be registered. To get mortality rates, we also need to know the population by age, sex, and race so as to be able to calculate the fractions who have died; these counts come from regular censuses of the population, which most countries carry out every decade or so (for some reason, almost always in years ending in either zero or one).

Sweden was one of the first countries to have a complete vital registration system, which is why we have Swedish mortality rates for as early as the eighteenth century. London started collecting "bills of mortality" in the seventeenth century, and parish registers in Europe go back even further. The Puritans in Massachusetts thought that registration should be the business of the state, not the church, and Massachusetts had a vital registration system by 1639. Yet it was only in 1933 that all American states had complete registration, itself an important marker of government capacity. Without comprehensive data on births and deaths, a society is ignorant of the most basic facts about its citizens, and many of the roles that government exercises, and that today we take for granted, become impossible. The Swedes in the eighteenth century and the Puritans in Massachusetts were visionaries and pioneers in good government.

The American life expectancy data in Figure 1 before 1933 refer only to the states with registration. For countries with less than complete vital registration, or that lack good census data—probably a majority of countries in the world even today lack the state capacity to maintain either—demographers have developed tricks and approximations for filling in the blanks. For infant and child mortality, which remains a common occurrence in many countries, surveys of mothers can tell us how many children have been born and how many have survived. The United States Agency for International Development funds an invaluable series of surveys—the Demographic and Health Surveys—which collect this information for many poor countries where vital registration either does not exist or exists but is ignored in practice. (Parents do not register the births of their children, and when children or adults die, they are buried or cremated according to local custom, without the information being gathered into any national database.)

For the deaths of adults, there remain substantial gaps in information in many countries—where even the best estimates are little more than guesses—and in those cases it is impossible to draw the complete mortality "swooshes" that appear in Figure 2. Life expectancy is a little easier to guess, because it is so heavily influenced by child mortality, but in countries where adult mortality is unusual or variable—such as those affected by the HIV/AIDS epidemic—life expectancy estimates also need to be treated very cautiously. For all of these reasons, it is useful to look at the health experience of the poorest countries separately from that of the rich countries, which is what I shall do in Chapters 3 and 4.

Life and Death in Prehistory

How did today's mortality patterns come about? What caused the huge increase in life expectancy in the twentieth century? What was life like in the past, what made it get better, and what lessons does the past hold for improving the health of the large fraction of the world's population that has not yet escaped from the tentacles of early death?

For perhaps 95 percent of the time that humans have existed, for hundreds of thousands of years, people lived by hunting and gathering. Today, when there are only a few hunter-gatherer groups left in the world, nearly all living in marginal environments such as deserts or the Arctic, it might seem strange that life among such people has any relevance for our health. But it was the hunter-gatherer existence that shaped us, if only because of the enormous spans of time involved. Human beings *evolved* to be hunter-gatherers, and our bodies and minds were adapted for success in such an existence. Humans have lived in modern circumstances, as farmers or city-dwellers, for "only" a few thousand years, and it helps in understanding our health today if we know something about the conditions for which our bodies were designed.

We cannot look back and know how our ancestors lived and died hundreds of thousands of years ago, but much has been learned from the archeological record, including the examination of skeletal remains (paleopathology), which provide an amazing amount of information about nutrition, disease, and causes of death. Paleopathology can also estimate age at death from even partial skeletons, so we know something about life expectancy. Anthropologists have been studying actual hunter-gatherer groups for much of the past two hundred years, though some of the best evidence—including medical evidence—comes from contemporaneous groups (with appropriate adjustments made for their contact with modern society). Taken together, the two sources of evidence have provided a remarkable amount of useful data.[3]

Diet is a good starting point. So is exercise. Hunter-gatherers did a lot of brisk walking, tracking down prey, perhaps ten or fifteen miles a day. Their diet contained mostly fruits and vegetables, which were typically more easily obtained than animals. Wild plants—as opposed to their cultivated descendants—are fibrous, so hunter-gatherers ate lots of roughage. Meat was highly prized but often scarce, although some of the most fortunate groups lived in times or places where large wild animals were plentiful. Meat from wild animals has a much lower fat content than the meat from the farmed animals we eat today. People ate a wide variety of plants and meat, more so than in many agricultural communities even today, so micronutrient deficiencies were rare, as were diseases associated with them, such as anemia. Work was a cooperative activity, carried out with family and friends, and people depended on others to be successful in obtaining food. All of this sounds just like what my doctor tells me at each annual physical: get more exercise; eat less animal fat, more fruits and vegetables, and more roughage; and spend less time by yourself in front of a screen and more with your friends having fun.

Although hunter-gatherers knew nothing of modern hygiene, their behaviors helped protect their health, at least to some extent. Fertility was low by the standards of the poorest countries today, with the average woman giving birth to about four children, widely spaced and breast-fed for long periods. Low fertility may have been aided by infanticide, but breast-feeding—which lowers the probability of conception—would also have helped, as perhaps did the fact that women, like men, got lots of exercise. The contamination of food or water by human excrement—what in polite circles is called the fecal-oral transmission route for disease—is an efficient way of passing infection from one person to another and would kill millions in later eras. The fecal-oral link is obviously less dangerous where population density is low, and many groups of hunter-gatherers did not stay in one place long enough for accumulated waste to become an unmanageable threat. Even so, around 20 percent of children died before their first birthday, a number high by modern standards but not very different from, and in many cases better than, that seen in now-rich (but then-poor) countries in the eighteenth and nineteenth centuries —not to mention a number of poor countries in the twentieth and twenty-first.

Exactly how hunter-gatherers were organized depended on where they lived and on the local environment. But we can imagine a hunter-gatherer band containing thirty to fifty individuals, many of whom were kin, and small enough for everyone to know everyone else well. The band might be linked with other such bands within broader networks of hundreds, or in some cases thousands, of individuals. Within the band, resources were shared remarkably equally, and there were no leaders, kings, chiefs, or priests who got more than their fair share or who told other people what to do. According to one account, anyone who tried to set themselves above others was laughed at and, if the behavior persisted, killed.[4] One reason why equal sharing might have been important is that most of the groups did not or could not store food. So if one hunter and his friends had successfully hunted a woolly mammoth (or a lizard weighing a ton, or a 400-pound flightless bird) they could eat until they could eat no more, but they would have no way of keeping the leftovers for days when no mammoth, lizard, or bird was to be found. One good workaround is to share the mammoth with the whole group, so that when someone else kills another large animal on another day, last month's mammoth-catchers will get a share too. Over hundreds of thousands of years, individuals and groups that were good at sharing would do better than individuals and groups that did not share, so that evolution could eventually produce a species with a hardwired belief in sharing. Our current deep-seated concerns with fairness, as well as our outrage when our norms of fairness are violated, are quite possibly rooted in the absence of storage options for prehistoric hunters. There is even some evidence that in places where limited storage was possible—in northern as opposed to equatorial latitudes—societies tended to be more unequal.

Hunter-gatherer societies were egalitarian societies that managed without rulers, but we should not regard them as paradises, as Gardens of Eden before the Fall. Encounters with other groups were frequently violent, sometimes to the extent of ongoing warfare, and many men died in battle. Because there were no leaders, there was no effective system of law and order, so that internal violence—often between men fighting over women, or as a result of disagreements—went unpoliced, another source of high adult mortality. Hunter-gatherers were exempt from some infectious diseases, though others, like malaria, have likely been present throughout human history. Small groups cannot maintain infectious diseases, such as smallpox, tuberculosis, or measles, that confer (sometimes limited) immunity upon recovery, but they are subject to zoonotic diseases whose normal hosts are wild animals or the soil, as well as to a range of parasites such as worms. Life expectancy at birth among hunter-gatherers, around 20–30 years depending on local conditions, was short by today's standards, although not by historical standards in the West, nor within living memory in countries that remain poor today.

The availability of food varied from place to place and time to time, so that there would have been inequality between groups, and the wealth and longevity of groups would have changed over time. There is skeletal evidence suggesting periods of plenty, particularly in places where there was an abundance of easily hunted large animals—buffalo in the American West or large flightless birds in Australia. In these places and times, hunter-gatherer groups were what the anthropologist Marshall Sahlins described as the original affluent societies.[5] Large wild animals provided a rich and well-balanced diet—their fat content was only 10 percent of that of artificially fed and rarely exercised modern farm animals—and could be killed with minimal work, so that people in such groups had a high material standard of living and lots of leisure. Yet this Garden of Eden, if such it was, was lost as many of the large animals were hunted to extinction, forcing people to switch to plants and seeds and to smaller, harder-to-catch animals like rodents. This prehistoric degradation reduced the standard of living, and the skeletons of people from this era—who got less to eat from childhood on—are shorter than those of their more fortunate predecessors.

The history of the wellbeing of hunter-gatherers—their nutrition, their leisure time, and their mortality rates—is important for the general themes of this book. We should not suppose that the wellbeing of mankind has steadily improved over time or that human progress has been universal. We spent most of our history as hunter-gatherers, and during that time, as food got scarcer and work got harder and longer, life got worse, not better. Worse was to come as people moved from foraging to farming. Although we are now used to better (where "we" refers to the privileged inhabitants of today's rich world), the capability to live such long and good lives is a recent gift that even now has not been bestowed on everyone in the world. The anthropologist Mark Nathan Cohen, whose *Health and the Rise of Civilization* is one of my main sources here, concludes his review by observing that "the undeniable successes of the nineteenth and twentieth centuries have been of briefer duration, and are perhaps more fragile, than we usually assume."[6]

We also learn from this distant past that inequality has *not* characterized all human societies. For most of history there was no inequality, at least within groups of people who lived together and knew each other. Inequality, instead, is one of the "gifts" of civilization. Again, quoting Cohen, "The very process that creates the potential of civilization simultaneously guarantees that the potential is unlikely to be aimed equally at the welfare of all of its citizens."[7] Progress in prehistory—like progress in recent times—is rarely equally distributed; a better world—if indeed a world with agriculture *was* a better world—is a more unequal world.

The invention of agriculture—the Neolithic revolution—began "only" about ten thousand years ago, a brief period indeed compared with the hunter-gatherer era that preceded it. We are accustomed to thinking of "revolutions" as transformative *positive* events—the Industrial Revolution and the germ-theory revolution are the two obvious examples. Yet it is unclear that agriculture was an advance to a higher plateau of wealth and health, as opposed to a retreat from an older way of living that had become unsustainable as animal stocks

and suitable plants ran out under pressure of rising numbers and rising temperatures at the beginning of the Holocene. Like the "broad-
spectrum" revolution that preceded it—the switch from large animals
to small animals, plants, and seeds—the turn to agriculture is perhaps
more accurately seen as an adaptation to the increasing difficulty of
foraging for food, as was argued many years ago by the economist
Esther Boserup.[8] Agriculture may have made the best of a bad job,
and giving up foraging for a sedentary life as a farmer may have been
better than living on increasingly hard-to-find and ever-smaller wild
seeds, but it should not be seen as part of a long-term trend to better
wellbeing. Hunter-gatherers who had access to wild game, worked
little, and thoroughly enjoyed the hunts were unlikely to have volun-
tarily swapped their lives for the drudgery of agriculture and what
The Communist Manifesto called the "idiocy of rural life." Morris sum-
marizes Sahlins's argument as, "Why did farming ever replace foraging if the rewards were work, inequality, and war?"[9]

Settled agriculture allowed food to be stored, in granaries and in
the form of domesticated animals. Agriculture allowed and was
made more efficient by the possession of property and the development of priests and rulers, towns and cities, and within-community
inequality. Larger settlements and the domestication of animals
brought new infectious diseases, such as tuberculosis, smallpox,
measles, and tetanus. The Neolithic revolution probably did little to
increase life expectancy and may actually have reduced it, if only
because children continued to die in large numbers, from malnutrition and from germs, as well as from the new diseases, and
because sanitation is harder to deal with and fecal-oral transmission
harder to prevent in large, sedentary communities. Immobile agricultural communities also limited the diversity of food, and domesticated crops are in many cases less nutritious than their wild progeni-
tors; stored food can also be spoiled food and yet another source of

disease. Trade between communities could offset the monotony of the local menu, but it also brought new threats of disease. These "new" diseases, transmitted from previously unconnected civilizations, brought infections against which local populations had no immunity; they could and did cause huge mortality, up to and including the collapse of whole communities and civilizations.[10]

There is no evidence of any sustained increase in life expectancy for thousands of years after the establishment of agriculture. It is possible that adult mortality rates fell somewhat as child mortality rates rose; with very high mortality among children, those who survive may be particularly hardy. Women in agricultural settlements had more children than their foraging ancestors, and although they also lost more, the switch to agriculture helped population numbers increase. In good times, or when productivity increased through innovations, the new possibilities led not to sustained increases in per capita income or life expectancy, but rather to increased fertility and expansions of population as the carrying capacity of the land increased. In bad times, in famines or epidemics, or when there were more people than could be fed, population decreased. This Malthusian equilibrium persisted for millennia. Indeed, it is possible that the decline in individual wellbeing that took place toward the end of the foraging period continued long after agricultural settlement, albeit with interruptions, right through until the last 250 years.

We are so used to thinking of progress in terms of rising incomes and extended lives that we can easily make the mistake of ignoring the increase in wellbeing that comes from simply having more people. If it is true that having more people in the world implies that there will be less for each person—because of diminishing returns, for example—then the highest possible per capita wellbeing would come about in a world with only one person—hardly what we think of as a good world. Philosophers have debated these issues for many years; one position, argued by the philosopher and economist John Broome, is that once people are above some basic subsistence point that makes life worth living, then having more such people makes the world a better place.[11] The world is supporting more total wellbeing. If so, and provided that life was worth living for most people—admittedly a large proviso—the long Malthusian era from the invention of agriculture up to the eighteenth century should be regarded as a period of progress, even if living standards and mortality rates showed no improvement.

Life and Death in the Enlightenment

Fast-forward a few thousand years to a period for which we begin to have good data on mortality. The British historical demographer Anthony Wrigley and his colleagues have reconstructed the history of English life expectancy from the parish registers that recorded the births, marriages, and deaths (hatches, matches, and dispatches) of the population.[12] These parish records are not as good as a vital registration system—the study covered only a sample of parishes, there are issues with people moving from one parish to another, newborns who died very soon after birth may not have shown up at all, and parents sometimes reused the names of such children—but they provide by far the best record that we have for any country before about 1750. The line in Figure 3 shows the estimates of the life expectancy of the general population of England from the middle of the sixteenth century to the middle of the nineteenth century. Although there are sharp fluctuations from year to year associated with epidemics—smallpox, bubonic plague, and the "sweating sickness" (possibly influenza, possibly some other virus that no longer exists)—there is no clear trend over the three hundred years of the reconstruction.

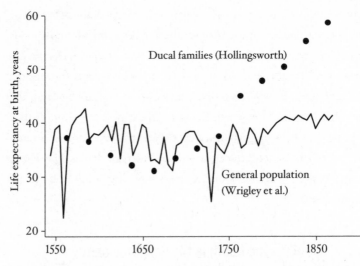

FIGURE 3 Life expectancy for the English population and for ducal families. (After Bernard Harris, 2004, "Public health, nutrition, and the decline of mortality: The McKeown thesis revisited," *Social History of Medicine* 17(3): 379–407.)

The circles in the figure show the life expectancy of the English aristocracy for each decade of the same three centuries; these data were assembled by the historical demographer T. H. Hollingsworth in the 1960s from the typically meticulous records of births and deaths kept by the British peerage.[13] The idea of superimposing the peers on the populace comes from the social historian Bernard Harris, who first drew this wonderfully informative diagram.[14] From 1550 to about 1750, the life expectancy of the dukes and their families was similar to, or perhaps a little lower than, that of the general population. This in itself is perhaps surprising; richer and higher-status populations often have better health than poorer and lower-status populations, a phenomenon that is known as the health "gradient"; there is evidence of this as far back as Ancient Rome. So the first lesson is that this "gradient" in health is not universal and was not present in Britain for at least two centuries.

There is little doubt that the British aristocrats got more to eat than did the common people; courtiers of Henry VIII at Hampton Court consumed 4,500 to 5,000 calories a day in the sixteenth century, and the king himself eventually became so obese that he could not move without assistance. Henry was not alone, and in some other European courts people consumed even more.[15] Yet more food—or at least more food of the kind that the aristocrats consumed—did nothing to protect against the bacteria and viruses that brought plague and smallpox, or from the poor sanitation that did away with their children. So the comparison with the peerage suggests that, in England from 1550 to 1750, it was disease, not lack of nutrition, that set the limits to life expectancy. Of course, disease and undernutrition compound one another—it is hard to digest food when you are sick—but there is no evidence that the consistently high nutrition levels of the aristocracy protected them or their children against the infectious diseases of the day.

After 1750, the life expectancy of the aristocracy pulled away from that of the general population, opening up a nearly twenty-year gap by 1850. After about 1770, there is also some upward movement in life expectancy for everyone. Looking at this figure alone, the movement looks comparable to other ups and downs since 1550, but it is significant in hindsight because of what was to happen after 1850—a sustained increase in life expectancy for the whole population, an increase that continues to this day. Life expectancy at birth in England and Wales was to rise from 40 years in 1850 to 45 in 1900, and almost 70 by 1950. The aristocracy not only opened up a health gradient in the last half of the eighteenth century, they also got a head start on the general increase in life expectancy that was to come.

We do not know for sure *why* the gap opened up, but there are many good guesses. This was the British Enlightenment, summarized by the historian Roy Porter as a time when people stopped asking "How can I be saved?"—a question that over the past century had brought little but mayhem, including a civil war—and asked instead "How can I be happy?"[16] People began to seek *personal* fulfillment, rather than seeking virtue through obedience to the church and "performing the duties appropriate to one's place in society."[17] Happiness could be pursued by using reason to challenge accepted ways of doing things, including obedience to the crown and the church, and by finding ways of improving one's life, including both material possessions and health. Immanuel Kant defined the Enlightenment by the mottoes "Dare to know! Have the courage to use your own understanding." During the Enlightenment, people risked defying accepted dogma and were more willing to experiment with new techniques and ways of doing things. One of the ways in which people began to use their own understanding was in medicine and fighting disease, trying out new treatments. Many of these innovations—in this earlier age of globalization—came from abroad. The new medicines and treatments were often difficult to obtain and expensive, so that, at first, few could afford them.

Inoculation for smallpox, or variolation, was one of the most important of these innovations.[18] Smallpox was a leading cause of death in Europe in the eighteenth century. In cities that were large enough for the disease to be permanently present, almost everyone caught smallpox in childhood, and those who survived had lifetime immunity. The inhabitants of towns and villages would often escape the disease for many years, but would have no immunity during an epidemic, and large numbers of both children and adults died. In Sweden in 1750, 15 percent of all deaths were due to smallpox. In London in 1740, there were 140 smallpox burials—mostly of children—for every 1,000 baptisms in the city.

Variolation is not the same as vaccination, which was developed by Edward Jenner only in 1799, was widely and rapidly adopted thereafter, and is credited with major reductions in mortality. Variolation was an ancient technique, practiced in China and India for more than a thousand years, and also long established in Africa. Material was extracted from the pustules of someone suffering from smallpox and scratched into the arm of the person to be protected; in the African and Asian versions, dried scabs were blown into the nose. The inoculee developed a mild case of smallpox but became immune thereafter; according to the History of Medicine Division of the U.S. National Institutes of Health, only 1–2 percent of those variolated died, compared with 30 percent of those exposed to smallpox itself.[19] The technique has always been controversial, and it is likely that some of those who were variolated could spread smallpox to others, and perhaps even start a full-fledged epidemic. No one would advocate the practice today.

The introduction of variolation in Britain is credited to Lady Mary Wortley Montague, who, as wife to the Turkish ambassador, had seen the practice in Constantinople and pressed for its adoption in Britain at the highest levels of society. Impressed, members of the royal family were variolated in 1721, although not before some condemned prisoners and abandoned children were pressed to serve as guinea pigs, variolated, and subsequently exposed to smallpox without ill effect. Variolation then spread widely among the aristocracy. The historian Peter Razzell has documented how, over the next three-quarters of a century, variolation started out as a very expensive technique—involving several weeks of isolation and substantial charges by the inoculators—and eventually became a mass campaign that inoculated ordinary people. Local authorities even paid to have paupers inoculated, because it was cheaper to inoculate them than to bury them. By

1800, the number of smallpox burials per baptism in London had fallen by half.

In the United States, variolation crossed the middle passage in the slave ships; the population of Boston was completely inoculated by 1760, and George Washington inoculated the soldiers of the Continental Army. Smallpox epidemics in Boston had killed more than 10 percent of the population in the late 1600s and in 1721, when variolation was first tried, but there were relatively few smallpox deaths after 1750.

The late eighteenth century saw other health and medical innovations, described by the medical historian Sheila Ryan Johansson.[20] Cinchona bark (quinine) was first introduced to Britain from Peru as a treatment for malaria, "holy wood" (guaiacum) was brought from the Caribbean and used as a treatment for syphilis (supposedly more effective, and certainly more expensive, than mercury), and ipecac was brought from Brazil as a treatment for "the bloody flux." Professional (male) midwives were used for the first time by the wealthy, an innovation imported from France. This was also the time of the first public health campaigns (for example, against gin), the introduction of the first dispensaries, and the beginnings of city improvement. In my home town of Edinburgh in Scotland, a New Town was built starting in 1765; the old city was not destroyed, but its central and heavily polluted North Loch was drained, and a new, spacious, and salubrious town was built to the north. Sir Walter Scott, who was born in the old town in 1771, lost six of his eleven brothers and sisters in infancy, and he himself contracted polio as a child, yet his family could not be described as impoverished; his mother was the daughter of a professor of medicine and his father, a solicitor.

We have no way of quantifying the effects of these innovations on mortality, and even the one most likely to have had the largest impact—variolation—remains controversial. Yet there is a plausible case that these innovations—all the result of better scientific knowledge, and born of the new openness to trial and error—were responsible for the better health of the peerage and the royal family at the end of the seventeenth century. At first, because they were expensive and not widely appreciated, they were confined to those who were wealthy and well informed, so that new inequalities in health were opened up. But those inequalities also signaled that general improvements lay just ahead, as the knowledge spread more widely, as the medicines and methods became cheaper, and as they led to new and related innovations that could cover the whole population, such as vaccination against smallpox after 1799 or the sanitarian movement that cleaned up the cities. We shall meet other examples of new knowledge opening up health inequalities that presaged general benefits, including the spread of the germ theory of disease at the end of the nineteenth century and the understanding of the health effects of cigarettes after the 1960s.

From 1800 to 1945: Nutrition, Growth, and Sanitation

If the improvements in life expectancy in the eighteenth century were muted and unequally distributed, no one could have missed the enormous and general improvements at the end of the nineteenth century and beginning of the twentieth. Figure 4 shows the progress of life expectancy for England and Wales, Italy, and Portugal; the data start earlier in Britain, with Italy following around 1875 and Portugal only in 1940. There are earlier data for the Scandinavian countries, and for France, Belgium, and Holland, but they would not be easily distinguishable from England on this graph. As we shall see, it is no accident that the countries that led the fight against mortality are those with the best and earliest data.

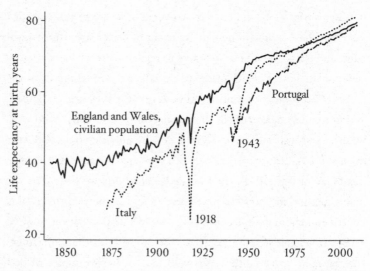

FIGURE 4 Life expectancy from 1850: England and Wales, Italy, and Portugal.

I focus on the English story here, but the diagram also highlights the diffusion of innovations, something we shall meet again and again. The English experience after 1850 is followed by other countries that got a later start (here Italy and Portugal), and what are initially very wide gaps in life expectancy—ten years between Italy and England in 1875 and about the same between England and Portugal in 1940—diminish over time, so that by the end of the twentieth century Italy had actually overtaken England, and Portugal was not far behind. As was the case for the peers and the people in England at the end of the eighteenth century, whatever happened in England—and shortly thereafter in the countries of northern and northwestern Europe, the United States, and Canada—generated a gap between them and the countries of southern (and eastern) Europe, as well as the rest of the world. Over time, those gaps have narrowed, as progress has spread and become more generalized—not evenly, not everywhere, and not completely, but eventually to the whole world. A better world makes for a world of differences; escapes make for inequality.

So what did happen in England? What caused life expectancy to double, from 40 years to almost 80 years, over a century and a half? Given the long history of thousands of years of stable or even falling life expectancy, this is surely one of the most dramatic, rapid, and favorable changes in human history. Not only will almost all newborns live to be adults, but each young adult has more time to develop his or her skills, passions, and life, a huge increase in capabilities and in the potential for wellbeing. Yet, perhaps surprisingly, this greatest of benefits is still less than fully understood and was little researched until late in the twentieth century.

A good starting point is life expectancy, not at birth, but at age 15, sometimes called adult life expectancy; this is defined as the number of *additional* years a 15-year-old can expect to live, calculated in just the same way as life expectancy at birth, but starting, not from zero, but from 15. Figure 5 shows life expectancy at birth as in Figure 4 (though I have taken the opportunity to switch to the total population, including armed forces, so that the mortality in World War I makes the dip in 1918 even larger), as well as life expectancy at age 15. At 15, people could expect to live for another 45 years in 1850, compared with 57 years a century later in 1950.

What is most notable about Figure 5 is that, until around 1900, adult life expectancy in Britain was actually *higher* than life expectancy at birth. In spite of having lived for 15 years, these teenagers could expect a longer future than when they were born. Because life as an infant or child was so dangerous, life expectancy shot up once you survived childhood. By the end of the twentieth century, the chances of dying in childhood have become very small—at least in the rich countries—so that the gap between adult life expectancy and life

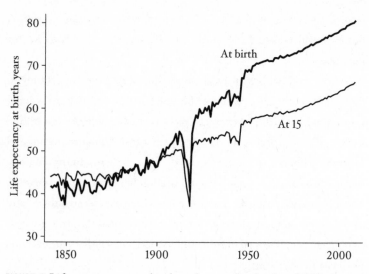

FIGURE 5 Life expectancy at birth and at 15: England and Wales, total population.

expectancy at birth has expanded, and it is now almost the full fifteen years that it would be if no one died before their fifteenth birthday. These patterns are similar in other countries for which we have data, although the date at which life expectancy at birth overtook adult life expectancy varies from country to country: up to ten years earlier in Scandinavia and ten to twenty years later in Belgium, France, and Italy.

Whatever caused the increase in life expectancy from 1850 to 1950 operated most powerfully by lowering the chances that children died. Factors that reduced mortality for adults, or factors that worked for both adults and children, were also important, but less dramatic in their effect.

Decreased child mortality cannot have had much to do with medical treatments, such as new medicines or drugs such as antibiotics, sulfa drugs, or streptomycin for tuberculosis, in part because most of the decrease in mortality took place long before such treatments were available, and in part because the introduction of the drugs did not result in any sharp changes in mortality from the diseases that they treat. The founder of social medicine, the Englishman Thomas McKeown, drew a series of famous diagrams showing for a whole series of diseases that mortality rates were falling *before* the introduction of the effective treatment, and continued to fall at much the same rate *after* its introduction.[21] McKeown, a physician himself, concluded that medicine was not very useful (he even argued that the higher the status of a doctor, the more useless he or she was likely to be)[22] and concluded that the roots of health improvement lay in economic and social progress, particularly in better nutrition and living conditions. McKeown was the first in a long line of physicians who came to feel that their own professional efforts could do little to improve public health, and who turned to more general social ills, such as poverty and deprivation, which they saw as the fundamental causes of poor health. McKeown thought that gradual improvement in the material conditions of life, such as better food and better housing, were much more important than either health care or even public health measures. McKeown's views, updated to modern circumstances, are still important today in debates between those who think that health is primarily determined by medical discoveries and medical treatment and those who look to the background social conditions of life.

Nutrition was clearly part of the story of early mortality decline. The population of Britain in the eighteenth and early nineteenth centuries consumed fewer calories than they needed for children to grow to their full potential, and for adults to maintain healthy bodily functioning and to do productive and remunerative manual labor. People were very skinny and very short, perhaps as short as at any previous (or subsequent) time. Throughout history, people adapted to a lack of calories by not growing too big or too tall. Not only is stunting a consequence of not having enough to eat, especially in childhood, but smaller bodies require fewer calories for basic maintenance, and they make it possible to work with less food than would be needed by a bigger person. A six-foot-tall worker weighing 200 pounds would have survived about as well in the eighteenth century as a man on the moon without a spacesuit; on average there simply was not enough food to support a population of people of today's physical dimensions. The small workers of the eighteenth century were effectively locked into a nutritional trap; they could not earn much because they were so physically weak, and they could not eat because, without work, they did not have the money to buy food.

With the beginnings of the agricultural revolution, the trap began to fall apart. Per capita incomes began to grow and, perhaps for the first time in history, there was the possibility of steadily improving nutrition. Better nutrition enabled people to grow bigger and stronger, which further enabled productivity to increase, setting up a positive synergy between improvements in incomes and improvements in health, each feeding off the other. When the bodies of children are deprived of the nutrients they need to grow, brain development is also unlikely to reach its full potential, so these larger, better-off people may also have been smarter, further adding to economic growth and speeding up the virtuous circle. Taller, bigger people lived longer, and better-nourished children were less likely to die and better able to ward off disease. This account has been developed over the years by the Nobel laureate economist Robert Fogel and his collaborators.[23]

There is no doubt that nutrition has improved and that people have become bigger, stronger, and healthier. But focusing entirely on food cannot provide a complete account of the decline in child mortality. Such an approach underplays the importance of the direct control of disease, and it focuses too much on the unaided role of the market economy and too little on the collective and political efforts that were behind the control of disease. The economist and historian Richard Easterlin has argued convincingly that, when we try to match the onset of economic growth with the improvements in health, the timing is wrong.[24] The improvements in child mortality across northwestern Europe were much too uniform to be explained by economic growth, which began at different times in different countries; we shall later see echoes of this in the twentieth century in the international synchronization of improvements in heart disease. And if food itself was so important, why did the British aristocrats, who had plenty of food, not do better than the ordinary people in the centuries before 1750? The demographer Massimo Livi-Bacci has documented similar cases in several European countries, including monasteries of well-fed monks, who ate rich and varied diets but died at the same rate as everyone else.[25] Food may protect against some diseases, but it is far from a universal prophylaxis. It may perhaps protect better against bacterial than viral diseases, but it is not clear that even that idea is correct.

The major credit for the decrease in child mortality and the resultant increase in life expectancy must go to the control of disease through public health measures. At first, this took the form of improvements in sanitation and in water supplies. Eventually science caught up with practice and the germ theory of disease was understood and gradually implemented, through more focused, scientifically based measures. These included routine vaccination against a range of diseases and the adoption of good practices of personal and public health based on the germ theory. The improvement of public health required action by *public* authorities, which required political agitation and consent and could not have been accomplished through the market alone, although rising real incomes certainly made it easier to fund often costly sanitary projects. At the individual level, the reduction in diseases—particularly diarrheal, respiratory, and other infections among children—improved nutrition and helped to account for the increases in height, strength, and productivity. Food intake is important, but more important is *net* nutrition, the amount of nutrition that is actually available to people after allowing for nutrition lost to disease, directly in the case of diarrhea, but also to fighting fevers and infections. The improvements in sanitation, followed by measures based on the germ theory of disease, were the major factors in improving life expectancy in northwestern Europe and in the British offshoot countries in the century after 1850. They spread to southern and eastern Europe in the early twentieth century, and eventually, after World War II, to the rest of the world, a development I shall discuss in the next chapter.[26]

The Industrial Revolution in Britain brought millions of people from the countryside to new cities like Manchester, where there were new livelihoods in manufacturing but little or no provision for dealing with the health hazards posed by so many people living in close quarters. Rural living can be reasonably safe in the absence of formal arrangements for the disposal of human wastes, but the same is not true in the cities. Domestic animals, horses for transport, cows for milk, and pigs for garbage disposal and food often lived in close proximity to their owners in the new cities. There were also dangerous wastes from factories and "nuisance" processes like tanning and butchery, and drinking water was often contaminated by human and other wastes. There were more public latrines in Ancient Rome than in Manchester during the Industrial Revolution.[27] When the same sources that provided drinking water were used to dispose of feces, the fecal-oral link that had been a problem since the Neolithic revolution was amplified to industrial strength. Life expectancy in the cities —as is still the case in some poor countries today—fell far below life expectancy in the countryside. Indeed, migration to the unhealthy cities helps explain why life expectancy of the general population was so slow to rise at the beginning of the nineteenth century, and why the general increase in life expectancy was postponed until after 1850. Eventually, these stinking and dangerous cities, the "dark, satanic, mills," provoked a public reaction beyond pronouncements about the sad moral state of the sufferers, and local authorities and public health officers began to provide public sanitation.

The sanitarian movement had no new science to guide its efforts. Indeed its theory of disease, the "filth theory" or the "miasma theory" —that if it smelled bad it was bad for health—was wrong and was no different from what public health authorities had believed in Italy when (mostly unsuccessfully) fighting the Black Death in the fourteenth century. Yet there was sufficient truth to the theory to make it effective if rigorously pursued. People are indeed less likely to get sick if human wastes are safely disposed of and if the city water does not smell bad. But the theory led to too much emphasis on sanitation and not enough on water supplies, so that, at one point, the health authorities in London were emptying the stinking cesspools in basements into the Thames, thus recycling cholera into the water supply. A few years later, in London's cholera epidemic of 1854, one of the two water companies supplying the city with drinking water from the Thames had its inlets downstream of the sewage discharges, recycling cholera bacteria from one generation of victims to the next. Indeed, the fact that the other major company had recently moved its inlet to purer water upriver enabled John Snow, then a physician in London, to map the cholera deaths and match them to the offending water company, and thus to demonstrate that cholera was spread through contaminated drinking water.[28] This was one of the first "natural experiments" in public health, and it gets my vote as one of the most important of all time. Yet Snow recognized that the experiment was hardly decisive—for example, it might have been that one water company might have served only well-to-do patrons, who were protected for other reasons—and went to great pains to rule out other potential explanations for his results.[29]

Snow's findings, together with the later work of Robert Koch in Germany and Louis Pasteur in France, helped establish the germ theory of disease, albeit with much resistance from holdout believers in miasma theory. One sticking point was why some people exposed to the disease did not become sick—a serious challenge to causality and understanding.[30] Indeed, Koch, who had isolated *Vibrio cholerae* in 1883, proposed four "postulates," all of which had to be satisfied if a microbe were to be safely identified as the cause of a disease. One was that, if the microorganism were introduced into a healthy person, the disease should follow. This gap in the theory was spectacularly demonstrated in 1892 when a prominent disbeliever and miasmatist, Max von Pettenkofer, then aged 74, publicly drank a flask of cholera bacteria, specially sent by Koch from Egypt, and suffered only mild negative after-effects. Exactly why he should have escaped is unclear—it was not stomach acidity, which he had neutralized—but many disease agents work only under suitable conditions, and von Pettenkofer had a theory of this kind, that the microorganism must first be converted to a miasma by putrefying in soil. This theory was proved tragically wrong in the Hamburg cholera epidemic in 1892; the neighboring city of Altona, which like Hamburg drew its water from the Elbe, filtered its water while Hamburg did not, and it escaped the epidemic. The swallowing of the bacillus came after the Hamburg epidemic and was something of a last act of defiance; von Pettenkofer shot himself in 1901.[31]

The discovery, diffusion, and adoption of the germ theory were the keys to the improvement in child mortality in Britain and around the world. The story also illustrates a number of themes that we shall meet again. Here was something new that had great potential for improving the wellbeing of mankind, in this case by saving children who would otherwise have died. The basic knowledge—that germs cause disease and, in the case of cholera, that the bacteria were spread through contaminated water—was free and available to anyone in the world without charge. Yet that did not mean that the policy measures that followed from the theory were adopted immediately or even quickly. For one thing, and as we have seen, not everyone was convinced. And even when people *were* convinced, there were all sorts of barriers. The knowledge might have been free, but adopting it was not. Constructing safe water supplies is cheaper than constructing sewage plants, but it is still costly, and it requires engineering knowledge as well as monitoring to ensure that the water is indeed uncontaminated. Sewage needs to be disposed of in a way that it does not pollute the supply of drinking water. Monitoring of individuals and of businesses is often difficult and often resisted, and it requires state capacity and competent bureaucrats. Even in Britain and the United States, the fecal contamination of drinking water was an issue well into the twentieth century. Turning the germ theory into safe water and sanitation takes time and requires both money and state capacity; these were not always available a century ago, and in many parts of the world they are not available today.

As always, there is the important matter of politics. The historian Simon Szreter describes how, in the cities of the Industrial Revolution, fresh water was widely available, but to factories as a source of power, not to the inhabitants of the cities to drink.[32] As is so often the case, the benefits of the new ways of doing things were far from equally distributed. And the factory owners, who were also those who paid taxes, had no interest in spending their own money on clean water for their workers. Szreter documents how new political coalitions of working men and displaced landholders successfully agitated to install the infrastructure for clean water, an agitation that was effective only after the Reform Acts enfranchised working men. Once the political balance had changed, the factory owners climbed on board, and cities began to compete with one another in advertising their healthfulness. (Princeton University, where I teach, did likewise at the same time, claiming that its elevation—all of 140 feet above sea level—made it a healthier environment for young men than the malarial swamps nearby.) Whenever health depends on collective action—whether through public works, the provision of health care, or education—politics must play a role. In this case, the (partial) removal of one inequality—that working people were not allowed to vote—helped remove another inequality—that working people had no access to clean drinking water.

Diffusion of ideas and their practical implementation take time because they often require people to change the way they live. Almost everyone in the rich world is now taught in school about the importance of germs and about how to avoid them by washing hands, by disinfection, and by the proper handling of foods and of wastes. But what we take for granted was unknown at the end of the nineteenth century, and it took many years before public and private behaviors could change to take full advantage of the new understandings.[33] The demographers Samuel Preston and Michael Haines have described how, around the turn of the century, there were sharp differences in infant and child mortality rates between ethnic groups in New York City, so that, for example, Jews, whose religious observances were health-promoting, did much better than French Canadians, who had no such protection.[34] But the children of physicians died at much the same rate as the children of the general population until the germ theory of disease was understood, after which physicians' children were much less likely to die. In the United States, hotels did not change the bed linen from one guest to the next. At Ellis Island, physicians examined potential immigrants for trachoma (an infectious eye disease) using a buttonhook-like implement that was not sterilized between examinees; the immigration authorities were *spreading* trachoma, not halting it at the border.[35] A more contemporary example comes from India, where the *dai,* a traditional birth attendant, is often brought in to help women deal with complicated pregnancies. One such woman was observed by an American obstetrician, who marveled at her manipulative skill at reorienting an unborn child, a skill that would have made her rich in the United States. Yet this highly skilled professional never washed her hands between attending one woman and the next.[36]

Scientific advances such as the germ theory are not single discoveries but clusters of related discoveries, and they usually depend on earlier advances. Germs cannot be seen without microscopes, and although Anthony van Leeuwenhoek had made microscopes and used them to see microorganisms in the seventeenth century, such microscopes provided highly distorted images. In the 1820s, Joseph Jackson Lister developed the achromatic microscope, which used a combination of lenses to remove the distortions or "chromatic aberrations" that made earlier microscopes close to useless. The germ theory itself led to the identification of a range of causative microorganisms, including the bacteria for anthrax, tuberculosis, and cholera in Koch's laboratories in Germany. Koch was one of the founders of the then new field of microbiology, and his pupils went on to identify the microorganisms responsible for many diseases, including typhoid, diphtheria, tetanus, and bubonic plague. In the next wave of discovery, Louis Pasteur in Paris demonstrated that microorganisms were responsible for the spoiling of milk and showed how to "pasteurize" milk to prevent it. Pasteur also showed how attenuated versions of infectious microorganisms could be used to develop a range of vaccines. (He also invented Marmite, a basic foodstuff without which life would be impossible for contemporary Britons; we shall meet it again in Chapter 6.) The germ theory also led Joseph Lister (son of

Joseph Jackson Lister) to develop antiseptic methods in surgery which, together with the development of anesthetics, made modern surgery possible. The work of Snow, Koch, and Pasteur not only established the germ theory but also showed how to put it into practice for the public good.

Scientific advance—of which the germ theory is such a singular example—is one of the key forces leading to improvements in human wellbeing. Yet, as the gradual adoption of the germ theory demonstrates, new discoveries and new technologies are not enough without acceptance and social change. Nor should we think of scientific advances as appearing out of nowhere, like manna from heaven. The Industrial Revolution and the urbanization that accompanied it created the *need* for the scientific advance—people were dying of diseases that had not been a problem in rural England—but also the conditions under which it could be studied. The industrial-strength fecal-oral link that was forged by putting the effluent of one generation of cholera victims into the mouths and guts of the next provided an opportunity for *someone* to figure out what was going on. Of course, there is nothing inevitable about the process—the demand for cures does not always produce a supply of cures—but need, fear, and, in some circumstances, greed are great drivers of discovery and invention. Science develops according to the social and economic environments in which it exists, just as those environments themselves depend on science and knowledge. Even the microorganisms that play the central role in the germ theory do not exist in some pristine state waiting to be discovered. Their propagation, their evolution, and their virulence develop alongside the people that they infect. The conditions of the Industrial Revolution changed the conditions of life of millions of people, but they also changed the microorganisms that infected them, and the way in which they infected them, as well as creating the conditions under which the germ theory could evolve.

THREE

Escaping Death in the Tropics

FOR THE MAJORITY OF the world's population not fortunate enough to be born in a rich country, the battles against infectious disease had hardly been joined by 1945. Yet history did not have to be relived, or at least not at the same glacial pace. In 1850, the germ theory had yet to be established. By 1950, it was common knowledge, so that at least some of the improvements that had taken a century in the leading countries could happen more quickly in those that followed. That India today has higher life expectancy than Scotland in 1945—in spite of a per capita income that Britain had achieved as early as 1860—is a testament to the power of knowledge to short-circuit history. The rapid if uneven reduction in infant mortality in poor countries allowed millions of children to live who would otherwise have died and caused the "population explosion"—from 2.5 billion in 1950 to 7 billion in 2011—an explosion that is today gradually coming to an end. Over the postwar years, life expectancies in poor countries moved closer to life expectancies in rich countries, at least until the 1990s, when HIV/AIDS in Africa undid the postwar progress in the most seriously affected countries. Inequalities in life expectancy, which had expanded from 1850 when the rich countries pulled away, decreased after 1950 as poor countries caught up, and then expanded again with the advent of the new epidemic.

There are many countries where large fractions of children still die, and there are three dozen countries where more than 10 percent die before their fifth birthday. They are not dying of the "new" diseases, like HIV/AIDS, or exotic tropical diseases for which there is no cure. They are dying from the same diseases that killed European children in the seventeenth and eighteenth centuries, intestinal and respiratory infections and malaria, most of which we have known how to treat for a long time. These children are dying from the accident of where they were born, and they would not be dying had they been born in Britain, Canada, France, or Japan.

What is it that maintains these inequalities? What is it that makes it so dangerous to be born in Ethiopia or Mali or Nepal, and so safe to be born in Iceland or Japan or Singapore? Even in a country like India, where mortality rates have fallen rapidly, large fractions of children remain malnourished; they are skinnier and shorter than they ought to be for their age, and their parents are among the shortest adults on the planet, perhaps even shorter than the stunted adults in eighteenth-century England. Even today, and in spite of India being one of the fastest-growing countries in the world, why is it that so many Indians are trapped in the destitution that was the ultimate outcome of the Neolithic revolution?

In the years after World War II, in what the United Nations (UN) calls the less-developed regions of the world, large numbers of infants and children continued to die. In the early 1950s, more than a hundred countries lost more than a fifth of their children before their first birthday. These countries included all of sub-Saharan Africa, South Asia, and South East Asia. In 1960, the World Bank estimates that forty-one countries had child mortality rates (death by age 5) of more than a fifth, and in a few the rates were close to two-fifths. In the 1950s and 1960s, most of the world had mortality rates not very different from those in Britain a hundred or two hundred years before. But change was on the way.

The most rapid increases in life expectancy came very soon after the war. The demographer Davidson Gwatkin reports that around 1950, countries such as Jamaica, Malaysia, Mauritius, and Sri Lanka saw *annual* increases in life expectancy of more than one year for more than a decade.[1] In Mauritius, life expectancy rose from 33.0 years in 1942–46 to 51.1 years in 1951–53; in Sri Lanka, it rose by fourteen years in the seven years after 1946. Of course, these dashes for immortality cannot continue forever, and they can come only from large, one-time reductions in infant and child mortality. They were caused partly by the introduction of penicillin, which had first become available during the war; partly by use of the somewhat older sulfa drugs; and probably in largest part by what is called "vector control," the chemical assault on disease-bearing pests, particularly mosquitoes and especially those of the genus *Anopheles,* which carry malaria. Much of the progress against malaria was later reversed when the mosquitoes became resistant and when the use of the highly effective insecticide DDT was stopped worldwide because of its environmental effects (largely from its overuse in agriculture in rich countries). Even if the effects on malaria were temporary, they were temporarily large, and subsequent advances in other directions, such as immunization campaigns, more than made up for the losses.

UNICEF, the arm of the UN responsible for the health and well-being of children, received the Nobel Peace Prize in 1965 for its work among the world's children. Immediately after World War II, UNICEF vaccinated children in Europe against tuberculosis, and it extended its reach in the 1950s to worldwide campaigns against tuberculosis, yaws, leprosy, malaria, and trachoma; it also sponsored clean water and sanitation projects. The Expanded Programme on Immunization

(EPI) of the World Health Organization (WHO) was launched in 1974; it promoted immunization against diphtheria, pertussis (whooping cough), and tetanus (the DPT vaccine covers all three), as well as measles, polio, and tuberculosis. Most recently the Global Alliance for Vaccines and Immunisation (GAVI Alliance) was established in 2000, in an attempt to reinvigorate the work of the EPI. The progress of immunization has slowed somewhat in recent years, perhaps because the populations that were the easiest to reach and the most willing have already been covered. Another important innovation to help maintain the rate of mortality decline was the demonstration of the effectiveness of oral rehydration therapy (ORT) during a cholera outbreak in Bangladeshi and Indian refugee camps in 1973. A solution of salt and glucose in water, taken orally, prevents the dehydration that kills many children with diarrhea. The treatment costs only a few cents a dose, and it was hailed by the medical journal *The Lancet* as "potentially the most important medical advance this century."[2] ORT is another good example of how a pressing need, together with scientifically informed trial and error, can sometimes lead to a spectacular life-saving innovation.

These medical and technical advances were implemented even in places where local capacity was limited. Mosquitoes could be sprayed by foreign experts or contractors directed by foreign experts, and immunization campaigns could be directed from WHO in Geneva as short-term, almost military-style operations using local paramedics to give the shots. Vaccines were (and are) cheap and were often centrally obtained by UNICEF or WHO at favorable prices. These health campaigns, known as "vertical health programs," have been effective in saving millions of lives. Other vertical initiatives include the successful campaign to eliminate smallpox throughout the world; the campaign against river blindness jointly mounted by the World

Bank, the Carter Center, WHO, and Merck; and the ongoing—but as yet incomplete—attempt to eliminate polio.

Medical and public health advances were not the whole story; better education and higher incomes have helped too. Rates of economic growth have been high by historical standards since World War II, and there have been improvements in education—not everywhere, but in many countries. Women are more likely to be educated than used to be the case. In Rajasthan in India, where I was involved in collecting data, almost all of the adult women we interviewed could neither read nor write. Yet we regularly passed lines of uniformed girls (locally referred to by the British term "crocodiles") setting off to school. Between 1986 and 1996, the fraction of rural Indian girls enrolled in school rose from 43 to 62 percent, and although the schools are sometimes terrible, even badly educated women are likely to be better and safer mothers than mothers who have no education at all. There is a large amount of research from India and other countries showing that the children of more educated mothers do better in both survival and subsequent outcomes; beyond that, educated women have fewer children and can devote more time and resources to each child. Lower fertility is good for mothers too, reducing the health risks of pregnancy and childbirth, and allowing women greater opportunities in their own lives.

Improvements in education may be the single most important cause of better health in lower-income countries today.

Economic growth puts more money into the hands of families, who are better able to feed their children, as well as into the hands of local and national governments, who are better able to make improvements in water supply, sanitation, and pest eradication. In most districts of India in 2001, more than 60 percent of households had access to piped water, while two decades before very few districts met this target; piped water is not always safe water, but it is much safer than water from most traditional sources.

Writing in 1975, the demographer Samuel Preston—the world's most acute observer of mortality—estimated that less than a quarter of the increase in life expectancy between the 1930s and the 1960s came from increases in domestic living standards, with the vast majority coming from new ways of doing things, vector control, new drugs, and immunizations.[3] Preston's calculations were for the limited group of countries for which he had data, several of which were not poor in 1945. His conclusion came from looking at graphs like Figure 3 in Chapter 1. He calculated how much life expectancy would have increased if the curve relating life expectancy to income had remained fixed and countries moved along it with economic growth (the contribution of income to better health), and how much of the gain came from the upward movement of the curve itself (the contribution of new methods that permit better health without any increase in living standards).

Later authors have split the credit between innovation and income differently, and there is no reason to suppose that the balance will be the same at all times, as Preston himself emphasized. The important new ways of saving lives—antibiotics, vector control, immunization— do not arrive evenly or predictably, and when one runs out of steam, there is no guarantee that there will be another waiting in the wings. Yet the big issues are always there: income on the one hand, treatment and innovation on the other hand, or the market versus public health, with education improving the effectiveness of both. If the diseases of poor countries are indeed "diseases of poverty" in the sense that they will vanish if poverty is reduced, then direct health interventions may be less important than economic growth. Economic growth would be "twice blessed"; it would increase material living standards directly *and* improve health as a bonus. If Preston's findings are still true today—a question I shall address later in this chapter—the magic of income will not be enough, and health must be addressed directly by health interventions. Note the similarity between Preston's findings and the conclusion of Chapter 2 that the mortality decline in Europe and North America from 1850 to 1950 was predominantly due to the conquest of disease by new ways of addressing health, with economic growth playing an important, but subsidiary, role.

Whatever takes the credit, there is no doubt about the extent of mortality reduction. The UN reports that, in the fifteen-year period from 1950–55 to 1965–70, the "less-developed regions" of the world saw an increase in life expectancy of more than ten years, from 42 to 53 years. By 2005–10, this had increased by another thirteen years, to 66 years. Although improvements continued in the "more-developed regions," they were much slower; see Figure 1, which shows the progress for selected regions of the world. The top line is for Northern

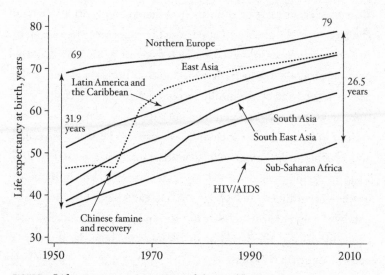

FIGURE 1 Life expectancy in regions of the world since 1950.

Europe, defined as the Channel Islands, Denmark, Estonia, Finland, Iceland, Ireland, Latvia, Lithuania, Norway, Sweden, and the United Kingdom. In these countries together, life expectancy started at 69 and gained ten years by the beginning of the twenty-first century; I shall look at how this happened in the next chapter. The other regions, East Asia (including Japan), Latin America and the Caribbean, South East Asia, South Asia, and sub-Saharan Africa, have all gained more than 10 years, so that the gaps between them and Northern Europe have decreased. Even for sub-Saharan Africa, which has gained the least, the gap between it and Northern Europe has narrowed, from 31.9 years in the early 1950s to 26.5 years in 2005–10.

Africa and to a lesser extent South Asia (which extends as far north as Afghanistan) are the regions where the most remains to be done. Even before the HIV/AIDS epidemic, life expectancy in sub-Saharan Africa was growing more slowly than elsewhere, and HIV/AIDS caused a further stalling that is clearly visible in the figure. With the advent in recent years of antiretroviral therapy, and with behavioral change, the UN estimates that African life expectancy has begun to rise once again. Yet in the most affected countries most or all of the postwar progress was lost; life expectancy in Botswana—one of the best-governed and economically successful countries in Africa—rose from 48 years to 64 years and then fell back to 49 years in 2000–05, while Zimbabwe's life expectancy—in one of the worst-governed and economically unsuccessful countries in Africa—was lower in 2005–10 than in 1950–55. Great epidemics that kill millions of people—according to WHO, HIV/AIDS had killed thirty-four million by the end of 2011—clearly did not end after the influenza epidemic of 1918–19, nor should we be complacent about the absence of new epidemics in the future.

Although no one knows exactly how the AIDS epidemic began, the same cannot be said of the Chinese famine of 1958–61, whose origins I discussed in Chapter 1 and whose effects are clearly visible in Figure 1. As we shall see shortly, one-party rule in China can be capable of promoting public health by adopting measures that would sometimes face decisive opposition in democracies. However, when policies are disastrously wrong, there is likewise nothing to stop their implementation, even when the result is catastrophe. A contrast is often drawn between China, with its lack of democracy but effective policy implementation, and India, which is a democracy with a free press but often ineffective policies. Yet India has had no famine since its independence, although there were many under the British Raj.

In spite of the great setbacks from HIV/AIDS and the Chinese famine, Figure 1 shows that life chances are *better* than half a century ago in most of the world. But how good (or bad) is today's situation, and what remains to be done? A useful way to understand today's mortality is to look at deaths around the world—what people are dying from in countries at different levels of economic development—and try to understand which of these deaths might be avoided given what we know. If people are dying of the exotic and incurable "tropical" diseases that often appear in scare stories in the media, we need new cures and new medicines. If, in contrast, people are dying of the same old diseases that have long vanished from rich countries, we need to ask why people are still dying of things we know how to prevent. As we shall see, while there is certainly a need for new and better treatments, the major problem lies in the fact that too many of the world's children continue to die from what should be readily preventable diseases.

Table 1 gives the facts about global mortality in 2008 from WHO. These numbers involve a lot of estimation and should not be treated

TABLE 1

Global mortality in 2008, and in the poorest and richest countries

	World	Low-income	High-income
Percentages of deaths (percentages of population)			
Ages 0–4	14.6 (9)	35.0 (15)	0.9 (6)
Ages 60 and above	55.5 (11)	27.0 (6)	83.8 (21)
Cancer	13.3	5.1	26.5
Cardiovascular disease	30.5	15.8	36.5
Millions of deaths			
Respiratory infections	3.53	1.07	0.35
Perinatal deaths	1.78	0.73	0.02
Diarrheal disease	2.60	0.80	0.04
HIV/AIDS	2.46	0.76	0.02
Tuberculosis	1.34	0.40	0.01
Malaria	0.82	0.48	0.00
Childhood diseases	0.45	0.12	0.00
Nutritional deficiencies	0.42	0.17	0.02
Maternal mortality	0.36	0.16	0.00
From all causes	56.89	9.07	9.29
Total population	6,737	826	1,077

SOURCE: World Health Organization, Global Health Observatory Data Repository, downloaded February 3, 2013.

NOTES: Cardiovascular disease includes stroke. Respiratory infections are mostly lower respiratory infections (*lower* refers to infections below the vocal chords, including pneumonia, bronchitis, and influenza, which can also affect the upper respiratory tract). Perinatal deaths are deaths of children at birth or immediately thereafter and include deaths associated with babies being premature and of low birth weight, babies who die during birth, and babies who die from infections immediately after birth. Childhood diseases are whooping cough, diphtheria, polio, measles, and tetanus. About two-thirds of deaths from nutritional deficiencies are due to deficiency of protein or energy, and one-third are due to anemia.

as accurate in detail, but the broad picture that they convey is reliable enough. The second column shows deaths for the world as a whole, the third for low-income countries, and the fourth for high-income countries. The division of the world by income comes from the World Bank, which divides the world into four categories: low income, lower middle income, upper middle income, and high income. Here I have shown only the top and bottom groups so as to focus on the inequalities in mortality between the richest and poorest. To give some idea of the countries involved, of the thirty-five low-income countries, twenty-seven are in Africa; the other eight are Afghanistan, Bangladesh, Cambodia, Haiti, Myanmar (Burma), Nepal, North Korea, and Tajikistan. India is no longer classed as a low-income country. There are seventy high-income countries, including most of the countries of Europe, North America, and Australasia; Japan; and a number of small oil-producing countries and a handful of island states.

The top part of the table shows how deaths divide up between children and the elderly, as well as the fractions that come from two of the leading noninfectious killers, cancer and cardiovascular disease. Deaths from cardiovascular disease include deaths attributable to diseases of the heart and of the veins, and so include strokes as well as heart attacks. The second column does the division for the world as a whole, the third and fourth for the low- and high-income countries. The bottom of the table shows raw counts in millions of deaths, focusing on the major killers in the low-income countries.

The top of the table shows in parentheses the percentages of the populations in each age group; the bottom of the table shows the population totals for each region. Note that most of the population of the world lives in the middle-income countries that are not shown here. The other key fact, in the top of the table, is that the low-income countries are much *younger* than the high-income countries. People have more children in poorer countries, and when populations are growing, each generation is larger than the previous one and the population is young. In some of the rich countries, baby boomers from the postwar years are now aging, which adds to the size of the 60-plus group. There are more than twice as many people aged 0–4 as people 60 and above in the low-income countries; in the high-income countries, there are more than three times as many elderly as children. Even if the risks were the same in poor and rich countries, there would be more deaths of children in the former, and more deaths of the elderly in the latter.

Infants and children account for 15 percent of all of the deaths in the world, while people aged 60 and over account for more than half. Yet that is not what happens in either poor countries or rich countries. In the poor countries, more than a third of deaths are of children under 5, and less than a third are of the elderly. In the rich countries, where the deaths of children are rare, more than 80 percent of deaths are of people 60 or older, and the vast majority of newborn children live to be old. In part, these differences are explained by the much larger fractions of old people in the rich countries, but not entirely—child deaths in relation to child populations are much higher in the low-income countries. The contrast between rich and poor comes from the epidemiological transition, according to which death itself "ages" as countries develop. The switch from death in childhood to death in old age also comes with a switch in the causes of death, from infectious disease to chronic disease. The fraction of people dying of cancer, stroke, and heart disease triples from low-income to high-income countries. In general, old people die of chronic disease, children of infectious disease.

The major killers in poor countries are largely the same diseases that used to kill children in the now-rich countries—lower respiratory infections, diarrhea, tuberculosis, and what WHO calls "childhood diseases": whooping cough, diphtheria, polio, measles, and tetanus; between them, these four categories still cause nearly eight million deaths a year. Other important causes of death are malaria and HIV/AIDS (for which treatment is still far from perfect), deaths at or near birth (perinatal deaths), deaths of mothers associated with childbirth, and deaths from nutritional inadequacies, of which the two most important are deaths from protein or energy insufficiency (not having enough to eat) and deaths from anemia (which comes from a diet that does not supply enough iron, often associated with vegetarianism). Apart from pneumonia, which causes 350 thousand deaths a year among the elderly in rich countries, essentially *no one* dies of any of these causes in rich countries, where better public health measures have greatly reduced the risk of children dying from diarrhea, pneumonia, and tuberculosis. Malaria is not a risk in rich countries, though it was in some countries until shortly after World War II; in poor countries, it mainly causes death among children. Antiretroviral drugs and changes in sexual behavior have greatly reduced deaths from HIV/AIDS. Near-universal immunization of children has largely eliminated the "childhood disease" category, and ante- and postnatal care have reduced perinatal and maternal mortality to very low levels. Few people in rich countries die from lack of food, and while anemia is not unknown, there are no large populations in the rich world that lack vital micronutrients such as iron.

So we have a puzzle. Why should children die in poor countries when they would not die if they had been born in rich countries? What is it that prevents the knowledge that is freely available and effective in the rich world from saving the lives of millions of people who die in the poor world? The most obvious candidate is poverty. Indeed the very classification I have adopted, between low- and high-income countries, suggests that income is what matters. Just as in the historical context, we think of diarrhea, respiratory disease, tuberculosis, and undernutrition as "diseases of poverty," as we think of cancer, heart disease, and stroke as "diseases of affluence." As was the case in the eighteenth and nineteenth centuries, income certainly must play a role; people who have money typically can get as much food as they need, and economic growth helps provide the funds that are needed for vector control, for sanitation and water treatment, and for clinics and hospitals. Even so, the poverty and income story is at best incomplete, and focusing too much on income may mislead us about both *what* needs to be done and *who* should do it.

As always, much can be learned from looking at what happened in China and India. The World Bank no longer counts them as low-income countries, but as lower-middle- (India) and upper-middle- (China) income countries. Both have grown rapidly in recent years, yet they were among the poorest countries in the world in the 1950s. More than a third of the world's population lives in one or the other, so that understanding what happened there is important by any measure. Figure 2 looks at economic growth and infant mortality in the two countries over the past fifty-five years. National income, or more precisely GDP per capita, is plotted on the right-hand vertical axis; once again I have used a log scale, on which a constant rate of growth would show up as a straight line. In fact, for both countries, growth has been *accelerating* over time, particularly—and spectacularly—for China. For India too, after forty years of anemic economic growth, there was acceleration after 1990, particularly at the very end of the period. Both countries instituted economic reforms that are credited with raising growth rates, China after 1970, when farm prices were raised and farmers were encouraged to grow and sell more, and India after 1990, when many of the old rules and regulations of the "license Raj" were scrapped.

Infant mortality rates have fallen as China and India have become richer. The patterns are very similar for child mortality (the 0–4 group), so I do not show them here. The decline in China was halted

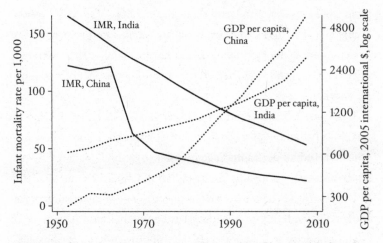

FIGURE 2 Infant mortality and economic growth in China and India.

by the famine, during which as many as a third of the birth cohort died (the figure shows five-year averages, so the effect is much smaller), but the famine aside, the general pattern is of rapid decline until about 1970, followed by much slower decline after 1970. This is precisely the opposite of what we would expect if the fall in infant deaths had been driven by economic growth, which would be the case if the death of babies were a direct consequence of poverty. What happened in China is no mystery. When the authorities decided to focus on growth, resources were switched to making money and away from everything else, including public health and health care. Even the people who were responsible for keeping mosquitoes under control were turned into farmers to join the dash for growth. In the early years, the Communist Party paid a great deal of attention to public health—*Away with All Pests* is the memorable title of an account of a British doctor working in China in the 1950s and 1960s[4]—but that focus was lost after the reforms. None of this means that the reforms were bad; the economic growth after the reforms raised millions of people out of poverty and gave them a better life. What it does show is that the growth does not bring any *automatic* improvement in the health component of wellbeing. In China, it was policy that mattered: in effect, the authorities decided to trade off one aspect of wellbeing for another.

In India, as always, events were slower and less spectacular. Growth was slower than in China, and the uptick after the reforms less pronounced; India's per capita income used to be higher than China's, but by the early 2000s was less than half of China's. (As we shall see in Part II, these comparisons are subject to *lots* of uncertainty.) Yet India's decline in infant mortality has been remarkably steady—not at all responsive to changes in the rate of growth—and the absolute decline, from 165 out of every 1,000 babies dying in the early 1950s to 53 in 2005–10, is actually *larger* in absolute numbers than the decline in China, from 122 to 22. While it is still more dangerous to be born in India than in China, India's health performance is not obviously inferior to China's, in spite of the very large differences in economic growth. India's success was also achieved without the coercion and loss of freedom associated with the Chinese one-child policy; indeed, as noted by the economists Jean Drèze and Amartya Sen, regions in South India are now doing substantially better than China.[5]

China and India are "only" two countries, and there is no reason why what is true there will also be true elsewhere, so that economic growth may still be the key to health improvements in Africa, or in countries that are much poorer than China and India are today. Yet there is very little evidence that countries that grow more rapidly have had faster declines in infant or child mortality. Figure 3 shows how little relationship there is between how quickly infant mortality has declined and how fast the economy has grown. In order to give the growth story a fair tryout, I look here only at longer-term changes. Rapid growth over a year or two might not do much to bring about

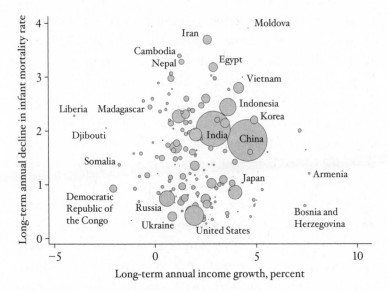

FIGURE 3 Infant mortality and economic growth around the world since 1950.

the improvements upon which child health depends; for example, a boom in the price of a commodity export might bring in a lot of money for a few people or for the government, but it would have little effect on general prosperity. However, if growth persists for a few decades, its effects should surely show up—if they are really there. The availability of data limits what can be done, but the figure shows growth and mortality decline over spans that are always at least fifteen years long—on average forty-two years long—beginning in some cases as early as 1950 and ending after 2005. The vertical axis shows the annual *decline* in the infant mortality rate, so that bigger is better. Since the infant mortality rate is measured in deaths per thousand, a number like 2 (for India, for example) means that over the years for which I have data (fifty-five years), India's infant mortality rate has fallen by 2 times 55, or 110 deaths per 1,000 births. I have included the rich countries in the picture, but, since they already had low rates of infant mortality, they had small declines over the period, and all cluster at the bottom near the center, so that excluding them would not have made much of a difference to the pattern.

The figure gives the impression of a positive relationship, but that is because I have followed my usual practice of plotting circles whose area is proportional to population. In this case, there are three big countries, China, India, and Indonesia, that have grown relatively quickly and that have had faster than average rates of mortality decline. However, to check the idea that it is growth that reduces mortality, we should not take population size into account. The question that we are asking is, "Do faster-growing countries have faster rates of decline of infant mortality?" In this respect each country is a separate experiment, and there is no reason to treat different experiments differently. When we look at the picture in that way, and give each country the same weight, there is no relationship at all. At least in the historical record, faster-growing countries did not improve their infant mortality rates at faster rates. The picture shows many examples. Haiti, whose economy actually shrank from 1960 to 2009, had a very respectable rate of infant mortality decline, faster than the rates in China or India. For the sixteen economies that got smaller, the average annual rate of mortality decline was 1.5 per year, slightly better than the rate for all 177 countries in the picture. It is certainly possible for infant mortality to fall even when there is no economic growth at all.

That there should be *no* relationship at all between growth and saving lives is surprising. We know from the historical evidence that other things—like disease control—are as or more important but, even so, it is hard to believe that money does not help at all. And indeed, there is reason to think that Figure 3 may be misleading, because it ignores feedback from the decline in infant mortality to the rate of economic growth. When children who would otherwise have died are saved, the population grows, and this may cause income per head to fall, or at least to grow less rapidly than it would have without the life-saving innovations. Eventually, these newly saved children will grow to be productive adults, and there is no reason to suppose, nor any evidence, that larger populations are inevitably poorer populations. Even so, in the first years of lower child mortality, the newly saved people are children, whose contribution to the economy mostly lies ahead of them, so that for a while lower child mortality might reduce each person's share of national income. This effect will work in a direction opposite to any effect of higher per capita income on child mortality and may even cancel it out, giving the lack of correlation in Figure 3.

Yet the evidence does not support this line of argument. It is true that the countries whose infant mortality rates fell most rapidly are also the countries whose populations rose most rapidly. Rich countries, whose infant mortality rates were already low, saw little decline in infant mortality and experienced low population growth. Poor countries saw much more rapid declines in infant mortality, and their population growth was more rapid. But *within* the poor countries, or within Africa, Asia, and Latin America, there is no relation at all between the decline in infant mortality and the rate of population growth, either because other factors were important or because over forty years fertility rates had time to adjust. As we can see in Figure 3, there is no relation between growth and mortality decline, even in the poor countries, and this absence cannot be explained by any obscuring effect of mortality decline on population growth.

If poverty is not the reason why so many children die in poor countries, and if economic growth does not automatically eliminate those deaths, why do they continue, even when most of them are preventable given current medical and scientific knowledge?

It is helpful to turn again to the causes of death listed in Table 1, and to think about how each might be dealt with, because different causes of death call for different solutions. For tuberculosis, malaria, diarrhea, and lower respiratory infections, the environment would need to be different. There would need to be better pest control, better water, and better sanitation, all of which require collective action, organized by central or local government. What might be called the physician-patient health-care system cannot do much about these problems. They are problems of public health, not private health care, even though health care can sometimes alleviate the consequences. Better living standards must surely help too, although, as we have seen from the data, this does not seem to be enough by itself.

Deaths from childhood diseases, from perinatal and maternal conditions, and from hunger could all be prevented by better ante- and postnatal care: giving a mother advice before and after the birth of her child, having health facilities available to deal with emergencies and complications, and having clinics and nurses that monitor young children to check that their immunizations are up to date, to ensure that they are growing as they should, and to advise parents. Children are particularly at risk in poor countries after weaning, when they switch from a relatively rich, complete, and safe diet—breast milk—to a diet that may be insufficient, unvaried, and unsafe. Educated mothers can do a lot by themselves, but doctors, nurses, and clinics can help children and their mothers get through this risky time. For these causes of death, therefore, the physician-patient health-care system is important. Yet many countries spend very little on their health-care systems, and it is close to impossible for a health service to do much good on the $100 per person that is typical for sub-Saharan Africa, a figure that includes private as well as public expenditures. For example, the World Bank calculates for 2010 that, in 2005 price-adjusted dollars, Zambia spends $90 a head, Senegal $108, Nigeria $124, and Mozambique only $49. In comparison, Britain spends $3,470 and the United States $8,362.

Why do the governments of poor countries spend so little when their citizens are in such poor health? Why do citizens in need not turn to private health care when the government is missing in action? And what about the foreign assistance that has been so important in improving some dimensions of international health?

Unfortunately, governments do not always act to improve the health or wellbeing of their citizens. Even in democracies, politicians and governments have a good deal of leeway to pursue their own ends, and there are often sharp political disagreements about what needs to be done to improve health, even when there is agreement on the need to do so. But many countries around the world are not democratic, and more broadly, many governments are not bound to act in the interest of their populations, whether by circumstance—for example the need to persuade citizens to let them raise revenue—or by effective constitutional rules or constraints. This is clearly true in dictatorial or military regimes, or in countries where repressive governments use the armed forces or secret police to control the population. In other cases, governments are well funded by the sale of natural resources—minerals and oil are notorious in this regard—so they have no need to collect revenue from the population. Since he who pays the piper usually calls the tune, governments can use such revenues to maintain a system of cronies and patronage that has little interest in popular health or wellbeing. In extreme cases, particularly in Africa, foreign aid has been significant enough to act in this way too, providing governments with resources but undermining their incentives to spend them in the right way. Even with the best will in the world, it has been difficult for donors to stop this from happening, a topic on which I will have more to say in the last chapter.

Governments do not bear all of the blame. In some places, people do not seem to understand that their health could be better—another place where education might help—or that the government might have the tools to help it improve. In Africa, the Gallup World Poll regularly asks people on what issues their governments should focus. Health concerns are not high on the list, and they appear long after anything to do with poverty reduction or providing jobs; governments that emphasize job creation, even useless jobs in a bloated civil service, may actually be doing what their constituents prefer. In our work in the Udaipur district of Rajasthan, we found that people knew they were very poor, but even though they suffered from a wide range of preventable sicknesses—what the economist and activist Jean Drèze calls "an ocean of sickness"—they thought their health was just fine. It is easy to tell that there are many people richer than you, but much harder to see that they have better health, or that their children are less likely to die; such things are not publicly visible in the way of wealth, housing, or consumer goods.

In Africa, where men and microbes coevolved, the fact that they are both still around is another way of saying that sickness has been man's companion throughout African history. More broadly, and as we have seen in Chapter 2, the escape from sickness and early death happened only recently *anywhere* in the world, and many people may still not understand that such an escape is possible, or that good health care might be a route to freedom. The Gallup World Poll regularly finds that the fraction of people who are satisfied with their health is much the same in poor countries as in rich countries, in spite of huge differences in objective health conditions. There are many countries in the world where people have great confidence in their health-care and medical system, in spite of poor outcomes and low spending. Americans, by contrast, have very low confidence in their health-care system, in spite of all the money that they spend; in one study, the United States ranked 88th out of 120 countries, worse than Cuba, India, and Vietnam and only three places ahead of Sierra Leone.[6]

A great scandal of government health care in many countries is that medical workers—nurses and doctors—are frequently absent from work. In Rajasthan, only about half of the small clinics were open at all when we made random checks, and while the larger ones were open, many of the health workers were not there. The World Bank has carried out surveys on absenteeism, and it turns out that in many countries—although certainly not all—absenteeism is a huge problem in both health care and education.[7] In some cases, these workers are not paid very much. It is as if there were an implicit contract between the workers and their employers; the government pretends to pay them, and they pretend to show up for work. But low wages are not always the reason. When people expect little of their health service, it is easy for absenteeism to flourish. In Rajasthan, it was hard to get people even to admit that a particular nurse had not shown up for weeks, and for many, this level of service is what they expect of the public system. But not everywhere. The Indian state of Kerala is famous for its grass-roots political activism, and for the robust protests that follow the failure of a clinic to be open. In Kerala, absenteeism is rare, and people expect their clinics to serve them. If we knew how to move Rajasthani attitudes closer to Keralan attitudes, a large part of the problem would be solved.

Private physicians often do a flourishing trade in poor countries, and their services often help make up for the deficiencies of state-provided (or not provided) health care. But the private sector has problems of its own. In particular, knowing what you need when you are sick is a problem for anyone who is not a trained physician. Buying health care is not like buying food when you are hungry; it is more like taking your car to the repair shop. The people who are better informed are the very people who are providing the care, and they have incentives and interests of their own. In the private sector, providers make more money if they provide more care or more profitable care; they also have incentives to give people what people think they want, whether or not they actually need it. In India, private practitioners routinely give people the antibiotics that they demand, often by injection, leaving them as satisfied consumers and feeling (temporarily) better. Intravenous drips are another favored item, and they are heavily advertised by health-care providers in India, just as complete body scans or PSA tests for prostate cancer are relentlessly marketed in the United States. Public doctors in public clinics and hospitals in India typically will not give antibiotic shots or intravenous drips on demand—a good thing—but they also do not have time to carry out tests to find out what a patient might actually need—not such a good thing. So the choice between a public and a private doctor is a matter of chance, though you are likely to *feel* better treated—at least in the short run—when you visit a private doctor.

All of this would be less of a problem if public-sector health care were trustworthy, or if private-sector health care were properly regulated. The problem in many countries is that neither condition applies. Indeed, even in the world's richest countries, the provision and regulation of health care is one of the most difficult, contentious, and politically charged functions of government. Most of the private "physicians" visited by the people we talked to in Rajasthan were not qualified doctors but quacks of one kind or another—what in Rajasthan are slightingly referred to as "Bengali doctors." Several "doctors" had not even graduated from high school. The lack of government capacity lies behind the failures of *both* private and public health care. The government is capable neither of delivering health care itself nor of providing the regulation, licensing, and policing that is required for an effective and safe private health-care system.

Money is a problem too, and it is probably true that India (and many countries in Africa) could not run a better health-care system without spending a great deal more than is currently spent. However, it is also easy to imagine a much more expensive system that is no better, in which absentee doctors get paid even more for not showing up for work. Without an educated population and without government capacity—an effective administrative structure, cadres of educated bureaucrats, a statistical system, and a well-defined and enforced legal framework—it is difficult or impossible for countries to provide a proper health-care system.

FOUR

Health in the Modern World

SINCE WORLD WAR II, people in poor countries have begun to see the health benefits that people in rich countries have long enjoyed. The germ theory of disease had made possible a great reduction in the burden of infectious disease, but the science and science-based policies took more than a century to spread from their origins to the rest of the globe. If this had been the whole story, the late adopters would have eventually caught up with the pioneers, and the history of global health would have been the story of the gradual elimination of the inequalities in international health that first appeared in the eighteenth century. But there were further escapes to be made, even in the pioneer countries, and the length of life continued to increase, even in the countries that had led the way and even after deaths of infants and children had become rare. Now it was the turn of the middle-aged and the elderly.

This chapter tells the story of how those further escapes came about, and what the future might hold for longevity in the rich world. It is also about the implications for health of a highly interconnected world in which it makes less and less sense to talk about the rich world and the poor world. With faster and cheaper transportation and communication, health innovations in one country have almost instantaneous implications for health in the rest of the world; the germ theory may have taken a century to spread, but modern discoveries travel much more rapidly. New diseases, like new treatments, also ride the global highways. In this age of globalization, international inequalities in longevity have been shrinking. However, longevity is not the only aspect of health that is important, and it is much less clear that international *health* inequalities are getting smaller; they certainly should not be thought of as relics ready to go quietly into the dustbin of history. Health is not only about living and dying, but about how healthy people are while they are alive. One measure of "living" health, which provides both an antidote and a complement to life expectancy, is human height—a sensitive indicator of the burden of undernutrition and disease, especially among children. We will see that most—but not all—of the people of the world are growing taller. Yet progress is slow; at current rates, it will take two hundred years for Indian men to grow as tall as Englishmen are now. And that is not the worst news; it will take nearly five hundred years for Indian women to catch up with English women.

The Elderly Can Escape Too:
Life and Death in the Rich World

Even in the rich countries, the health improvements that came from the germ theory were far from complete by 1945; the infant mortality rate in Scotland in that year was as high as it is in India today. Yet, after World War II, increases in longevity in the pioneer countries came increasingly to depend on reductions in mortality among the middle-aged and elderly, and less on reductions in mortality among infants and children. Today, the leading causes of death are no longer tuberculosis, diarrhea, and respiratory infections, but heart disease, stroke, and cancer. Yet life expectancy is still increasing (albeit more slowly than it did before 1950), driven upwards not by cleaner water and more complete vaccinations but by medical advances and changes in behavior.

By 1950, the rich countries of the world had done most of the work of escaping from childhood infectious disease, and by 2000, the job was essentially complete. As I write, in 2013, around 95 percent of all newborns in rich countries can expect to reach their fiftieth birthday. In consequence, further increases in longevity now depend on what happens to the middle-aged and elderly. Here too there has been much progress in the past fifty years.

Figure 1 shows what happened to life expectancy at age 50 in fourteen of the world's rich countries. Life expectancy at 50 is defined as the number of years that someone on his or her fiftieth birthday can

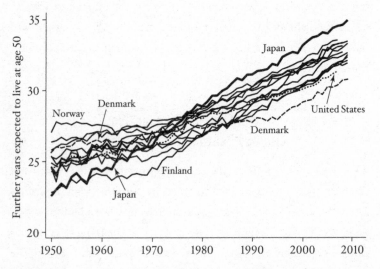

FIGURE 1 Life expectancy at 50 in wealthy countries (men and women together).

expect to live, so if life expectancy at 50 is 25 years, the 50-year-old can expect to live to age 75; as with life expectancy at birth, the calculation assumes that mortality rates will remain constant. The figure shows the average for men and women; as always women do better, but here I simply want to show the rate of progress for everyone, rather than looking at differences between the sexes. Even in 1950, the 50-year-olds in all of these fourteen countries could expect to live at least a couple of years beyond the biblical threescore and ten; this was true even in Japan, which was then the worst-performing country in the group. There was substantial inequality across countries in 1950, from 27.0 years in Norway to 22.8 in Finland and 22.6 in Japan. In the 1950s and 1960s, progress was different in different countries, but after 1970, the rate of increase in longevity speeded up. It was also much more closely synchronized across countries. Whatever was making people live longer seemed to be working in much the same way everywhere. Between 1970 and 1990, life expectancy at 50 in these countries rose by nearly three years. Progress continued after 1990, but now there were more differences across countries; some, like Japan, did extraordinarily well, while others, like the United States and Denmark, lagged behind.

The main message of the figure is that the middle-aged and elderly everywhere saw big reductions in mortality rates after 1950. As we saw in Chapter 2, nothing like this happened prior to 1950, when the improvements were mostly among children, with less of a gain in life expectancy at higher ages. The second message is that some countries have done better than others. Japan, which was last in 1950, is now first. Denmark, which was among the early leaders, is now last, and the United States, which started out in the middle of the pack, is now second from the bottom.

What made this happen? One reason transcends the specifics of diseases and their treatment. People do not want to die, and they will devote great resources—both their own and those of their governments—to trying to escape death. When large fractions of children die before they become adults, doing something about child mortality is the first priority for parents and for society as a whole. But as people live longer, the "next" disease becomes the most important one, and the "next" disease typically means the next major killer that afflicts people at an older age than did the "last" one. Having slain the first monster in the labyrinth, the next priority is the monster that lurks behind it, whose presence becomes much more important once we have figured out how to dispose of the first one.

With child mortality and infectious disease largely behind us in the 1960s and 1970s, the next monsters were the chronic diseases that killed people in middle age: heart disease, stroke, and cancer. *Chronic* in this context applies to diseases that last for a while— conventionally more than three months—and is the opposite of *acute,* referring to diseases that threaten to carry you off quickly, as happens with many infectious diseases. (Perhaps more accurate would be the descriptors *noncommunicable* and *infectious.*)

As we shall see, there has been progress against all three of the major chronic diseases, particularly heart disease and stroke, which both fall into the category of cardiovascular disease. At least some of this progress came from people being prepared to spend large sums of money, partly on treatment, but more importantly on the research and development that unraveled the basic mechanisms of the diseases and thus allowed the design of better treatments. As cancer and cardiovascular disease recede in importance—as we can reasonably hope they will—new urgency will be focused on disorders such as Alzheimer's disease, a condition that was much less of a priority in 1950, let alone 1850, because so few people lived long enough to suffer from it. Just as in the nineteenth century, new diseases demand new cures and offer new opportunities to discover them. Today, as death itself ages, the challenging diseases are those that afflict older and older people.

Cigarette smoking is one key to understanding recent mortality trends in high-income countries.[1] The patterns are not the same everywhere, but the spread of smoking in the first half of the century happened everywhere, with subsequent declines in many, if not all, countries. At first, women were much less likely to smoke than men, so that women became smokers later and, in countries where smoking is now declining, have been slower to quit than men. Smoking brings benefits to people in straightforward enjoyment, and it was a cheap and sociable pleasure for poor and rich alike. For many poor people, it was an easily available and affordable activity that provided a temporary escape from busy and often difficult lives. But it also brought disease and death. Lung cancer is most strongly associated with cigarette smoking because very few people who die of lung cancer did not smoke, although not everyone who smokes gets lung cancer. Deaths from lung cancer typically lag behind smoking trends by about thirty years, so that the mortality from smoking continues long after the behavior has changed. But cigarettes likely kill more people through cardiovascular disease than lung cancer, and there are other unpleasant consequences, such as respiratory diseases. The most important among these is chronic obstructive pulmonary disease, which includes both bronchitis and emphysema; the disease makes it difficult to breathe and is a major cause of death.

In the United States, the publication in 1964 of the surgeon general's *Report on the Health Consequences of Smoking* (for men!) is often seen as the hinge moment for behavioral change; many older Americans will say that they smoked until the report came out, but then either quit, or at least resolved to do so, immediately thereafter. There was no better example than that of the surgeon general himself, Dr. Luther Terry. In an attempt to minimize public attention, the press conference for the release of the report was scheduled for a Saturday morning in Washington, D.C., and as he traveled to the conference in his limousine, Dr. Terry was smoking. To his intense irritation—"that is none of their business"—an aide warned him that the first question would be whether or not he himself was a smoker. Indeed it was, and Terry replied with an unhesitating "No." "For how long?" was the follow-up. The answer: "Twenty minutes." Millions of Americans followed the surgeon general's example in the years that followed. Sales of cigarettes peaked in the early 1960s at around eleven per day for each adult, when about 40 percent of the population smoked, each consuming more than a pack a day.

That the surgeon general's report by itself changed everything can reasonably be doubted. There had been many earlier reports on the health consequences of smoking —indeed, my mother was ordered by her doctor in Edinburgh in 1945 to quit smoking during her pregnancy, which may be why I am writing this book—and even in the United States, the 1964 peak was largely coincidental. Smoking among men had been declining well before 1964, and women's smoking had been rising for some time; it was only the sum of the two that peaked in 1964.

Knowledge about the harmful effects of smoking is now widespread, at least in rich countries, so one might think that smoking should have declined everywhere. Yet there remain significant differences across countries and between men and women. Incomes and the local cost of cigarettes vary from one country to another, and different countries have different attitudes about health warnings and restrictions on smoking in public places. None of those factors does much to explain the differences between men and women. In some countries, it was socially disreputable for women to smoke—in Scotland in the 1950s women who smoked on the street were regarded (at least by my mother) as little more than prostitutes—and the right to smoke became associated with movements for equal rights for women. In the United States, as in Britain, Ireland, and Australia, women's smoking caught up with or even exceeded that of men, although today the prevalence of smoking is falling in both sexes. In Japan, the rate of smoking among men has been extraordinarily high (close to 80 percent in the 1950s), though it is declining now; very few Japanese women have ever smoked. In continental Europe, smoking is also generally declining, but there are many exceptions, especially among women. As someone once joked, the surgeon general's report was not translated into "foreign" languages.[2]

There is a parallel between the spread of smoking and the spread of the germ theory of disease less than a century before. Cigarettes are, or were, part and parcel of the way people lived, and they are, or were, an important source of pleasure. The knowledge that cigarettes are harmful makes people less likely to smoke, but there are offsetting considerations—not to mention a habit that is difficult to break. Knowledge of the germ theory needed to be embodied in day-to-day housekeeping and hygiene, and it too involved habits and ways of living that were difficult and sometimes costly to change. In both cases, gender roles were important. Women were primarily responsible for the housekeeping and childrearing tasks that were important for implementing measures against the spread of germs, and in many families, women became the household "germ police."[3] In the case of cigarettes, smoking was linked first to the oppression and later to the liberation of women. It is also important to keep in mind that cigarettes are *not* analogous to cholera bacteria or the smallpox virus, in spite of the current demonization of tobacco and the frequent use of the terms *plague* or *epidemic* to describe smoking. Certainly smoking is harmful to health, but it also brings benefits, something no one ever claimed for the bubonic plague or, for that matter, for breast cancer. It is not a mark of insanity if a person decides that the pleasures of smoking more than compensate for the health consequences. Many localities in the United States are currently raising substantial sums of money from the predominantly poorer people who choose to smoke; these funds are largely used to offset property taxes for better-off people. It is far from clear that any overriding public health interest justifies this taxing of the poor to benefit the rich.

The rise and fall of cigarette smoking is echoed in the rise and fall of deaths from lung cancer in Figure 2.[4] The graphs show the mortality rate for people aged 50–69 from lung cancer since 1950 for Australia, Canada, New Zealand, the United States, and the countries of northwestern Europe. The United States is shown as the heavy line in both graphs. In the graph for men, we see an explosion of mortality, peaking around 1990, about two to three decades after the peak in smoking, and then falling back. On the right, because women took up smoking much later, the fall is confined to only a few countries, and the graph looks like the open jaws of a crocodile.

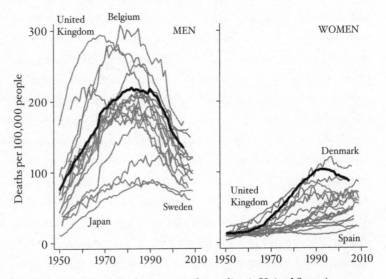

FIGURE 2 Mortality from lung cancer (heavy line is United States).

Among women, the explosion in smoking is still going on, although for a few countries, including the United States, lung cancer mortality has begun to fall. Women never smoked as much as men, so their mortality rates are lower, in line with their smoking rates in earlier years, with the countries in which women smoked experiencing higher death rates. Note finally that, although lung cancer is an important cause of death, only a small fraction of the 40 percent who used to smoke actually died (or will die) of lung cancer; the average annual mortality rate in the United States in the worst years was just over 200 per 100,000 people, or a fifth of 1 percent.

Although smokers are ten to twenty times more likely to die of lung cancer than nonsmokers, the vast majority of smokers do not die of the disease; the Memorial Sloan-Kettering Cancer Center has an online calculator that estimates the risks.[5] For example, a 50-year-old man who has smoked a pack a day for thirty years has a 1 percent chance of developing lung cancer if he quits now and a 2 percent chance if he does not. Before anyone takes too much comfort from this information, it should be remembered that lung cancer is neither the only nor the most prevalent risk from smoking.

Cigarette smoking is the main reason that women's life expectancy has been rising less rapidly than men's in recent years, not only in the United States but also in a number of other countries where women started smoking early, including Britain, Denmark, and the Netherlands. American women are paying quite a price for the tobacco companies' successful attempt in the 1960s and 1970s to link women's liberation to cigarette smoking. American smoking prevalence is the single biggest reason why life expectancy at 50 has been growing less rapidly in the United States than in a number of other rich countries, such as France and Japan. Recent calculations estimate that without smoking, life expectancy at 50 in the United States would be 2.5 years longer than it is.[6]

Even more important than the decline in lung cancer has been the decline in deaths from cardiovascular disease, a term that covers diseases of the heart and veins, including stroke, atherosclerosis (the accumulation of plaque that blocks arteries), coronary artery disease, heart attack, congestive heart failure, and angina. The reduction in smoking among men has helped relieve this burden too, but there have also been important advances in effective medical treatment, something that has not so far been true for lung cancer.

Figure 3 shows mortality from cardiovascular disease since 1950 for middle-aged to older men between the ages of 55 and 65. In the left panel, I show only the United States and Britain; in the right panel, I show mortality in the same rich countries included in Figure 2. These numbers are *huge*—about *five times* the mortality rate for lung cancer. In the 1950s, between 1 and 1.5 percent of these middle-aged and older men could expect to die in any given year. Cardiovascular disease was then, and remains today, the leading cause of death in

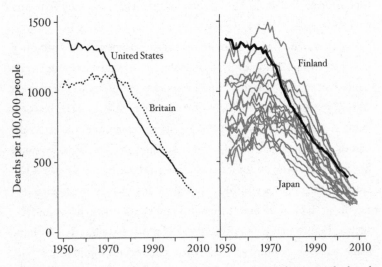

FIGURE 3 Mortality from cardiovascular disease (heavy line in right-hand panel is United States).

high-income countries. In the 1950s and 1960s, mortality from cardiovascular disease was higher in the United States than in Britain, rising slowly in Britain and falling slowly in the United States. Among other rich countries, the United States had the highest risk, and there was considerable variation across countries, with Iceland and the Netherlands at the bottom of the graph. Until about 1970, each country went its own way, with no obvious coordination across countries. Whatever the cause of cardiovascular disease, it was—like smoking, which is indeed one of its causes—different in each country.

Everything changed after 1970. With the United States leading the way, mortality from cardiovascular disease started to fall—later in some countries than in others; Britain, for example, was seven or eight years behind—and there was an internationally synchronized collapse of mortality from cardiovascular disease. Even Finland— once the home of mortality from cardiovascular disease, with annual mortality of 1.5 percent in 1970—rapidly fell into line, so that in the first years of the twenty-first century not only has the mortality rate fallen by a half to two-thirds, but there has also been a convergence of rates across different countries. Nearly all of the diversity of experience in the 1950s has vanished.

What happened? Quitting smoking was part of the explanation, but as we have already seen, behavior varies from country to country even now, and behavioral change is unlikely to be so fast and so coordinated across countries. It is not as if there were some international health authority—and the World Health Organization is hardly a likely candidate—that ordered all its member countries to change at the same time. A much better candidate is a medical innovation, especially one that is both cheap and effective, so that it can quickly move from one country to the next.

One key innovation in managing cardiovascular disease was the discovery that diuretics—cheap pills, sometimes called "water pills" because they increase the frequency of urination—are effective antihypertensives, meaning that they reduce high blood pressure, one of the major risk factors for heart disease. According to the Mayo Clinic, "Diuretics . . . help rid your body of salt (sodium) and water. They work by making your kidneys put more sodium into your urine. The sodium, in turn, takes water with it from your blood. That decreases the amount of fluid flowing through your blood vessels, which reduces pressure on the walls of your arteries."[7] An important randomized controlled trial from the U.S. Veterans Administration was published in 1970,[8] and thereafter practice changed quickly in the United States.

One of the characteristics of the U.S. health-care system is that innovations tend to be introduced very quickly—not only the good ones like antihypertensives, but also many that are of dubious value. Britain, with its cash-constrained and centrally run National Health Service, tends to be much slower and more cautious about introducing medical innovations—today it has a National Institute of Clinical Excellence, with the splendid acronym NICE, to test new products and new procedures and make recommendations—so even the cheap and effective diuretics took a while to be adopted. The right-hand side of Figure 3 shows that the same happened elsewhere; the United States led the way, and other countries followed after a time that varied with local institutions and health-care systems.

Diuretics were the first antihypertensives and they were followed by a series of others—with names like ACE inhibitors, calcium channel blockers, beta-blockers, and angiotensin antagonists—so that physicians now have a large cast of characters from which to select the one that best suits a specific patient. Cholesterol-reducing drugs—statins—have also contributed to the mortality reduction, by one account by as much as drugs that reduce blood pressure.[9] These preventive measures are designed to reduce the chance that people get sick in the first place, but there have also been innovations in treatment. One important—and also very cheap—treatment is to make sure that people who are brought to a hospital after a heart attack are immediately given aspirin. There are other, higher-tech innovations for treating heart disease—bypass surgery and the like—which are decidedly *not* cheap, and which may also have contributed to the decline in mortality. One clinical trial showed that on average there were mortality reductions for middle-aged people who took a "baby" aspirin every day, but it has subsequently become clear that while such a treatment saves some, it kills (a smaller number of) others—a good example of what is often a sharp conflict between the average and the individual. Even so, the innovations in treatment and prevention have collectively saved millions of lives, greatly reducing mortality from the leading cause of death; leaving millions of middle-aged men who would otherwise have died to continue working, earning, and loving; and making it more likely that they will get to meet and know their grandchildren.

What about women? As is the case for lung cancer, the mortality rates from cardiovascular disease are *much* lower for women, generally half of those for men. But those rates too have been decreasing, by around a half depending on the country, and with a similar degree of international coordination, so that international variations in women's mortality rates from cardiovascular disease today are much lower than was the case in the 1950s. Although they had lower risks to begin with, women have shared with men the benefits of declining risks of dying from heart disease. For women, as for men, cardiovascular disease is the leading cause of death. While breast cancer is (rightly) seen as an important and specific threat to women, fewer women die of breast cancer than die of heart disease.

The innovations that have helped prevent and treat cardiovascular disease are unusual because they did *not* generate cross-country inequality among the relatively rich countries—rather the reverse.

Rates of mortality from heart disease are much more similar across countries now than they were half a century ago, so the important innovations that drove the decline did not generate the international inequality in health outcomes that was brought about by the germ theory of disease a century ago. Perhaps because the important innovations were cheap and easily imitated, countries could quickly bring them into their health services. But cheapness does not seem to have helped guarantee complete diffusion *within* countries, and progress against cardiovascular disease has likely caused some widening of health inequalities across income and education groups. The part of the treatment that depends on the individual—in this case regular visits to a physician to have blood pressure taken and cholesterol measured—were adopted more quickly by the more educated, the better off, and those who were already healthier.[10]

Cancer is the second major killer after heart disease. After lung cancer, the most important forms of the disease are breast cancer (almost entirely among women), prostate cancer (entirely among men), and colorectal cancer (which affects both men and women). At least until the 1990s, there was little progress in treating these cancers, and mortality rates did not fall. In spite of a multi-billion-dollar war on cancer in the United States, people went on dying at about the same rates, and the most authoritative reviews concluded that the war was being lost, or at least not won.[11] Throughout this book, I have emphasized that the discovery of new knowledge and the invention of new ways of saving lives are responsive to the need for them. But demand does not *always* create supply, nor do billions of dollars or the declaration of war on a disease necessarily cure that disease—as evidenced by the failure to find a cure for cancer.

Yet, once again, there is evidence that, at last, progress is being made, and that mortality rates for all three kinds of cancer have begun to fall.[12] This decline may have been going on for some time, but, perhaps paradoxically, it might have been disguised by falling rates of mortality from cardiovascular disease. If we get better at dealing with the first monster in the labyrinth, the monster behind it claims more victims, and it will kill more even if it is not as deadly as it once was. People who were saved from heart disease became available to be afflicted by cancer, and if some of the risk factors (perhaps obesity) overlap, then successes in preventing cardiovascular disease should raise mortality from cancer. That this did *not* happen, that the dog did not bark in the night, might then be counted as evidence of progress against cancer. But recent reductions in cancer mortality provide more direct evidence of success. Screening for all three diseases—with mammograms, PSA tests, and colonoscopies—is often given some of the credit, though its role, especially that of mammograms and PSA tests, cannot be very large. For example, with the rise in mammography, there was an enormous increase in early-stage diagnoses, but no sign of the corresponding decline in late-stage diagnoses that should have been the consequence; over the past thirty years breast cancer screening has detected cancer in more than a million women who would never have experienced any symptoms.[13] Improvements in treatment have likely been more important, such as the use of tamoxifen for breast cancer. In his biography of cancer, *The Emperor of All Maladies,* oncologist and historian Siddhartha Mukherjee argues that, after generations of what was essentially trial and error in surgical and chemical treatment, a better scientific understanding of the origins of individual cancers is slowly emerging and is beginning to pay off in new and more effective treatments.[14]

In contrast to many of the most effective new treatments for cardiovascular disease, the new chemical and surgical treatments for cancer are often very expensive, and that expense will limit the speed with which they are transmitted to other countries. Screening itself is not very expensive, but it can cause great subsequent psychic and monetary expense. A prime example is the situation in which screening detects not a disease itself but a risk factor for a disease, such as high blood pressure, high cholesterol, or even a genetic predisposition. Treating those in whom such risk factors are detected—with antihypertensives, statins, or in extreme cases with prophylactic surgery, such as breast removal for women with a genetic risk of breast cancer—will save the lives of a few of those treated, while treating a much larger number of healthy people who would never develop the disease.[15] When screening is effective, it can also introduce inequalities if the more educated and the better informed adopt it first. Even so, there is hope that screening will become more effective over time, that overscreening will be better controlled, and that drugs and procedures will become cheaper as they are more widely prescribed. If so, there is a good hope that cancer will follow cardiovascular disease as one of the success stories of science and medicine. One more bar of the prison of poor health will have been removed, giving people more capabilities to lead better lives for more years.

Many other factors affect mortality rates, though these are typically less clear or more controversial than the ones that I have discussed. One is our old friend, more and better food. Better nutrition is more plausible as a factor driving down mortality rates in the nineteenth century, when hunger was more common than it is today; today we tend to worry about people eating too much, not too little. Even so, it is possible that one of the reasons that mortality rates are falling among the elderly today is improvements in their nutrition seventy years ago, when they were being conceived, born, and nurtured as children. Finland, which had the highest mortality from cardiovascular disease in the 1970s, was one of the poorest countries in the world around the time of World War I, when the 55-year-olds of the 1970s were born.

Another piece of evidence that supports the food argument is a remarkable finding by the demographers Gabriele Doblhammer and James Vaupel.[16] They calculated that in the Northern Hemisphere life expectancy at 50 is half a year higher for people born in October than for people born in April. The pattern is reversed in the Southern Hemisphere, except for those born in the North and who later emigrated to the South; they too show the Northern pattern. One plausible reason for their finding is that, even in now-rich countries, green leafy vegetables, chicken, and eggs used to be readily and cheaply available only in the spring, which meant that nutrition in the womb was better for unborn children whose due date was in the autumn. As might be expected, this effect has become smaller over time, as seasonal differences in food supply have become less pronounced.

Declining mortality is a great boon—we all want to live longer—but it is not the only kind of health improvement. We also want to live better and healthier lives, so we should not focus only on mortality and ignore *morbidity*. People who are physically or mentally disabled, or who suffer from chronic pain or depression, have fewer capabilities to do the things that make life worth living. There have been important improvements here too. One is the development—essentially through trial and error—of joint replacement, particularly hip replacement, which is now a routine procedure that relieves what would otherwise be a lifetime of pain and immobility.[17] Hip replacement is one of those "magic" surgeries that turns a difficult, painful, and limited life into one in which original function is almost completely restored. Similarly, modern cataract surgery restores or even improves vision. Such procedures restore a whole range of capabilities that would otherwise be lost. Pain medication is much better than it was; ibuprofen (available since 1984) provides relief in situations where aspirin does not, and health professionals now understand much better how to allow patients to control their own pain medication in more serious situations. New drugs for the treatment of depression have improved many people's lives. Access to health professionals is important even when they can do nothing, because they can at least reassure people who are concerned about their own or their loved ones' health; and even if they cannot, they can help resolve the uncertainty that is a source of distress on its own.

Physician care and treatment cost money—from either individuals, their insurers, or the state. The United States spends a uniquely high amount on health care—currently about 18 percent of national income—but it is not unique in facing challenges in paying for ever more expensive and, in many cases, *effective* new techniques. In some cases, in order to save money, states place restrictions on access. In one famous story, the British National Health Service in the 1970s severely limited the availability of kidney dialysis, restricting it to those who were deemed young enough to benefit and excluding those in their 50s, who were described as "a bit crumbly" and not worth the cost.[18] In some periods, Britain has also had long waiting lists for hip and knee replacements. In such cases, inadequate provision of health care raises morbidity and mortality rates, and access to kidney dialysis and joint replacement is currently much less restricted in Britain. Yet Britain has not abandoned its attempts to control the introduction of new drugs and procedures. I have already referred to its NICE, which tests medical innovations and issues detailed reports on how well they work and whether they offer value for money. Such an institution is strongly opposed by the pharmaceutical industry and by device manufacturers. At least one pharmaceutical company threatened to withdraw from Britain after an early adverse decision, but Tony Blair, then the British prime minister, held his ground.[19]

There is disagreement among both economists and doctors on how much health care is too much or on the necessity for some form of rationing. Some point to the enormous successes of medicine; they argue that if we put reasonable values on morbidity and mortality reductions—which doctors hate to do, and which is an imprecise and controversial art at best—we need more health care, not less, even in the United States. Spending twice as much money and getting twice as much mortality and morbidity reduction, they argue, would still be a good deal. Some of these calculations make the mistake of crediting *all* mortality reductions to health care—ignoring, for example, the large effects of reductions in cigarette smoking—but even with a more reasonable attribution, a case can be made for spending more, not less. As we get richer, this argument goes, what better way to spend our money than on achieving better and longer lives? And if health care costs more in the United States than in Europe, that is in part because health care is more luxurious in the United States—more private or semiprivate rooms in hospitals, shorter waits for diagnostic tests and screening—which makes sense, given that Americans are on the whole richer than Europeans and can afford such things.

The opposing argument concedes that health care has delivered great benefits but focuses on the waste in the system, which affects the level of expenditure, and on the lack of a NICE-like approval process, which allows new procedures to be introduced whether or not they are beneficial and accelerates the rate of growth of spending. One of the star witnesses in making the case that many health expenditures are unnecessary is the Dartmouth Atlas, which documents spending by Medicare, the program that covers health care for the elderly in the United States. The atlas is a map of the United States that shows extraordinary variation in health-care expenditures from place to place, a variation that is linked neither to medical needs nor to better outcomes. Indeed, there is a *negative* correlation between expenditures and the quality of outcomes.[20] The most plausible interpretation is that some doctors and hospitals are much more aggressive than others in ordering tests and treatments and that those additional expenditures produce little or no benefit and in some cases may actually harm patients. If this is true, health-care expenditures could be greatly reduced without harming health.

Given that health care is of high quality and helps maintain and improve health, it is an important instrument of wellbeing. But health care is expensive, so there is a potential trade-off between greater health care spending and other aspects of wellbeing. If Americans spent twice as much on health care, they would have to reduce expenditures on everything else by a quarter. Or if we could follow the Dartmouth recommendations in reducing expensive, low-value programs, and cut health-care expenditure by, say, half, we could have an increase of almost 10 percent in everything else. These sorts of trade-offs happen all the time in daily life, and we do not usually worry too much about whether people are, for example, spending too much on books or electronic gadgets so that they have too little left to spend on summer vacations. So why is health care different?

The problem is that people are not actually *choosing* how much to spend on health care in the way that they choose how much to spend on books or on vacations. Indeed people may not even be aware of what they are paying for health care, or what they are giving up to get it. In the United States, most health care for the elderly is paid for by the government through Medicare, and most (59 percent) of the nonelderly have coverage through their employers. Many of these think that their employers are *paying* for their health care at no cost to themselves. Yet most studies have shown that it is not employers that ultimately pay, for example through lower profits, but employees, through lower wages.[21] As a result, typical earnings, and the family incomes that depend on them, have grown more slowly than would have been the case if health-care costs had not grown so rapidly. But people do not see it that way, and do not think to blame rising health-care costs for the slow growth in their incomes. As a result, they fail to see the cost of health care as the problem that it really is.

Similar problems arise when the government provides health care, as in Europe, or in Medicare, which pays for health care for the elderly in the United States. When people press for the government to provide additional health-care benefits—coverage for prescription drug benefits, for example—they tend not to think about what has to be given up in exchange. The doyen of American health economists, Victor Fuchs, gives the example of an elderly woman for whom Medicare will provide expensive surgery at no cost to herself, even surgery that might not be urgent or necessarily effective, but whose pension check is not enough to allow her to buy a plane ticket to attend her granddaughter's wedding or to visit a new grandchild.[22] These trade-offs have to be made through the political process by some sort of democratic debate, but that is a difficult, contentious, and often ill-informed process. It is also a process that, at least in some countries, is deeply influenced by the providers of health-care services, who have an interest in over-provision—an interest that becomes stronger and better financed the more that is spent.

Income and health are two of the most important components of wellbeing, and the two with which this book is mainly concerned. We cannot think about them one at a time, or allow doctors and patients to lobby for health improvements and economists to lobby for economic growth, each group ignoring the other. When health care is as expensive and as effective as it is today, trade-offs need to be made; in Fuchs's words, we must take a holistic view of wellbeing. Some process needs to be put into place to allow us to take that view collectively, almost inevitably involving an institution like Britain's NICE, as well as a greater and more widespread public understanding of the threats to other aspects of wellbeing that come from the unlimited growth of health-care costs.

What about the future? Can we expect life expectancy to continue its rise in the high-income countries? The negative view, often associated with the demographer and sociologist Jay Olshansky, starts from the observation that it is getting harder and harder to increase life expectancy. This is something we have already seen; saving children's lives has a dramatic effect on life expectancy, because they have so many years to live, but once nearly all of the children have been saved, saving the elderly makes less of a difference, at least to life expectancy. Figure 1 in Chapter 2 shows the distinct slowdown in the rate of increase in American life expectancy after 1950, and the argument is that we can expect a similar slowdown in the future, even if innovations continue, because the lives saved will be of ever-older people. Even if cancer were eliminated in the United States, life expectancy would increase by only four or five years. The pessimists also note that the rise in obesity in most rich countries may raise mortality rates in the future. Perhaps, but there has been little evidence of it so far. This may be because, with better treatments for cardiovascular disease—including drugs to control cholesterol and hypertension—the risks of obesity are lower now than when they were first studied.[23]

On the other side, the demographers Jim Oeppen and James Vaupel published in 2002 a remarkable diagram that calculated the world's highest life expectancy for women in each year from 1840, and showed that this measure—which can be thought of as the maximum possible life expectancy in each year—has risen at a constant rate for 160 years.[24] For every four years of calendar time, the world's highest life expectancy increased by a year. Oeppen and Vaupel see no reason why this long-established rate of progress should not continue. Their diagram also marks the many previous estimates of the maximum possible life expectancy, each of which was swept away by actual events; many previous sages have forecast that the gains to life span will slow or stop, and they have all been wrong. Further supporting the optimistic argument in favor of a continued rise in life expectancy is the fact that people do not want to die any earlier than they must; that as they get materially richer they have more income to spend trying to avoid that outcome and will likely be prepared to devote a larger and larger share of their incomes to staying alive; and there is no reason to suppose that they will not succeed in the future as they have in the past.

I find the optimistic argument the more compelling: ever since people rebelled against authority in the Enlightenment, and set about using the force of reason to make their lives better, they have found a way to do so, and there is little doubt that they will continue to win victories against the forces of death. That said, it is too optimistic to think that life expectancy in the future will grow at the same rate as it did in the past; falling rates of infant and child mortality make life expectancy grow rapidly, and that source of growth is largely gone, at least in the rich countries. During the 160 years when top life expectancy grew by a year every four years, a substantial contribution came from saving the lives of children, and that will not continue. Once again, there is good reason *not* to focus on life expectancy as the measure of success. Eliminating cancer and other diseases of the elderly would eliminate great suffering and improve millions of lives. That it would have a modest effect on life expectancy is largely beside the point.

Health in an Age of Globalization

I have looked at rich countries (in this chapter) and poor countries (in Chapter 3) as if they were separate worlds. Now it is time to look at them together, and to think about how the two groups affect one another. The past half-century has seen an unparalleled integration of the world—a process often referred to as globalization. This is certainly not the first instance of globalization in history, although the current episode is one of the most far reaching. Transport is faster and cheaper than ever before, and information moves faster still. Globalization has affected health in many ways: directly through the spread of disease, information, and treatment, and indirectly through economic forces, particularly increased trade and higher economic growth.

There have been many periods of globalization in history—sometimes through war, conquest, and imperialist expansion, sometimes through new trade routes, bringing new products and new riches. Disease usually came along for the ride, with consequences that reshaped the world. The historian Ian Morris has described how increased trade around the second century CE merged previously separate disease pools that, since the beginning of agriculture, had evolved in the West, South Asia, and East Asia, "as if they were on different planets." Catastrophic plagues broke out in China and in the eastern outposts of the Roman Empire.[25] The Columbian exchange after 1492 is an even better-known example.[26] Many historical epidemics started from new trade routes or new conquests. The plague of Athens in 430 BCE was attributed to trade, and bubonic plague was brought to Europe in 1347 by rats aboard trading ships. The cholera epidemic of the nineteenth century is thought to have come from Asia thanks to the activities of the British in India, and its subsequent spread through Europe and North America was speeded by the new railways. An infected person could be in another city before he or she knew of the infection, and cholera spread along the railway lines; today, someone can move from one hemisphere to another in the time it used to take to go from one city to another.

Yet globalization also opens its routes to the enemies of disease. We have already seen how the germ theory of disease—a set of ideas and practices developed in the North—spread rapidly to the rest of the world after 1945. Knowledge about drugs to control high blood pressure spread rapidly across the world after 1970, producing the synchronized declines in mortality plotted in Figure 3. That cigarette smoking caused cancer did not have to be rediscovered country by country. While the origins of HIV/AIDS are in dispute, there is no dispute about its rapid spread from one continent to another. The scientific response—the discovery of the virus, the deduction of its means of transmission, and the development of chemotherapy that is transforming the disease from a fatal to a chronic condition—was extraordinarily rapid by historical standards, although hardly rapid enough for the millions who died as they waited. Today's understanding of the disease, although still incomplete, has underpinned the response—not just in the rich world—and in the worst affected African countries rates of new infection have fallen in the past few years, and life expectancy is beginning to rise again.

Successes against cardiovascular disease and cancer are spreading, not just from one rich country to another, but throughout the world. As mortality from infectious disease has fallen, noncommunicable diseases are becoming more important as the children who did not die become adults and live long enough to encounter them. Except in Africa, noncommunicable disease is now the leading cause of death everywhere in the world, and cheap and effective preventative drugs like antihypertensives should spread just as vaccines did in the past. Here, once again, the constraint is likely to be the capacity of some governments to organize and regulate a physician-based system of health care. Advances that are more expensive, such as some cancer treatments or joint replacement, are also spreading, but they are typically available only to the well heeled or well connected in a limited number of poor countries.

The contributions of rich-country to poor-country health have not always been benign. Health researchers, unlike economists, often think of globalization as a negative force. There is deep concern about cigarette smoking, and the activities of the tobacco companies whose products, no longer welcome in much of the rich world, are finding a safe haven in poorer countries whose governments, once again, may not have the capacity for or an interest in regulation. The patent system that makes drugs temporarily very expensive has been vociferously challenged, though it is not clear whether patents are the real problem. Again, local capacity for delivery is an issue and, in any case, nearly all of the drugs that the WHO lists as "essential medicines" are off patent; even so, the list might be longer if more drugs were cheaper. Small poor countries often find themselves at a disadvantage when negotiating bilateral trade deals with large rich countries. The latter are much better supplied with lawyers and lobbyists, including pharmaceutical lobbyists, whose interest is not to protect poor-country health. First-world medicine has certainly sharpened local health inequalities in poor countries. In cities like Delhi, Johannesburg, Mexico City, and São Paulo, first-world state-of-the-art medical facilities treat the wealthy and powerful, sometimes within sight of people whose health environment is not much better than that of seventeenth-century Europe.

What has happened to global health and global health inequalities since 1950? In Figure 1 of Chapter 3, we saw that regional inequalities in life expectancy have narrowed, so that the regions with the lowest life expectancy have drawn closer to the regions with the highest life expectancy. Now I look at countries, not regions, as units. Figure 4 shows how life expectancy is changing in the typical country, how the worst and best countries are doing, and whether inequality in life expectancy is getting larger or smaller. The graph looks like a series of organ pipes, though it is actually known as a "box-and-whisker" plot. The vertical axis shows life expectancy, and the pipes (or boxes) show

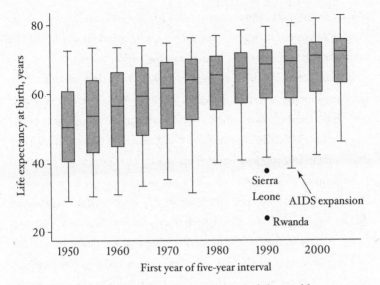

FIGURE 4 Life expectancy and its dispersion around the world.

where countries' life expectancies line up; the first message from the graph is that the pipes are rising from bottom left (1950–54) to top right (2005–09) as longevity increases around the world. Each shaded box contains half of all countries, and the line across the middle marks the middle country in terms of life expectancy. These horizontal lines are rising over time—life expectancy in the middle country is going up—albeit at a rate that is somewhat slower now than fifty years ago. Once again, the reason is that we have moved from the large increases in life expectancy that come from saving children to the smaller and more hard-won gains that come from saving the elderly. The top and bottom "whiskers," shown as lines coming out of the pipe with bars on the end, are designed to capture all countries except those that are really extreme in their longevity. The figure shows only two countries that are extreme in this way, both of which were in the midst of civil wars between 1990 and 1995: Rwanda and Sierra Leone. A total of 192 countries are plotted for each period, and some of the estimates are speculative, especially in the earlier years.

The figure shows the pipes getting smaller over time, so that countries are moving toward the middle of the crowd. The dispersion of life expectancy across countries is narrowing, and this measure of the international distribution of health is becoming less unequal. The explosion of international health inequality that began 250 years ago is beginning to be reversed. The narrowing has not been entirely even, and we can see the widening in 1995–2000 that comes from AIDS deaths in Africa, after which the narrowing resumes. The bars in the middle of the boxes are getting progressively closer to the tops of the pipes, and to the top whisker, which tells us that the gap between life expectancy in the middle country and the top countries —like Japan—has also been narrowing over time. There is now only a 10.5-year gap between the middle—more precisely the median— (72.2 years) and the top (Japan at 82.7 years). Yet this narrowing is leaving a longer tail of countries behind it. Even ignoring the horrors in Rwanda and Sierra Leone in the early 1990s, the gap from middle to bottom has grown from 22 to 26 years.

Once again we must ask ourselves whether life expectancy is a good measure for thinking about health inequalities across countries. This chapter has shown that the gains have come from saving children in poor countries and from saving the middle-aged and elderly in rich countries. When we use gains in life expectancy to compare across rich and poor, we give greater weight to the poor countries, because saving a child has a much larger effect on life expectancy than saving a 60-year-old. And indeed, this is the main reason why inequality in life expectancy has declined. Yet it is not obvious that saving a child is indeed better than saving an older adult, a judgment that is built in to this measure of inequality. This point can be argued either way. Some would argue for saving the child—because, even if he or she does not yet have much stake in the world, so many future years are gained—and others for saving the adult—because he or she has a larger stake, albeit with fewer years left. But there is nothing that says that using life expectancy to look at inequalities solves this conundrum in just the right way, and weighing lives differently could make the reduction in inequality larger or smaller, or might even reverse it.

The reductions in global inequalities in life expectancy do not automatically mean that the world is a better place, because life expectancy does not capture all the aspects of health—or even of mortality—that we care about. Certainly, we live in a world in which child mortality is falling in poor countries, and middle-aged and elderly mortality is falling in rich countries. Whether those trends make the world a more equal place is a debatable issue that depends on how much we care about each kind of mortality decline.

The philosophical arguments do not stop there. The reductions in infant and child mortality have been followed by reductions in the number of children that people choose to have. In Africa in 1950, each woman could expect to give birth to 6.6 children; by 2000, that number had fallen to 5.1, and the UN estimates that it is 4.4 today. In Asia as well as in Latin America and the Caribbean, the decline has been even larger, from 6 children to just over 2. Fertility did not fall immediately after mortality rates fell, which is why there was an explosion in population. Yet in time, as parents came to believe that not so many children would die, they stopped having so many babies, though they may have had as many or more who survived to adult-hood. One way of thinking about this change is that babies, who would have been born and quickly died, are now not being born at all. Who are the beneficiaries of this change? Again, it depends on how we choose to weigh lives, a question that has engaged philosophers for a long time. Yet it is clear that *mothers* benefit a lot; they do not have to be pregnant as often to have the same number of children who survive, and they—and their husbands—are spared the agony of having their children die. Lightening this burden on women not only removes a source of pain, it also frees them to lead fuller lives in other dimensions, becoming more educated, working outside of the home, and playing a fuller role in society.

Changing Bodies

There is much to cheer about in global health since 1950. But I want to conclude with a somewhat less cheery set of observations that focus not on the Great Escape from death—which has been impressive in most places, and perhaps even equalizing—but on the less impressive and less equal progress in the Great Escape from malnutrition. One good way to look at malnutrition is to see what has happened to human height.

Height, in and of itself, is not a measure of wellbeing. Other things equal, there is no reason to suppose that someone who is over six feet tall is any happier, richer, or healthier than someone who is six inches shorter. Nor is height a part of wellbeing in the way that income and health are parts of wellbeing. Yet when a *population* is short, it indicates that its members were nutritionally deprived in childhood or in adolescence, either because they did not get enough to eat, or because they lived in an unhealthy environment where disease, even if it did not kill them, left them permanently stunted. While height depends on genes for each individual, so that taller parents have taller children, it is now believed that this is not true for (sufficiently large) populations, and that variations in average height among populations are good indicators of variations in the degree of deprivation. In the past, we thought that genetic differences were the main source of differences in heights across populations. But as conditions improved, and one "short" country after another has grown taller, sometimes quite quickly, these views have been discarded.[27]

We are now beginning to understand that deprivation in childhood can have serious and long-lasting consequences. Shorter people earn less than taller people, not only in agricultural societies, where strength and physique are useful in the labor market, but also among professionals in rich countries such as Britain and the United States. One reason is that cognitive function develops along with the rest of the body, so that shorter people, *on average,* are not as smart as taller people—a statement that tends to call forth howls of outrage. Two of my Princeton colleagues who investigated this question[28] were denounced, bombarded with hate-filled emails, and subjected to demands by alumni that the university dismiss them. So let me try to explain carefully.

In an ideal environment where everyone gets enough to eat and where no one ever gets sick, some people will be short and some tall, according to their genetic makeup, but there will be *no systematic difference* in cognitive function according to height. In the actual sublunary world, some people will be deprived in childhood, and those people will be overrepresented among the short, which is why short people, on average, have poorer cognitive function. This may be simply a matter of insufficient calories, or of fighting off one too many childhood diseases, an important drain on calories. The deprivation can also be more specific; for example, children's brains need fat to develop properly, and there are millions of people in the world whose diets contain *too little* fat, in contrast to the more familiar millions whose diets contain too much.

Nutritional deprivation wears off as populations become richer and get enough to eat, and as childhood disease is banished through sanitary improvements, pest control, and vaccines. Even so, the effects of nutritional deprivation on heights may take many years to wear off, if only because tiny mothers cannot have large children. The rate of height increase in a population is subject to this biological limit, so that it may take many generations for populations to grow to their full potential, even after the nutritional and disease constraints have been removed; biology limits growth to avoid problems that would result from fast catch-up.[29] But over time we would expect to see the people of the world getting taller. It turns out that some have and some have not.

Europeans have become *much* taller. The economists Timothy Hatton and Bernice Bray have assembled data on men's heights from various sources for eleven European countries going back into the late 1850s or early 1860s.[30] Unfortunately there are very few historical data on the heights of *women*, because the information on men's heights typically comes from measurement during recruitment for armies. For those born in the middle of the nineteenth century, the height of the average European adult man was 166.7 centimeters (cm), or 5 feet 5.5 inches. For those born a little over a hundred years later, in the five years from 1976 to 1980, the average was 178.6 cm, or 5 feet 10.5 inches. In the country that grew the least—France—the rate of growth was 0.8 cm for each decade; in the fastest-growing—the Netherlands— the rate of growth was 1.35 cm for each decade. Men in most of the other countries grew taller by something close to 1 cm for every decade. Hatton has tracked these improvements back to their underlying causes and, in line with the arguments of this chapter, finds that the reduction in infant mortality—an indication of an improved disease environment—was the most important factor, with growth in income in second place.[31] As Europe made its escape from too little food, and the "cloacal infernos"[32] created by the Industrial Revolution, people's bodies began to grow toward the heights that had always been possible but were previously unachievable.

For most of the world today, there is only fragmentary historical information, but we do have good information on the heights of women from many of the Demographic and Health Surveys discussed in Chapter 2. (The most recent of these surveys measured men too.) Each survey gives us historical information because it measures people aged 15 to 49. Because people's heights do not change once they reach their adult height (or at least not until they start shrinking after age 50), each survey gives us the average adult heights of people born over a period of twenty or more years. So not only do these surveys give us the average heights of female adults in the country at the time of the survey, but by comparing older and younger women we can also see how fast heights are growing. In countries that are doing well, the older women will be a centimeter or two shorter than the younger women.

Figure 5 shows women's heights around the world. Each of the points in the figure is for a "birth cohort" of women for a country; it is the average height in centimeters of all the women born in a particular year, say 1960. That average is plotted against average national income in that country in the women's year of birth, and once again I have used a log scale for income. At the top right of the picture, for example, we see European women getting taller as their national incomes rose; women born earlier are at the bottom left of the European group, and women born later are at the top right. The United States is shown as a spur on the right; Americans have been growing taller but not as quickly as Europeans. In the middle and to the left of the diagram we see the women of poor and middle-income countries. The dark circles are for Africa and appear mostly to the left, because African countries were poor when these women were born, just as they are poor today. (The rich Africans on the right of the diagram live in Gabon, whose oil exports give it a high per capita income, although most of its inhabitants remain poor.) Nestled among the

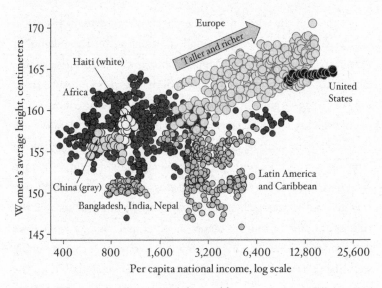

FIGURE 5 Women's heights around the world.

Africans are Haitians (white circles), most of whom are of African descent, and whose heights and incomes give them much in common with Africans in Africa. China (in gray) is also on the left, and Bangladesh, India, and Nepal are on the bottom at the left. Remember that we are looking at incomes in the years in which these now-adult women were born, typically 1980 or earlier, so that China and India show up as much poorer than they are today. Latin American and Caribbean women, who live in middle-income countries, appear in the lower middle part of the figure.

Perhaps the most startling feature of the diagram is the enormous inequality of average heights around the world. For women born in 1980, the average adult Dane was 171 cm, the average Guatemalan was 148 cm, the average Peruvian or Nepali 150 cm, and the average Indian, Bangladeshi, or Bolivian 151 cm. If the shortest populations in the world were to grow at the European rate of 1 cm every decade, it would take 230 years for the Guatemalan women to be as tall as Danish women are today. Today, a Danish woman visiting a Guatemalan village would tower 9 inches above her hosts, a modern Gulliver in a modern Lilliput.

Looking from bottom left to top right, people in better-off countries are taller than people in poorer countries, which is what we might expect if higher incomes come with better sanitation, lower rates of childhood disease, and more to eat. But things are not quite so simple. Imagine the figure redrawn with Europe and the United States blanked out. For the rest of the world, the relationship between height and income goes the wrong way, with the *taller* people living in the *poorer* countries. A lot of this has to do with Africa. There is a lot of variability across African populations—think of Dinka basketball players from southern Sudan or the bushmen of the Kalahari—but on average African women are tall, not relative to Europeans but relative to South Asians and many Latin Americans. This negative relationship between heights and incomes is not about to go away any time soon, because Indian children born today are *still* very short, in spite of the rapid growth of the Indian economy in recent decades.

Why Africans are so tall is not well understood. One reason is that, in much of the continent, food is neither so scarce, nor so heavily vegetarian, as in much of South Asia, particularly India. Obviously, this is not true in some places—the Kalahari Desert, for example—but in most African countries, people eat a varied diet that includes meat and animal fats. There is also great variability in Africa, depending on local food availability and local disease environments. At the same time, mortality rates among children are extremely high, and if the shorter children are weaker and more likely to die, the survivors will be relatively tall. For this to produce a tall population, mortality has to be very high, high enough to sweep away a large enough fraction of short children and to overcome the stunting effect of living through a dangerous disease environment in childhood. Sanitation may be another factor; in places where people defecate in the open, and where population density is high, child growth is stunted by chronic exposure to fecal germs. Africa, with its much lower population density, does better than India.[33]

The fact that residents of many African nations are taller than those of India, or of several countries in Latin America, should help us resist the superficially attractive idea that population average heights can be used as some overall measure of wellbeing or of the standard of living. Mortality and income are two of the most important influences on adult height, and they are also crucial for wellbeing. But there is no guarantee that the way that disease and poverty affect height is the same as the way that they affect wellbeing. And as the map of Africa attests, many local factors—such as variations in diet—affect height, and these local factors may or may not affect wellbeing. Recall too that it can take many generations for populations to grow taller, because the mothers have to grow before the children, the grandmothers before the mothers, and so on. It is not just today's nutrition and today's diseases that determine today's height; history matters too. All of this means that average height is not a sensible measure of wellbeing.

The fact that South Asians are so short is perhaps the most informative part of the whole picture. Because we do not have historical data on European women, we do not know how far we have to go back to get to modern Indian heights. However, the latest Indian data include men, and it turns out that the average height of Indian men born in 1960 was 164 cm: 2–3 cm shorter than the European average in 1860, similar to European heights in the eighteenth century, and only 5 cm taller than the lowest figures in the literature, 159 cm from contemporary bushmen and from Norway in 1761.[34] In Sikkim and

Meghalaya, states in northeastern India, the average heights of men born in 1960 are actually less than 159 cm.

It is possible that the deprivation in childhood of Indians born around midcentury was as severe as that of any large group in history, all the way back to the Neolithic revolution and the hunter-gatherers that preceded them. Life expectancy in India in 1931 was 27, also reflecting extreme deprivation. Indians, even in the twentieth century, lived in a Malthusian nightmare. As in Malthus, death and deprivation kept the population in check, but even for the survivors, the conditions of life were terrible. Not only was there insufficient food to maintain good health, but its makeup also lacked important nutrients. Most people ate a monotonous diet of a single cereal, supplemented by a few vegetables, lacking iron and adequate fat. In order to survive at all, even with a life expectancy in the 20s, the whole population had to be short, just as were the populations of England in the seventeenth and eighteenth centuries. The Malthusian imperative trades off more people for shorter people.

India is today escaping from this nightmare, but it still has a long way to go. Indian children are still among the skinniest and shortest on the planet, but they are taller and plumper than were their parents or grandparents, and the signs of gross hunger, such as marasmus, are now rarely seen in nutritional surveys. Indians too are now growing taller, decade by decade, though not as quickly as happened in Europe, or indeed as is now happening in China, where people are growing at about (the now familiar figure of) a centimeter every decade. Yet the Indian escape is only half as fast—about *half* a centimeter a decade—and that figure is for *men;* Indian women are growing too, but at a much slower rate, so that it takes them sixty years to grow a centimeter.[35]

We do not know why Indian women are doing so much worse than Indian men; the reason is surely linked to general patterns of favoring sons in north India, though exactly how this works is not known. In south India, in Kerala and Tamil Nadu, which have no tradition of bias against girls, both men and women are growing taller at the standard centimeter-a-decade rate, but in the north, women are growing more slowly than men, who are themselves growing less fast than their counterparts in the south. An irony of this sort of discrimination against women is that it rebounds against the men, because men, just like women, have unduly small and undernourished women as mothers, compromising their own prospects for physical and cognitive development.

In Africa, although people are taller on average, women in some places are actually getting *shorter*.[36] Although, as we have seen, it is not always true that better-off people are taller, there is a strong correlation around the world between getting richer and getting taller. This is most obviously true in Europe, and the growth has been sufficiently prolonged for it to be visible in Figure 5, but it is also true in modern China, India, and elsewhere. So the most likely reason that African women are shorter than their mothers is falling real incomes in Africa in the 1980s and early 1990s.

The world's peoples are not just living longer or getting richer; their bodies are getting taller and stronger, with many good consequences, including even possibly an increase in cognitive ability. But as with mortality and money, the distribution of benefits has been unequal. At current rates, it will take centuries for the Bolivians, Guatemalans, Peruvians, or South Asians to become as tall even as Europeans are today. So while many have made their escape, millions more are left behind, resulting in a world of difference in which inequality is apparent even in people's bodies.

PART II MONEY

FIVE

Material Wellbeing in the United States

STARTING IN THE MIDDLE of the eighteenth century in Britain, longevity slowly began to improve in countries around the world. As people made their escape from disease and early death, living standards began to improve too, and, to a large extent, health and the level of living moved in parallel. The ideas of the Scientific Revolution and the Enlightenment eventually brought a revolution in material wellbeing, just as they brought a revolution in the length of life. These parallel revolutions, driven by the same ultimate causes, brought better and longer lives for many, but also created a world of difference through what the economist Lant Pritchett has memorably called "Divergence, big time."[1] Economic growth brought better living standards as well as a reduction in poverty. It is hard to measure any of this precisely—a situation about which I will have more to say—but one careful study estimates that the average income of all the inhabitants of the world increased between seven and eight times from 1820 to 1992.[2] At the same time, the fraction of the world's population in extreme poverty fell from 84 to 24 percent. This historically unprecedented increase in living standards came with huge increases in income inequality, both between countries and between individuals within countries. The *nature* of inequality also changed. In the eighteenth century, most inequality was *within* countries, between the rich land-owning aristocrats on the one hand and the common people on the other. By the year 2000, by contrast, the biggest gaps were *between* countries, the end result of the "big-time" divergence. In contrast to the shrinking gaps in longevity that we have already seen, the income gaps between countries show no sign of diminishing today.

I start with the material wellbeing of the United States, focusing on the past hundred years. I have chosen the United States because the story is a dramatic one and because it illustrates the central themes of this book. When wellbeing improves, not everyone benefits equally, so that the improvement often (although not always) widens gaps between people. Change, positive or negative, is often unjust. What happens to inequality matters not only for how we should judge the improvement—who is reaping the benefit and who is being left behind—but also because inequality has its own effects. Inequality can sometimes spread growth, if it shows a way for others to benefit from the new opportunities. But it can also undercut material improvement and even threaten to extinguish it altogether. Inequality can inspire or incentivize those who are left behind to catch up, generating improvements for them and for others. Or inequality can become so severe, and the gains so concentrated in the hands of a few, that economic growth is choked off and the workings of the economy are compromised.

I have also chosen to start with the United States because the data are good and are easy to understand. Everyone knows what a dollar is, we do not need to convert currencies, and we can rely on data provided by a first-class statistical system. None of these luxuries will be available when we come to look at the world as a whole. Similarly, when we look far back in time, the data are weaker and the basis for comparison more tenuous. Comparing the twenty-first and nine-

teenth centuries is in many ways as difficult as comparing two different countries. The people are different, what they spend their money
on is different, and the standards of value are different; "the past is a
foreign country." The ease of working with data from the United
States gives me a familiar environment in which I can also develop
some concepts and try to clarify what economists and statisticians
mean when they talk about and try to measure income, poverty, and
inequality.

Economic Growth in the United States

The familiar concept of gross domestic product (GDP) is a good place
to start (though it would be a very poor place to stop). The top line of
Figure 1 shows what has happened to GDP per capita in the United
States since 1929, when the modern statistics begin. GDP is a measure
of how much a nation produces and is the basis for national income. It

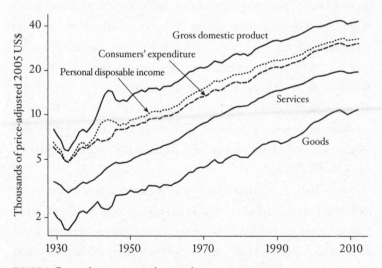

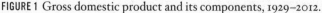

FIGURE 1 Gross domestic product and its components, 1929–2012.

was just over $8,000 per head per year in 1929, fell to $5,695 in 1933 in the depths of the Great Depression, and increased—with a few hiccups—to $43,238 in 2012, a more than fivefold increase since 1929. These numbers are corrected for increases in prices over time, so that they are measures of *real* income per head, measured in dollars at the prices of 2005. The figure for 1929 tells us that average national income in 1929, which was $805 in the much lower prices of the time, would have been worth $8,000 in 2009.[3]

The hiccups in GDP are times when progress stopped or was reversed; such hiccups have become less frequent and less severe over time—itself a measure of progress. The Great Recession that followed the financial crash of 2008 barely shows up in this history, in spite of the misery that it has caused, especially for the millions who became unemployed and remain so as I write. After 1950, the graph is close to being a straight line, which means a constant rate of growth at 1.9 percent per year, or a little more than 2 percent a year if we stop in 2008. Although the data get shakier as we move back in time, the growth rate of per capita national income has not changed very much over the past century and a half. At 2 percent growth, income doubles every thirty-five years, so if each couple had two children at age 35, each generation would have double the living standards of its parents. For those of us who are alive today, this seems like the natural order of things, yet it would have astonished our ancestors, who for thousands of years saw no progress at all, or who saw progress lost in subsequent setbacks. For all we know, it might also surprise our children and grandchildren.

As we shall see, GDP is a poor indicator of wellbeing, but it is limited even as a measure of income. It includes income generated in the United States that belongs to foreigners; it includes incomes in the form of undistributed corporate profits (which ultimately belong to shareholders) as well as surpluses run by federal, state, and local government. The part of national income that is available to families, after taxes have been paid and any transfers received, is *personal disposable income,* which is the second line from the top. It is a good deal smaller than GDP, but the historical picture of growth and fluctuation is very similar. Much the same is true if we look, not at what people get, but at what they spend. This is *consumers' expenditure,* the third line. The difference between personal disposable income and consumers' expenditure is the amount that people save, and the figure shows that the fraction of their income that Americans save has been falling, especially over the past thirty years. We don't know exactly why this has happened, and there are several possible explanations: it is easier to borrow than it used to be; it is no longer as necessary as it once was to save up to make the deposit on a house, a car, or a dishwasher; Social Security has perhaps reduced the need to save for retirement; and the average American benefited from increases in the stock market and in house prices—at least until the Great Recession.

Capital gains can be cashed in and spent, or they can be used to build wealth even when people are not saving. In the economists' lexicon, saving is defined as the *difference* between income and consumption, both of which are flows of money per unit of time. *Wealth* is not a flow but a *stock,* the total in a ledger at a moment of time. It is increased by capital gains and decreased by capital losses—many Americans lost around half of their wealth after the financial crash in 2008; it also increases when people save and decreases when they "dissave," spending more than they earn, for example in retirement or during a temporary period of unemployment.

The figure also shows what people spent their money on, split into two broad categories, goods (more than a third of the total in 2012) and services. The largest two items in services are housing and utilities, currently about $2 trillion a year or 18 percent of total consumers' expenditure, and health care, running at about $1.8 trillion, or 16 percent of the total. About a third of expenditure on goods is on durable goods—motor vehicles, furniture, electronics, and the like—and two-thirds is on nondurable goods—things like food and clothing. Americans today spend only 7.5 percent of their budget on food, or 13 percent once we add in expenditures on food consumed away from home. These expenditures are the stuff of material wellbeing, and their growth in Figure 1—and for the previous century—tells the tale of the increasing material prosperity that has accompanied increasing life spans. Life is not only longer, it is better.

Material wellbeing, and measures of it—GDP, personal income, and consumption—have recently received a bad press. Spending more, we are often told, does not bring us better lives, and religious authorities regularly warn against materialism. Even among those of us who endorse economic growth, there are many critics of GDP as it is currently defined and measured. GDP excludes important activities, such as services by homemakers; it takes no account of leisure; and it often does a poor job of measuring those things that *are* included. It also includes things that arguably should be excluded, like the cost of cleaning up pollution or building prisons or commuting. These "defensive" expenditures are not good in and of themselves but are regrettably necessary to enable things that are good.[4] If crime goes up, and we spend more on prisons, GDP will be higher. If we neglect climate change, and spend more and more on cleaning up and repairing after storms, GDP will go up, not down; we count the repairs but ignore the destruction.

GDP is notably silent on who gets what; Figure 1 tells us that there is more of everything to be had, but it does not tell us who is getting it. These issues of measurement and definition are serious, and I will come back to them. Who gets what is of the first importance, and much of this chapter is devoted to it. However, I want to start by defending the importance of material living standards and of economic growth against claims that they contribute little or nothing to wellbeing.

Economic growth requires investment in things—more machines, more basic facilities like highways or broadband—and in people, who need more and better education. Knowledge needs to be acquired and extended. Some of that extension is the product of new basic science, and some of it comes from the engineering that turns science into goods and services, and from the endless tweaking and improvement of design that, over time, turned a Model-T Ford into a Toyota Camry, or my clunky personal computer of 1983 into the sleek, almost weightless, and infinitely more powerful laptop on which I am writing this book. Investment in research and development enhances the flow of innovation, but new ideas can come from anywhere; the stock of knowledge is international, not national, and new ideas disperse quickly from the places where they are created. Innovation also needs entrepreneurs and risk-taking managers to find profitable ways of turning science and engineering into new products and services. This will be difficult without the right institutions. Innovators need to be free from the risk of expropriation, functioning law courts are needed to settle disputes and protect patents, and tax rates cannot be too high. When all of these conditions come together—as they have in the United States for a century and a half—we get sustained economic growth and higher living standards.

Is any of this worth having? Even beyond the point of having escaped from poverty and deprivation, new goods and services enable people to do things that were previously impossible, and these new possibilities make life better. Take a few examples and think about life before they existed. A host of domestic appliances free people, especially women, from soulless drudgery. Washing clothes used to be a whole-day activity every week, with coal-fired boilers, scrubbing of clothes, hanging them out to dry, and ironing. One Scottish advertisement in the 1950s claimed that a new improved washing powder "saved coal every Monday." Running water and good sanitation were well known to the Romans, but it took rising incomes to make them available to us all. More and better modes of transport provide personal freedom, widen the choices of places to live, and allow a new range of leisure activities, including making it easier to spend time with friends and family, activities that are often emphasized by antimaterialists. Air travel has made the country and the world accessible to a large fraction of the population. All of us can remain in touch with our children and friends throughout every day, we can develop and enjoy close friendships with people who live thousands of miles away, and we can enjoy contemporary and classical literature, music, and movies at any time and in any place. The Internet provides a cornucopia of information and entertainment, much of it for free. New medical treatments—such as the antihypertensive drugs documented in Chapter 4—have given us more years to enjoy these possibilities, while other treatments—such as hip replacements and cataract surgery—have reduced the morbidity that prevents their full enjoyment. That we are paying too much for health care does nothing to gainsay its achievements. No one denies that economic growth has negative side effects, but on balance it is enormously beneficial.

Depending on one's point of view, this recitation—the counting of the blessings from material innovation—may be seen as either trite and commonplace or not commonplace enough. But either way, such lists reveal just how implausible are claims that none of these advances contribute to human wellbeing or that we want these things only because our neighbors have them.

What about the evidence that, in spite of all of the growth documented in Figure 1, Americans are no happier than they were fifty years ago? Do these findings not contradict the idea that economic growth is good? Not necessarily. As we saw in Chapter 1, asking people whether or not they are happy yields results very different from those obtained by asking them whether or not they are satisfied with their lives; Figure 7 in Chapter 1 showed that Danes and Italians experience less happiness than Bangladeshis or Nepalese, even though they think that their lives are very much better. We do not know how Americans would have responded if asked to rate their lives over the past hundred years; the data do not exist. More importantly, we must think about the distribution of income. As we shall see, the economic growth graphed in Figure 1 greatly overstates what has happened to the typical American family, especially since the mid-1970s. The problem for them is not that they have seen lots of economic growth and been dissatisfied with it, but that they have seen little or no growth at all. It is hardly a surprise that they are no happier with their lives.

Growth of income is good because it expands the opportunities for people to live a good life. That said, it is also important to recognize what is covered by the measures in Figure 1 and what is not. Leisure time is not counted at all; if people decide to work less, and take more time for things they value more than work, national income and consumers' expenditure will fall. One reason that French GDP per capita is lower than American GDP per capita is because the French take longer holidays, but it is hard to argue that they are worse off as a result. Nor do we count services that are not sold in the market, so that if a woman works at home to care for her family, it is not counted, but if she works in someone else's home to care for *their* family, it *is* counted, and national income will be higher. If leisure is improved because, for example, the Internet provides quality entertainment at low cost, we have no way of counting those benefits. There are good (if somewhat technical) reasons for doing things this way, but these examples show that there really is a problem with GDP as an indicator of wellbeing.

One reason to worry about leaving out leisure is that there have been big changes in the way that Americans allocate their time over the past fifty years. The biggest change of all is that more women now go to work—especially women who are married to highly educated men. If we think of leisure as good and work as bad, these women are worse off on account of the leisure they have lost. For some women—those who are forced to take a second or third low-paying job to make ends meet—this makes sense, and if we count the extra income and ignore the loss of free time, we are overstating how well they are doing. But for many women, being able to work outside the home is a joy that was not available half a century ago. We should also be careful not to count the "leisure" of the unemployed as a benefit. Those who have lost their jobs are not *choosing* to spend more time at home, and study after study has documented that unemployed people are among the most dissatisfied with their lives. So the data in Figure 1 would not be improved by any mechanical adjustment for the value of leisure.

About two-thirds of Americans live in their own homes and pay no rent. Yet they receive a valuable service—living rent-free in their homes—and the national accountants include a value for this in consumers' expenditure, in personal disposable income, and in GDP. In effect, the accountants have decided that those of us who live in our own homes pay rent to ourselves, and they include this very large amount ($1.2 trillion in 2011) in both our income and our spending. The British government used to levy "real" taxes on this "imaginary" income as part of the income-tax system, and I remember that when he would receive the bill, my law-abiding and typically meek father would fly into an uncharacteristic anti-government rage. The accountants are correct to include these amounts—although the government today is probably wise not to try to tax them—but this and the many other "imputations" that are made to income drive a wedge between the way in which people perceive their incomes and the way in which the national accountants do. Personal income and expenditures also include the amounts that the government pays for health care on behalf of consumers, but, for obscure technical reasons, they do *not* include what the government pays for education on behalf of consumers.

If a politician tells you that "You never had it so good" and your reply is "Not around here; I just don't see it," you are unlikely to buy the explanation that you are doing well because the rent that you are paying to yourself has gone up, or because the government is buying more health care for the elderly!

Health-care expenditures are almost as large as those for housing, and measuring the value of health care is even harder. We know what health care *costs,* but the benefits it provides are both uncertain and difficult to value. If health care were sold in the market like cans of tuna or iPads, we could value it at what consumers pay for it. But health care is mostly paid for by insurance companies or by the government, which tells us nothing about its worth to the people who receive it. The national accountants, with no better option, measure health care by what it costs. Those who think that health care is worth more than every penny it costs argue that this understates its contribution, while those who emphasize the waste in the system argue the opposite. There is agreement only on the fact that the value of health care is poorly measured.

My counting of the blessings of economic growth made much of new goods. Yet many economists believe that the value of new goods, especially radically new goods, is not fully captured in the national accounts. The same goes for quality improvements in existing goods —shirts that no longer need to be ironed, phones that can understand speech, safer cars, or faster computers. The national accountants make allowances for all of these things, but no one thinks that we know exactly how to get it right. Some economists argue that economic growth used to be mostly about producing *more* things—more houses, more skirts and shirts, more tables and chairs—while today, it is mostly about producing *better* things. But measuring "better" is much harder than measuring "more," so that it is at least possible that the statisticians are missing more and more as time goes on. Perhaps the majority of economists think that the numbers underlying Figure 1 tend to understate how well people in the United States have been doing—though no one has come up with a convincing way of making a correction. And not all goods and services are better than they used to be. Banking is better since ATMs replaced having to visit a teller inside your own branch, but it is hard to believe that the predatory and misleading lending that led up to the recent financial crisis benefited bank customers.

The golden apple of material progress contains a worm that is just about apparent in Figure 1: average progress is slowing down, so that the gap between parents and their children is not what it used to be. If we look closely at the GDP figure, and compare its slope before and after 1970, we can see the decline, even if we ignore the last few years of the Great Recession. The decline is clearer in figures: in the decade from 1950 to 1959, GDP per capita grew at 2.3 percent a year; in the 1960s it grew at 3.0 percent; in the 1970s, at 2.1 percent; in the 1980s, at 2.0 percent; in the 1990s, at 1.9 percent; and in the first decade of the twenty-first century, at only 0.7 percent a year. Even if we exclude 2008 and 2009 from the last figure, we get only 1.6 percent. The difference between 3.0 and 1.6 percent might not seem very dramatic, but the power of compound growth means that, over a generation of twenty-five years, it is the difference between living standards more than doubling and living standards growing by less than 50 percent. An expanding economy means there is more for everyone (at least potentially), and the faster the cake expands, the less difficult are the conflicts over who gets what; everyone can get more without someone else having to get less.

The slowdown seems real enough, but if it is true that we are missing some of the improvements from better goods and services, we might be overstating its extent or even seeing a slowdown where there is none. Because services are a growing share of total GDP, and because services are the hardest to measure, the national accountants might be missing more and more over time. The same is true for all of the new Internet-based and electronic goods that have only recently become available and whose benefits are almost certainly not fully captured in the statistics. Health care is certainly becoming more effective, and the increased longevity that it brings is nowhere valued in the accounts. Yet to say this is also to see the problems that could come from a clumsy correction. As we saw in Chapter 4, some of the improvements in longevity have come from health care, but more have come from behavioral change, such as people stopping smoking. So if we assign a value to additional years of life—itself a difficult and controversial calculation—and attribute all of those years to health-care expenditures—we can easily, but *incorrectly*, increase the rate of growth of GDP. Once again, the statistical cure is likely to be worse than the statistical disease. Even so, the issue of understatement is not about to go away, and it will come up at several later points in this chapter.

Poverty in the United States

Just how the slower growth in GDP worked out for the worst-off can be seen by looking at what has happened to the number of people in poverty. Figure 2 shows the official poverty rates, published each year by the Bureau of the Census. The heavy line at the bottom is the percentage of all Americans who live in poverty, starting at 22 percent in

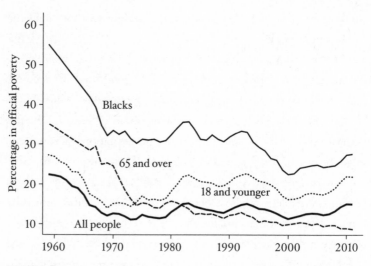

FIGURE 2 Poverty rates, 1959–2011.

1959 when the data begin, falling to a low of 11 percent in 1973, and then fluctuating around a gently rising trend. In 2010, 15 percent of the population was poor, about 2.5 percentage points higher than before the financial crisis. There is much to criticize in the way that these numbers are constructed, but on the face of it there is an aston-ishing contradiction between the *positive* picture of progress in Figure 1 and the *negative* picture of poverty in Figure 2, especially after the slowdown in economic growth that began in 1970. The econ-omy did not stop growing after 1973; income per person grew more than 60 percent between 1973 and 2010. Yet none of this growth made a dent in the poverty rate. Wherever the higher incomes were going, it was not to those who are officially classified as poor. And although there are the usual measurement difficulties—the incomes that go into the poverty statistics are not defined in just the same way as the incomes that go into GDP—that is not the explanation of why eco-nomic growth has not eliminated poverty.

Poverty rates are different for different groups, especially before the mid-1970s. Today, African-Americans and Hispanics (not shown in the graph) have (by far) the highest rates of poverty, and the elderly have the lowest rates, though poverty rates for all three groups have declined dramatically, especially in the early years. The reduction in poverty among the elderly is often cited as one of the great triumphs of the mature Social Security program, which guarantees price-adjusted payments for those aged 65 and over. Children are more likely to be in poverty than adults, but they, like other groups and like the population as a whole, have seen little or no reduction in poverty rates in the past thirty years. Note that the figure shows the *fractions* of people who are poor, so that, because the population is growing, the *number* of poor people is rising faster than the poverty rate. Indeed, in 2011, there were 46.2 million Americans in poverty, up by 6.7 million from 1959.

It is good to ask whether these numbers, showing increasing or at best stagnant poverty in a growing economy, are credible, or whether there is something wrong with the calculations. In fact, there are good reasons to be concerned about the way in which people are identified as being poor. While the basic idea is very simple, its implementation is not. Among the most difficult issues is how to choose the poverty line, and how to update it over time.

The poverty line in the United States was set in 1963–64 by Mollie Orshansky, an economist working for the Social Security Administration. She calculated how much a family of four—two adults and two children—would have to spend on food to just get by, and then she multiplied that amount by three on the grounds that the typical family spent about a third of its income on food. The number she came up with was $3,165 in 1963 dollars. In August 1969 that figure was officially adopted as the U.S. poverty line; apart from adjustment for changes in prices, it has been unchanged since. Its value in 2012 was $23,283. Keeping the line fixed in this way is really very odd; why not retain the original procedure and redo Orshansky's calculation for each subsequent year? Instead, the 1963 line has been retained, adjusted only for inflation.

Orshansky's "scientific" derivation of the poverty line—based on the superficially sensible and rhetorically appealing idea of nutritional needs—was little more than a smoke screen. Economists in the Johnson administration, preparing for what was to become the War on Poverty, needed a poverty line, and they were using $3,000 because it seemed like a sensible number. Orshansky's task was to provide something more readily defensible than a number plucked out of the air around the water cooler. Her first, and preferred, calculation was based on the Department of Agriculture's "low-cost food plan" and came in just above $4,000. A more stringent "economy food plan" produced the line of $3,165, which was adopted, not because it was more soundly or more scientifically based, but because it was closer to the original $3,000![5]

This story is not meant to illustrate the perfidy of the economists in the Johnson administration and even less to impugn the scientific integrity of a distinguished civil servant. The point is that the bureaucrats were right: the poverty line needs to make sense and to be acceptable to the public and to policymakers. Indeed Gallup polls at the time asked people what they thought the poverty line should be and the typical response was around $3,000.[6] The food rhetoric was (and remains) convenient because people tend to equate poverty and hunger, and they are perhaps more willing to go along with transfers to the poor when they think they are making transfers to people who do not have enough to eat. The nutritionally based calculations make the line seem like an "expert" line, though in truth there are no experts on what a poor family "needs"—except perhaps the poor family itself.

That the rhetoric and the reality gave the same answer was convenient in 1963 when the line was drawn, but less convenient in later years when different approaches to updating the line started to give different answers. If Orshansky's procedure was the right one, the poverty line should have been recalculated each year with a new economy food plan and a new multiplier. If we like the Gallup procedure, we should update using what people say the line ought to be. (The latter is my personal favorite: if we are going to label people as poor and treat them differently because they are poor, for example by giving them food subsidies, the opinion of the general public—whose taxes are being used for the purpose—should have something to do with where the line is set.) In fact, neither option was followed. Apart from some minor technical fixes, and apart from adjusting for price increases, the line today is the same as the line that Orshansky—or at least Johnson's economists—chose in 1963. If the Orshansky procedure had been updated —as she herself advocated over the years—the poverty line would have risen and would be much higher today than it actually is. The Gallup polls also show that people think the poverty line *should* have increased, pretty much in line with increases in real wages. Either way, the line should have risen over time, and poverty rates would have risen *more rapidly* than actually happened. It is certainly hard to argue that the failure of the American economy to reduce poverty more rapidly is a consequence of inappropriate updating of the poverty line; quite the opposite is true.

The American poverty line has become what is known as an *absolute* poverty line: one that stipulates a fixed amount of money needed to escape poverty, updating only for changes in prices. It does not depend on what other people get, nor on the prevailing standards in the economy. An absolute line makes most sense when there is a well-defined basket of goods that people need to survive. The poverty line is then just the cost of that basket, and such a line does not need to be updated over time except to account for price changes so that the basket is always affordable. This approach might make some sense for poor countries in Africa or South Asia, but poor American families are not close to this sort of subsistence now, nor did they *require* $3,165 to survive in 1963. The reality of poverty in America is about not having enough to participate fully in society, about families and their children not being able to live decent lives alongside neighbors and friends. Not being able to meet those social standards of decency is an *absolute* deprivation, but avoiding this absolute deprivation requires an amount of money that is relative in the sense that it must adjust to local standards.[7] In wealthy countries like the United States, it is very hard to justify anything other than a *relative* poverty line. And a relative line means that, compared to 1963, both the level and the rate of growth of poverty are being understated.

In a world in which general living standards are rising, an absolute poverty line means that those who are poor are drifting further and further below the mainstream of society. In the United States, as elsewhere, the poverty line is used as a standard of eligibility for a range of benefits and subsidies, and if it is not updated with general progress, benefits are effectively being more and more tightly restricted over time.

The failure to update the line is one of many flaws in poverty measurement in the United States. Another is that the official statistics use income *before* taxes and subsidies to figure out whether or not people are poor. This is a crippling defect. The many government programs to relieve poverty, including food stamps (officially the Supplemental Nutrition Action Program or SNAP) and cash grants paid through the tax system, are ignored. This has the absurd consequence that such policies, no matter how effective in reducing *actual* poverty, cannot reduce *measured* poverty. Even if an imaginative and effective administration managed to *eliminate* poverty through such schemes, the official counts would not show it. Such a failure is more than a theoretical possibility. Better calculations show that the rise in the overall poverty rate after 2006 (though not the earlier rises) would have been a good deal less had a more inclusive measure of income been used. Once again, this failure should not be attributed to the Census Bureau statisticians; the problem has been understood for a long time, and the Census Bureau has led the way in developing better measures.[8] The problem is that the original procedures did not take subsidies or tax credits into account because neither existed in 1963, and very few poor people paid taxes, so that the errors were inconsequential at the start. In later years, politics took over. Changing the procedure for counting the poor—even when fixing a flaw that everyone agrees is a flaw—is difficult to do without opening up a Pandora's box of difficult, controversial, and deeply partisan issues—and few administrations have shown an appetite for the task.

What can we say about poverty rates in the United States since the late 1950s? We know a lot about incomes at the bottom of the distribution, so that even if the official poverty line is itself flawed, we can still see what has happened. The decline in general poverty from 1959 until the mid-1970s was certainly real, as was the particularly rapid improvement among the elderly and among African-Americans. There is also no doubt that progress after the mid-1970s has been slowed or halted. For those who think that a fixed poverty line is the way to go, as in the official measures, poverty rates have been stagnant, in spite of the substantial economic growth over the period.

One escape route from this negative conclusion is to argue, once again, that progress is being understated because quality improvements and new goods are not being adequately captured in the statistics. That would mean that inflation is being overstated, because some of the increase in prices comes from better things, not just from dearer things. If so, the poverty line is being increased too fast, and an ever-increasing proportion of the poor are not poor at all. If we buy this argument—and there is no way of knowing by how much the poor are benefiting from unmeasured quality improvements—we might be winning the war on poverty after all.[9] Working in the same direction is the failure of the official measure to incorporate taxes and transfers that are designed to benefit the poor. Doing so not only moderates upticks during recessions, as we have seen for the recent recession, but also would have resulted in a larger decline in poverty over the longer run.[10]

However, if you believe, as I do, that the poverty line should move up with the living standards of typical households in the population, poverty rates have increased over the past four decades, in stark contrast to the growth of the average economy. More broadly, postwar economic growth in the United States was widely shared until the 1970s. Since then, economic growth has been slower, and it has no longer been shared with the people at the bottom of the distribution. Postwar history is divided into two periods: one with relatively rapid, widely shared growth and one with slower growth together with a growing gap between the poor and everyone else.

Poverty measurement in the United States has much in common with poverty measurement elsewhere, including the measurement of world poverty. The choice of a poverty line is almost always controversial, and there are often technical—and less publicly visible—questions of how to define and measure income. The question of how to update poverty lines is difficult, in part because of philosophical and political differences, but also because changing who is poor often involves changes in benefits, from which some gain and some lose. Any change in how poverty is calculated—even one that is designed to fix an obvious and universally recognized flaw, like not counting food stamps—will provoke political opposition to the change. Poverty statistics are part of a state's apparatus for governing, for redistribution of income, and for trying to stop people from falling into destitution in the face of misfortune; they are part of the machinery of justice. Their existence marks the acceptance by the state of responsibility for addressing poverty and for offsetting its worst consequences. They allow states to "see" poverty and are part of the apparatus that allows what the political scientist James Scott has memorably called "seeing like a state."[11] As always, just as it is hard to govern without measurement, there is no measurement without politics. The "stat" in statistics is not there by accident.

The Distribution of Incomes in the United States

The evolution of income can be looked at from three different perspectives: growth, poverty, and inequality. Growth is about the average and how it changes, poverty about the bottom, and inequality about how widely incomes are spread across families or people. The spread is often measured by the *Gini coefficient,* named after Corrado Gini, an Italian economist who worked in the first half of the twentieth century. Gini's coefficient, or simply the Gini, is a number that lies between 0 (perfect equality—everyone has the same) and 1 (perfect inequality, with one person having everything). It measures how far people are apart on average. (If you really want know the details, it is the average difference in income between all pairs of people divided by twice the average income. If there are two of us, and you have everything, the difference between us is twice the mean, and the Gini is 1. If we both have the same, the difference between us is 0, and so is the Gini.)

The Gini was roughly constant from the end of World War II until the mid-1970s, and it has grown since then; this was also true for the income share of the top 10 percent, and it is true whether we look at pre- or after-tax incomes. Average income has grown while bottom incomes have stagnated, and this can happen only if nonpoor incomes have pulled away from the incomes of the poor. Such descriptions are correct, but they are not very helpful for telling us what has been going on or why. Instead, we need to look at all incomes, where they come from and the forces that have been shaping them; there has been much more going on than can be summarized by two or three statistics. The incomes of Americans can be thought of as a broad river, whose average rate of flow tells us little about what is happening on one side or the other, in the eddies, or in the stagnant pools.

Figure 3 makes a start by showing what has happened to average incomes at various points in the distribution. The Census Bureau calculates these numbers from an annual survey that asks families about their incomes in the previous year; the last numbers shown come from more than 87,000 families surveyed in March 2011 and asked about their incomes in 2010. The graph shows the average incomes (adjusted for inflation at 2010 prices and on a log scale) of families in each fifth

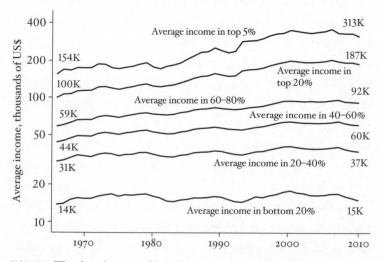

FIGURE 3 The distribution of family income in the United States.

of the income distribution. The top line shows the average incomes of the top 5 percent of families. The average income of families in the top 5 percent was eleven times the average income of families in the bottom 20 percent in 1966. By 2010, the ratio had risen to twenty-one times. All of these numbers are before taxes and subsidies, and they make no allowance for those items—such as a great deal of health care—that are provided to households by the government; some of those omissions are important, as we shall see. Those items *are* included in the income figures in Figure 1, which is one of the reasons why it paints a somewhat rosier picture than Figure 3.

The figure shows one of the main facts about the distribution of family income since the late 1960s. All families shared in the rising prosperity until the mid- to late 1970s. Since then, incomes have pulled apart. As we already know from the poverty numbers, the bottom fifth of families gained very little. The growth in their average incomes was less than 0.2 percent a year over the past forty-four years and, even before the recession, their real incomes were no higher than they had been in the late 1970s. Average incomes of the top fifth, by contrast, grew more quickly, at 1.6 percent a year, though not as quickly as those of the top 5 percent, whose average incomes grew at 2.1 percent a year. Once again, if we roll out the argument about unmeasured quality change, progress would be greater in the bottom fifth, though the *differential* rates of progress between the bottom and the top would be unaffected.

As we shall see later, this figure is deficient in two respects: it doesn't go back far enough, and because the survey sample is too small it doesn't capture the incomes of the very rich. Neither Bill Gates nor Warren Buffett has much chance of ever being included in the survey. I shall address both of these deficiencies later, but, for the moment, I want to focus on the past forty years and on the broad swathe of families who are not earning millions of dollars a year.

Inequality at Work

The labor market is a good starting point for thinking about incomes; most families get their incomes from what people earn, so that jobs and wages exert a profound effect on family incomes. But the labor market is only one of the forces shaping family incomes. Many people—homemakers, retirees, children, the unemployed, or the disabled—have no earnings and depend for a living on other members of their families, on pensions, or on government. Some people own businesses from which they draw an income, and this income is partly earnings from labor and partly a return from the capital invested in the business. Some people receive income from capital, the dividends and interest on wealth that they, their parents, or their grandparents have accumulated in the past.

Many families have more than one person who receives income, so that the way that people live together shapes the way that individual incomes are converted into family incomes. This is the effect of *demographic characteristics* on the distribution of incomes. A world in which men work and women do not is different from one in which "power couples" each earn top salaries, and changing demographics have been part of the story of growing inequality. Government policy is also important. National and local governments decide how much of income is to be taxed, set the rules for social security (state pensions) and for much of health care, and set and enforce a multitude of rules and regulations that affect the operations of firms and of labor markets. Politics settles conflicts over who gets what, and government is a battleground for constituents, as well as for interest groups and lobbyists who strive to increase the shares of their clients. Changes in the size and power of these groups—labor unions, the elderly, immigrants, and even prisoners—have all shaped the way that incomes in America have evolved. All of this happens against a background of changing technology, changing international trade and migration, and changing social norms.

The distribution of income cannot be boiled down to one mechanism, such as supply and demand in the labor market, nor can it be measured by a single measure of inequality like the Gini coefficient. It is the result of many different processes working together. History matters, as do the market, politics, and demography.

Jan Tinbergen, one of the two economists who shared the first Nobel Prize in Economic Sciences, saw the evolving distribution of income not as it might have been seen in the past, as a battle between labor and capital, but as a race between technological development and increases in schooling.[12] The Harvard economists Lawrence Katz and Claudia Goldin have used this analogy to describe recent developments in the American labor market.[13] The technology used at work requires skill and training or perhaps just the adaptability that comes from a good general education. If the education of workers falls behind what the market is looking for, the price of education will rise, the earnings of more educated workers will pull ahead, and inequality will increase. When education runs ahead—for example, when the Vietnam War drove young men to go to college who would not otherwise have gone—the supply of skill rises and its price—the premium to a college education—falls, and wage inequality declines.

In the early part of the twentieth century, the main educational distinction was between those who had or had not graduated from high school; today, when the average level of education is much higher, it is between those who do and do not have a college education. Changes in the technology of production have consistently favored those with more skills; this trend is described by the term *skill-biased technical progress*. Once upon a time, the upgrade was from farm work to an assembly line; today, it is the ability to write code for computers to undertake new tasks. Better-educated workers can better use new technologies as they come along and are better able to adapt, improve, or tweak the new methods.

Over most of the past century, Americans have been acquiring more education, so that the supply of skill to the labor market has increased. If nothing else had happened, this chain of events would have reduced the value of education and driven down the gap in wages between those with and without a college degree. Yet the gap has risen, not fallen, and it has done so particularly rapidly since the late 1970s. When price rises even though supply has risen, we know that demand must be rising even more rapidly. Economists attribute this rise to the relentless increase in the skills required to work with new, information-based technologies. They believe that the acceleration in skill-biased technical progress over the past thirty years is the main engine driving increased inequality in earnings. The growing premium to getting a college education is the way the market tells young people that changing technology is making it more and more worthwhile to go to college, and the increase in the average level of education shows that people have been paying attention.

Rapid changes in the way that computers are used, in the Internet, and in the ready availability of information have created an accelerating demand for those who can use that information in decision making and in business, and, at least since the late 1970s, education has not been keeping up. Of course, this trend may not go on indefinitely. If the educational system becomes flexible enough to produce the new skills as quickly as the need for them grows, the increase in inequality will eventually come to an end.[14]

As always, changes in ways of doing things should not be thought of as scientific breakthroughs that drop from the sky at random or that pop into the minds of lonely geniuses. Instead, they usually respond to needs in the economic and social environment. Sometimes the basic science is already in place and the blueprints already on the shelf, but their application requires entrepreneurs and engineers to see profitable opportunities and shape them for the market. The economist Daron Acemoglu has argued for the importance of this sort of "directed" technological change, emphasizing that many new methods become viable only when there is a sufficient supply of skilled workers to implement and develop them.[15] As he notes, this is hardly to argue that the skill expansion triggered by the Vietnam War caused the computer to be invented, but he envisages a cumulative process in which the skill premium from earlier technical change provides incentives for more people to go to college, the greater supply of college-educated workers speeds up the rate of technical progress, thus raising the skill premium, and so on. The process will stop only when we have done everything that can be done with the new information technologies, and inventive attention will move on to some other part of the economy, just as it moved on from railways to automobiles and from automobiles to electronics. Rising wage inequality is a by-product of this mechanism and plays a key role in raising the supply of skills. So while the inequality is not particularly welcome in its own right, it is part of a system that is raising living standards for everyone.

A nice analogy is when parents tire of perpetually messy rooms and decide to reward tidiness by linking their children's allowances to the state of their bedrooms. Such schemes typically have at least some of their desired effect, making the house more livable, parents less irritated, and children more aware of the pleasures of an orderly room. Yet there are perils too. If one child is more readily incentivized than her siblings, or one is just naturally tidier no matter what the incentives, initially equal allowances will soon become persistently unequal. In an ideal family, all the children would keep their rooms perfectly tidy and receive their full allowances. In real families, as in real economies, sharper incentives mean more inequality. Some parents may not see this as a problem; each child, after all, has perfect equality of opportunity and should learn to live with the consequences of his or her actions. Other parents may be more sympathetic; may understand that each of their children is differently endowed with the ability to be tidy and that everyone makes mistakes from time to time; and may share the likely perception of their children that the new inequality is unfair. Equality of opportunity does not guarantee outcomes that are transparently just.

If the family incentive scheme runs long enough, inequality may be increased even more if the children save part of their allowances. Even if all children save the same share of their allowances, one is regularly adding more to her wealth than the others, and she will get steadily richer than her siblings. Saving will ramp up the inequality in the allowances, and inequality in wealth will soon dwarf the inequality in allowances, just as, in the actual economy, inequality in wealth dwarfs inequality in earnings. This ramping up of inequality will be even faster if the children who are naturally inclined to be tidy are also those who are naturally inclined to save for the future. In the society at large, the same forces are at work if those who are more oriented to the future and have more self-control are the same people who are more able to benefit from education and more likely to accumulate wealth from their education-enhanced earnings. There is a deep conflict between incentives and inequality, in families and in countries.

Is the explosion of new technologies really making everyone better off? It certainly holds out that possibility: better ways of doing things mean that more total income is potentially available for distribution. And even if the premium for skill is increasing, the process should not, by itself, lower the wages of the unskilled. While Figure 3 does not show any decline of family *incomes* in the bottom 20 percent, the picture is different for the lowest *wages,* which have indeed been declining in real terms. Family incomes have kept up only because more women have been participating in the labor force, so that more families now have more than one earner. What then has been keeping wages down?

Globalization is a part of the story; the manufacture of many goods that used to be made in the United States by low-skilled workers has moved to poorer countries, and many companies have sent offshore jobs that used to be done domestically, including "back-office" work (like claims processing) and customer call centers. Legal and illegal immigration has also been blamed for downward pressure on low-skill wages, though such claims remain controversial, and some credible studies show that the effect is small. The rising cost of medical care has also been important; most employees receive health insurance as part of their overall compensation, and most research shows that increases in premiums ultimately come out of wages.[16] Indeed, average wages have tended to do badly when health-care costs are rising most rapidly and to do better when health-care costs are rising more slowly.[17] The share of GDP going to health care, only 5 percent in 1960, was 8 percent in the mid-1970s but had risen to nearly 18 percent by 2009.

Even among low-skill jobs, how people have fared depends on just what kind of skill they have. The worst situation is to have been a clerk in a mechanical office job that can be (and has been) performed by a computer, or has been outsourced to lower-cost workers in poorer (though not the world's poorest) countries. Even so, among the occupations with some of the lowest average wages, both wages and employment have been rising. These are service jobs in retail, restaurants, or health care—jobs that require human contact, though often not a high level of cognitive skills (the kind that are learned in college), and that cannot be performed by computers. Women have traditionally done many of these jobs, and this has put further pressure on the men whose jobs have been lost. The much richer people who have been doing really well (on which more below) also want services, from restaurant workers, daycare workers, nannies, doulas, dog walkers, cleaners, and personal shoppers all the way to private chefs, chauffeurs, and pilots. In this respect, we have recreated something like the old European aristocracy, in which great landowners employed armies of retainers—Downton Abbey in the Hamptons or Palm Beach.[18] To the extent that these service groups remain at the bottom of the distribution, earnings and jobs have been polarized, expanding at the very top and at the very bottom, but not at all in the middle.[19]

Politics and Inequality

Politics has affected wages among low-paid workers. The minimum wage is set by Congress—in 2013 it was $7.25 an hour or $14,500 for a two-thousand-hour year—and some states have their own minimum wages, eighteen of which are higher than the federal rate. The key point is that the federal minimum wage is *not* automatically adjusted for inflation or for growth in market wages. In consequence, the real value of the minimum is on a constant downward trend punctuated by upward adjustments whenever Congress acts; when real wages are growing, the ratio of the minimum wage to the average wage declines even faster.

Changing the minimum wage is nearly always contentious; it pits labor against employers, and each is well represented in politics. As a result, the minimum wage can be constant for long periods of time; it was $3.35 from January 1, 1981, until April 1, 1990, it was $5.15 from September 1, 1997, to July 24, 2007, and the current (2013) rate has been in place since July 24, 2009. Even when changes were made, they were often not large enough to make up for price increases; the minimum wage of $2.10 in 1975 had a purchasing power that was a third greater than the minimum wage of $7.25 in 2011. Put differently, someone paid at minimum wage in 1975 would have earned $4,200 a year, which was the official poverty line for a three-person family. By 2010, earnings would have been $14,500, while the three-person poverty line had risen to $17,374. This long-term erosion, punctuated by occasional and only partial restorations, is a measure of the declining political power of those workers whose earnings are at or close to the minimum wage.

The effects of the minimum wage have been controversial among economists as well as politicians. Standard—and only mildly simplistic—theory predicts that if government raises the wage above its free-market value, employers will fire some of the newly expensive workers because their contribution is now less than what they cost. Empirical work by the Princeton economists David Card and Alan Krueger in the early 1990s suggested that these effects were nonexistent, at least for *small* increases in the minimum wage.[20] Such heresy generated heated denunciations, not only from those whose interests were directly affected, but also from enraged economists. Nobel laureate James Buchanan wrote in the *Wall Street Journal* that allowing the evidence to contradict the theory in this way implied that "there is no minimum scientific content in economics," so that "economists can do nothing but write as advocates for ideological interests." He concluded by congratulating most economists who "have not yet become a bevy of camp-following whores."[21]

While there is little empirical evidence in economics that cannot be challenged, claims of ideological bias and of self-proclaimed scientific integrity—hardly confined to one side of the argument—are especially common when, as here, there is a confrontation between political interests. Even so, in this case one part of the empirical evidence is not at all controversial. Among those who actually have jobs, a decline in the minimum wage increases inequality in wages because it allows some low wages that otherwise would not exist. This effect will not be important for groups or occupations in which people are relatively well paid, so that there are few people below the minimum, but it will be important in low-wage areas, in low-wage occupations, or among groups, such as women or African-Americans, whose wages are relatively low.[22]

If the erosion of the minimum wage since the 1970s has been partly responsible for the overall decline in real wages among low-wage workers, why didn't politics stop it from happening? One reason is the decline of labor unions, especially in the private sector. The fraction of private-sector workers who were union members declined from 24 percent in 1973 to only 6.6 percent in 2012. Although the unionization of public-sector workers increased in the 1970s, it has been stagnant since 1979; the majority of union members are now in the public sector. The declining political clout of unions is made worse by the fact that there are other groups that can't vote at all. Illegal immigrants obviously do not vote, but neither do legal immigrants who are not citizens. Between 1972 and 2002, the ratio of noncitizens to the voting-age population rose fourfold at the same time as they became poorer relative to the general population. As immigration policies changed, legal immigrants moved from being relatively well heeled to being relatively poor; their political voice was quieted even as the political power of unions declined.

Yet another important group has been disenfranchised, in spite of being citizens. Only Vermont and Maine allow felons to vote from jail, but ten states disenfranchise felons for life, even after they have served their sentence and parole. In 1998, the Sentencing Project of Human Rights Watch estimated that 2 percent of the voting-age population was currently or permanently disenfranchised. One-third of those were African-American men, so that 13 percent of the African-American male population could not vote; in Alabama that rate is estimated to be more than 30 percent, and it is almost as high in Mississippi. Even in a relatively liberal state like New Jersey, which does not disenfranchise people for life, 18 percent of black males cannot vote. While many of the people so disenfranchised are not very likely to vote in any case, they are *potential* voters, and their exclusion from participatory politics precludes their ever being organized into an effective political force, so that politicians have no reason to pay any attention to what they want.

Retired people are not immediately affected by what happens in the labor market, although their pensions depend on their work history, their own savings, their or their past employers' contributions to pension plans, and the rules of the Social Security system, which makes payments to retirees. These payments are another arena for politics and the exercise of political power. Although the elderly are not particularly wealthy, they are large in numbers (increasingly so as the baby boom generation ages), they vote, and their lobbying organization, AARP, is one of the most powerful (and most feared) in Washington.

The contrast between what has happened to minimum wages on the one hand and to Social Security on the other is a testament to the declining power of unions and the rising power of the elderly. The elderly also receive (increasingly) expensive benefits through Medicare, the government program that provides health care for them; if the cost of this program is counted as part of the income of the recipients, the elderly have done even better than is indicated by their cash income alone. Once again, the political power of the elderly has been and remains important in maintaining these benefits, although other powerful lobbies—such as those for health-care providers, insurers, and pharmaceutical companies—are also at work.

Taxes are the very stuff of politics. Income taxes are progressive, taking more from the rich than from the poor, who may even receive tax credits, so that the after-tax distribution of income is, by design, more equal than its pretax distribution. The progressiveness of the tax system is continuously contested, for example in debates over whether capital gains or dividends should be treated like other income, or whether fairness demands redistribution (from the left) or that everyone pay their share (from the right).

About half of American families pay no federal income taxes. Even so, taxes have not played a very large part in shaping the changes in inequality since the 1970s, most of which have been driven by pretax income. In the 1980s tax policy widened disparities somewhat, by means of tax reductions that favored the better-off, while in the 1990s the opposite was true, with tax increases at the top and expansions in the Earned Income Tax Credit, which provides benefits at the bottom. Since 2001, tax cuts have once again favored high-income taxpayers. The Congressional Budget Office estimates that, between 1979 and 2007, income inequality (measured by the Gini coefficient, though on a slightly different basis) increased by about a quarter for pretax income and by about a third for after-tax income (including the value of Medicare). This large discrepancy is driven in part by the tax system becoming less progressive over the whole period, but also by the movement of transfers up the income distribution, as transfers to the (politically powerful) elderly grew relative to transfers to the (politically weak) poor.[23]

Earnings and Families

People bring home their paychecks and share them with other family members, some of whom may have earnings of their own. Many families do not have an earner, including those who are retired and live on private or government pensions. How people live together and who is working further shape the distribution of family incomes over and above what happens to earnings in the labor market. Some trends, such as the increase in women's earnings relative to those of men, and the increase in earnings of blacks relative to those of whites until 1985, have offset the increases in wage inequality from the labor market. If we look at the earnings of all people, whether or not they have a job, and irrespective of their race and sex, the increase in earnings inequality is much less than if we confine our attention to those who are working. The widening earnings inequality among workers has been partially offset by the movement into the workforce of people who were previously not working and earning nothing, particularly married women. And while inequality of earnings has increased within groups, such as white males in full-time employment, there has been some reduction in inequality between groups, with women's earnings rising relative to men's and earnings of African-Americans rising relative to those of whites.

Other changes have worked to spread family income out even more than earnings. Highly educated men tend to marry highly educated women. While this has been true for a long time, fifty years ago the wives of high-earning men were less likely to work than the wives of low-earning men. These women were often highly educated, but in keeping with the custom of the time they were homemakers for their successful husbands. Today, husbands and wives are still matched on education, but the spouses of high earners are now more, not less, likely to be high earners themselves. "Power couples," both earning top salaries, help stretch out the top of the (family) income distribution beyond the top of the (personal) earnings distribution. One way of showing this is to take the survey data, divorce (only statistically!) all married couples, randomly remarry them to other spouses, and recalculate the distribution of family income. Doing this does not eliminate the rise in inequality of family income, but it substantially reduces it.

While the top of the income distribution is being stretched out by power couples, the bottom is being stretched out by people who are not partnered at all, particularly households headed by single women, whose numbers have risen much more rapidly than the total number of households, and who are significantly more likely to be in poverty.

For the vast majority of families in America, the impersonal forces of the labor market have been the most important influence on their incomes and on how their incomes compare to those of other people. Changing family composition has also widened the gaps between families, as have the actions of policymakers responding to political pressure from those who have political power. In the labor market, the interplay between technology and education has been the lead actor, with smaller but still important parts played by globalization and the decline in minimum wages. The rapidly rising costs of health care have been a persistent drag on wage rates. Incentives for education have sharply increased, as have the corresponding penalties for ignoring the incentives, which have hurt those who chose not to be educated, or whose lack of ability or background prevented them from becoming educated. Just as in the parable of the tidy and the untidy children, sharper incentives have brought wider inequalities. The inequalities in the labor market have created new jobs at the top and bottom of the market and hollowed out the middle. The poor have also lost out in the political game, as unions have lost members and political clout, as poorer nonvoting immigrants rose as a share of the workforce, and as African-Americans either did not vote or were precluded from voting. The not-so-poor elderly have done increasingly well as their numbers, voting power, and political representation have risen. However, the most successful group, both in the market and in politics, is the group at the very top of the income and earnings distribution, and it is to them that I turn next.

Top Incomes in the United States

The study of income inequality was transformed by a 2003 study by two economists, Thomas Piketty, now of the Paris School of Economics, and Emmanuel Saez of the University of California at

Berkeley.[24] It had long been known that the data on incomes from household surveys were not very useful for looking at very high incomes; there are too few such people to show up regularly in nationally representative surveys. (Even if approached at random, they might also be less likely to answer.) Piketty and Saez greatly extended a method that had been originally used in 1953 by Nobel laureate economist Simon Kuznets, who worked with data from income-tax records.[25] The rich, like everyone else, have no choice but to file tax returns, and so they are fully represented in the income-tax data. Piketty and Saez's results have changed the way that people think about income inequality, particularly at the top of the distribution. Later studies have looked at comparable data from other countries around the world, so that we can extend these insights beyond the United States.

Within this chapter I have saved this material until last because I want to give it particular attention and because of its enormous importance for understanding what has happened in the labor market, the capital market, and in politics. I also believe that top incomes have special importance, just because of the enormous sums of money that are involved.

Figure 4 is an updated version of one of the key graphs in Piketty and Saez's paper.[26] The data go back to the introduction of the income tax in the United States in 1913 and run to 2011, during the Great Recession. They include both world wars, shown in light shading, and the Great Depression, shown in a darker shade. The three lines show estimates of the percentage share of total personal income (including capital gains) that went to the top 1 percent of all tax units (the top line), the top half of 1 percent (middle line), and the top tenth of 1 percent (bottom line). The dollar amounts on the right show the average incomes of those in each group in 2011: $1.1 million for the top 1 percent, $1.7 million for the top 0.5 percent, and $5 million for the

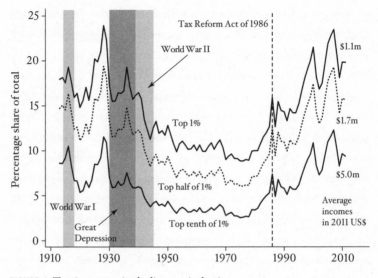

FIGURE 4 Top incomes, including capital gains, 1913–2011.

top 0.1 percent. For the top 0.01 percent (not shown here), average income in 2011 was more than $24 million, and between them they received 4.5 percent of total income. More modestly, the top 10 percent of tax units in 2011 commanded 47 percent of all income, with an average income of $255,000. (A tax unit is not identical to a family, nor is income for tax purposes the same as other measures of income, but the overlaps are big enough that these trends are not misleading.)

The figure shows that the share of top incomes was U-shaped over the past century. The top shares declined sharply during both world wars—the taxes that funded the American contribution to the wars fell heavily on corporations and resulted in sharp reductions in dividends to the rich—as well as during the Great Depression. After World War II, there was a further but gentler decline, which was eventually reversed toward the end of the 1970s and early 1980s. There was a sharp rise in top shares in 1986, followed by further increases, so that by 2008 the richest taxpayers were receiving about the same share of total income that they received on the eve of World War I. A major tax reform in 1986 changed the definition of taxable income and caused the blip in that year.

Not only have there been major swings in top incomes, but the kind of people who receive them has also changed. In the early years, top incomes were derived from capital, and the richest people were what Piketty and Saez call "coupon clippers," who received most of their incomes from dividends and interest. The fortunes underlying these receipts were eroded over the century by increasingly progressive income and estate taxes. Those who used to live off their (or their ancestors') fortunes have been replaced at the top by *earners,* people like CEOs of large firms, Wall Street bankers, and hedge fund managers, who receive their incomes as salaries, bonuses, and stock options. Entrepreneurial income was important a hundred years ago and remains important today, and the share of such income among top incomes has remained relatively constant. This is in contrast to the big story—the replacement of the coupon clippers, or the "idle rich," by the "working rich." At the dizzying heights of the top tenth of 1 percent, capital income still accounts for a larger share than among the top 10 percent but wage income is now the largest share: nearly three-quarters in the top 10 percent and 43 percent of income among the top tenth of 1 percent. In 1916, only 10 percent of income in this elite group came from wage income. Dividends and interest are still important, but they are more widely distributed because so many stocks are owned by pension funds.

The past thirty years show a particularly marked contrast between the material wellbeing of the majority of the people and that of those at the top. Since 1980, the bottom 90 percent of taxpayers have seen their inflation-adjusted pretax incomes grow at less than a tenth of 1 percent a year, for a *total* increase of 1.9 percent over twenty-eight years. Each generation is barely holding on to the living standards of its parents. On an after-tax basis, and particularly after adding imputations for their share of the cost of Medicare, the bottom 90 percent did somewhat better. The Congressional Budget Office reports that between 1979 and 2007, the bottom 80 percent of households saw growth of about a quarter in after-tax income, less than 1 percent a year.[27] Medicare is a valuable program, but the benefits go to the elderly, and the money cannot be used to pay the rent or to put food on the table.

Among the top 1 percent, by contrast, pretax incomes have grown by *2.35 times;* for parents and children who had the good fortune to be in the top 1 percent in both 1980 and 2011, there has been progress indeed. At the very top, and beyond what is shown in the figure, the average incomes of the top 1 percent of the top 1 percent have grown more than four times. These numbers refer to *pretax* incomes, so that, with the reductions in taxes on top incomes since 2001, the top income earners have done even better in after-tax dollars. These sharp contrasts in experience between the majority and the fortunate minority do much to explain the apparent contradiction between Figures 1 and 2—how it can be that, in an economy that has seen substantial economic growth, there has been so little progress against poverty. They also show that it was not *only* the poor who saw little improvement in their living standards.

What Happened and Why Does It Matter?

Did the rich get richer at the expense of everyone else, or was it simply that they, like other highly educated and talented people, became more productive, for example by inventing new and better ways of doing things that benefited everyone? In such a world, in which everyone is doing well, but some more so than others, do complaints about inequality have any legitimacy, or are they simply an expression of envy? Why do we care about inequality anyway? If everyone starts out with an equal chance, why should we worry if those who work harder do better? Or if people do not start out with equal chances, perhaps we should worry about equality of opportunity, not equality of outcomes.

There is much to be said for equality of opportunity, and for not penalizing people for the success that comes from their own hard work. Yet, compared with other rich countries, and in spite of the popular belief in the American dream that anyone can succeed, the United States is in fact not particularly good at actually delivering equal opportunities. One way of measuring equality of opportunity is to look at the correlation between the earnings of fathers and sons. In a completely mobile society, with perfect equality of opportunity, your earnings should be unrelated to what your father earned; by contrast, in a hereditary caste society, in which jobs are handed down from one generation to the next, the correlation would be 1. In the United States, the correlation is about 0.5, which is the highest among the OECD countries and is exceeded only by those of China and a handful of countries in Latin America. Indeed, countries with a lot of income inequality are countries where father's and son's earnings are closely related;[28] the unequal countries, including the United States, are the countries where there appears to be the least equality of opportunity. Even if we believe that equality of opportunity is what we want, and don't care about inequality of outcomes, the two tend to go together, which suggests that inequality itself is a barrier to equal opportunity.

What about envy of the rich? Economists have a strong attachment to something called the Pareto principle, which we first met in the Introduction: If some people are made better off and no one is made worse off, the world is a better place. Envy should not be counted. This maxim is often cited as a reason to focus on poverty and not to worry about what is happening at the top. In the words of

Martin Feldstein, a Harvard economist, "income inequality is not a problem in need of remedy."[29] There is a lot to be said for the Pareto principle, but, as we shall see, it does not imply that rising income inequality is not a problem. But to get there, we need to know more about *why* the top incomes have risen so rapidly in recent years, and what the consequences were.

One story is that the top is not so different from the rest of the distribution, only more so. New technologies have provided new opportunities for the more educated and more creative and, in extreme cases, have provided extraordinary fortunes to the most highly educated and the most creative, or at least to the luckiest members of that group. The exemplars are people like Bill Gates at Microsoft, Steve Jobs at Apple, and Larry Page and Sergey Brin at Google. Entertainers or great athletes can now be appreciated by the whole world, not just their local audiences, and they get paid in proportion to that audience. Globalization allows successful entrepreneurs, like successful entertainers, to extend their reach and enlarge their profits. And indeed, many more people around the world can now enjoy their extraordinary talents.

Another group that is well represented among the highest-paid is the senior management of banks and of hedge funds. They too are very highly trained, and they have also used their training and creativity to produce new products. There is no unanimity among economists on the extent to which these new financial instruments have a social value that matches the profits that they generate for their inventors. It is hard not to sympathize with Paul Volcker's statement that the last truly useful financial innovation was the ATM machine. If bankers and financiers have private incentives that exaggerate their social incentives, we will get too much banking and financing, and there is no defense for the inequality that they cause.

Financial services have played an important role in financing innovation throughout the economy, and the efficient allocation of capital is one of the most valuable tasks in a market economy. But there is widespread suspicion that some highly profitable financial activities are of little benefit to the population as a whole, and may even threaten the stability of the financial system—what investor and businessman Warren Buffett has called financial weapons of mass destruction. If so, the very high payments that come with them are both unjust and inefficient. The heavy recruitment of the best minds into financial engineering is a loss to the rest of the economy, likely reducing innovation and growth elsewhere. What is much less controversial is that the implicit guarantee that the government would bail out the largest and most highly interconnected institutions led to excessive risk taking that was highly rewarded, even though it led to collapse and to misery for the millions who lost their jobs, faced reductions in incomes, or were left with debts that they could not hope to repay. That people playing with their own and their clients' money should get rich is one thing; that they should do so with public money is quite another. If these activities cause widespread social harm, the situation is intolerable.

Large increases in compensation have not been confined to financial companies and to a few super-creative innovators, but instead have spread to the senior executives of many American corporations. Once again, some have argued that the nature of senior management has changed, that corporations are bigger and that changes in information technology have allowed senior executives to manage larger groups of people. Yet there is a good deal of doubt that this trend can explain the increase in top-level compensation. For one thing, the changes in Figure 4 are too rapid to be plausibly explained by technical progress. For another, as we shall see in the next chapter, several other Western economies have had much smaller increases, or even no increases at all, in compensation for top managers, although they too have access to the new management technologies and are competing in the same global markets. One possible story is that globalization most favors the managers who are native English speakers because English is the language of the global economy, and because English-speaking managers can sell their services to the highest bidders in many countries. Indeed, the increases in top incomes have been larger in English-speaking countries than elsewhere.

One study showed that top executives in oil companies were paid more when the price of oil was high, suggesting that the rewards were paid because the money was there, not because the recipients had done anything to earn it.[30] When corporations are lucky, they pay their top management more, but when the luck runs out, there is no matching reduction. Compensation committees typically set top salaries, and their members are nominally independent directors. But, as has been noted by Warren Buffett among others, the members of these boards often receive a large share of their own total income from board membership and are effectively under the control of the CEO. Buffett has also drawn attention to the role of firms of compensation consultants ("Ratchet, Ratchet, and Bingo!"), who help spread giant packages from one company to another. The use of these firms, together with the common practice of CEOs sitting on each other's boards, might explain how jumbo compensation packages spread from financial firms to the broader corporate world. At the same time, the social norms that led to sharply progressive taxation and equalization after World War II had largely been eroded by the end of the century, and very large incomes have become more socially acceptable than would have been the case fifty years ago.

Government has also helped in promoting the rapid increases in top incomes. The "too big to fail" promise and the hundreds of millions in earnings that it allowed was a failure of government regulation. The economists Thomas Philippon and Ariell Reshef have shown how compensation in the financial sector, which was high in the 1920s, fell in the wake of post–Depression era regulation, and then rose again, especially after 1980.[31] They show that changes in four kinds of financial regulation and deregulation—allowing banks to have multiple branches, the separation of commercial and investment banks, interest rate ceilings, and the separation of banks and insurance companies—can together match the patterns of compensation in the financial sector. The imposition of the Glass-Steagall Act in 1932 and its eventual repeal in 1999 are the bookends in the saga.

Congress does not impose and repeal such laws in a vacuum. Lobbying by potential winners and losers is intense, and well-financed interests know how to use money to support or punish political campaigns. The political scientists Jacob Hacker and Paul Pierson argue that political lobbying has played a key role in the increase in top incomes.[32] They note that the number of firms represented by registered lobbyists in Washington increased from 175 in 1971 to 2,500 in 1982, in large part a reaction to the wave of government regulation of business associated with the Great Society. Changes in what might appear to be arcane or obscure rules on how markets operate, on what firms can and cannot do, or on accounting rules can mean immense sums to particular interests. This was true of the repeal of Glass-Steagall, and there are many other examples over the period leading up to and after the Great Recession. A spectacular example was the semipublic mortgage finance company Fannie Mae, which was run by well-connected political operatives who enriched themselves and their senior executives through ultimately catastrophic risk taking while keeping regulators at bay by means of well-funded campaigns of political influence.[33]

If these accounts are even partially correct, there is a danger that the rapid growth of top incomes can become self-reinforcing through the political access that money can bring. Rules are set not in the public interest but in the interest of the rich, who use those rules to become yet richer and more influential. The countries in the OECD that have seen the largest increases in shares of income at the very top are the countries that have seen the largest cuts in taxes on top income.[34] Studies of congressional voting by the political scientists Larry Bartels and Martin Gilens have documented how votes in Congress from both sides of the aisle are sensitive to the wishes of rich constituents and not at all to the wishes of poor constituents.[35]

And just as the diversion of talent to socially questionable financial engineering is a loss to the economy, so is the diversion of talent to lobbying. It has long been understood that these "directly unproductive profit-seeking activities" have been a serious obstacle to economic growth in many developing countries—India before the 1990s, with its famous License Raj, is a classic example—and the immense payoffs and relatively low costs of lobbying activity attract talent away from the production and innovation on which economic growth depends.[36] The expense of government and the escalating costs of elections is a frequent topic of comment, but even the costs of recent presidential elections are dwarfed, for example, by the annual advertising budgets of car manufacturers. Political favors come amazingly cheaply relative to the potential benefits.

On a flight from Delhi to Jaipur in Rajasthan one day, I sat beside a manufacturer of some product (I never discovered what exactly, except that it needed to be protected against foreign imports), who explained to me at length the wickedness of government regulators, and how much of his time was spent—as on this trip—applying for licenses, regulatory forbearance, and favorable interpretations of rules. His contempt for these individuals knew no bounds. As we parted, after he had bought me a fine breakfast in the five-star Rambagh Palace Hotel, and he set off to meet the despised bureaucrat, he whispered, "Ah-hah, Professor Deaton, the profits, the profits!" Sanford Weill, whose creation of Citigroup was made possible by the repeal of Glass-Steagall, might have said very much the same.

The process of cumulative causation, through money and politics, is far from fully documented, although both political scientists and economists have begun to show serious interest. What we are currently lacking are good notions of the *size* of the various effects—what fraction of the increase in top compensation comes from lobbying or other political activities, what fraction can be attributed to the high productivity of top earners, and just how much of political activity comes from those interests as opposed to the many others, such as unions, that are also well represented in Washington. We also don't understand why these influences should have become so much more powerful over time, if indeed they have. The answers to those questions are central for deciding just how much we should be worried about the rise in top incomes and why worrying about the rich getting richer is a good deal more than envy.

If democracy becomes plutocracy, those who are not rich are effectively disenfranchised. Justice Louis Brandeis famously argued that the United States could have either democracy or wealth concentrated in the hands of a few, but not both. The political equality that is required by democracy is always under threat from economic inequality, and the more extreme the economic inequality, the greater the threat to democracy.[37] If democracy is compromised, there is a direct loss of wellbeing because people have good reason to value their ability to participate in political life, and the loss of that ability is instrumental in threatening other harm. The very wealthy have little need for state-provided education or health care; they have every reason to support cuts in Medicare and to fight any increases in taxes.

They have even less reason to support health insurance for everyone, or to worry about the low quality of public schools that plagues much of the country. They will oppose any regulation of banks that restricts profits, even if it helps those who cannot cover their mortgages or protects the public against predatory lending, deceptive advertising, or even a repetition of the financial crash.[38] To worry about these consequences of extreme inequality has nothing to do with being envious of the rich and everything to with the fear that rapidly growing top incomes are a threat to the wellbeing of everyone else.

There is nothing wrong with the Pareto principle, and we should not be concerned over others' good fortune if it brings no harm to us. The mistake is to apply the principle to only one dimension of wellbeing—money—and to ignore other dimensions, such as the ability to participate in a democratic society, to be well educated, to be healthy, and not to be the victim of others' search for enrichment. If an increase in top incomes does nothing to reduce other incomes but hurts other aspects of wellbeing, the Pareto principle cannot be called on to justify it. Money and wellbeing are two different things!

Even if we focus only on incomes, and ignore harms in other dimensions, our view of whether or not income inequalities are unjust depends on whether or not increases in top incomes benefit everyone or only those who receive them. The public grieving at the death of Steve Jobs is unlikely to be replicated if one of the nation's prominent bankers were to follow him into an early grave.

America today is a sharp illustration of the themes of this book. The American economy has grown since World War II, not at its highest rate ever, but at a pace that is more than respectable by historical standards. The goods and services that were produced by this expansion improved the lives of many. This was hardly an escape from poverty and degradation—the United States was already wealthy by historical standards in 1945—but the effects of growth on wellbeing should not be understated. People are safer and better housed, they can travel in ways that were impossible for their grandparents, they have access to a significant fraction of the world's information and entertainment (something previously available to only a tiny minority), and they can communicate with one another in undreamed-of ways. Yet, as is so often the case, growth has created divisions, and some have done better than others, especially since the mid-1970s, when growth has been slower and much less inclusive. Those divisions can be productive and, as we have seen in many cases, they create both the opportunities and the incentives for catch-up and for spreading the benefits from the few to the many. In recent American history, this is encapsulated in the "race between education and technology" and the substantial increases in the numbers of Americans who are educated.

Growth, inequality, and catch-up are the bright side of the coin. The dark side is what happens when the process is hijacked, so that the catch-up never comes. The historian Eric Jones has written eloquently about why, over the long run of history, the West developed after 1750 and the East and South did not. It was not, he argues, that growth never happened in the rest of the world; rather it did, over and over again.[39] But it was always snuffed out by powerful rulers or priests who either appropriated the innovations for themselves or banned the activity altogether because it threatened their own positions. Either way, sustained growth never became established, and the goose that might have laid the golden eggs was throttled at birth. The extreme inequality of power in such societies led to an environment in which growth could not become established and a permanent escape route was cut off.

The economic historians Stanley Engerman and Kenneth Sokoloff tell another version of the inequality to (lack of) growth story.[40] In countries where power was concentrated in a few hands—for example, in plantation economies, in Latin America, or in the American South versus the American North—the rich opposed the enfranchisement of the majority and restricted education to the elite, to which they themselves belonged. Those failures of politics and of broad-based education deprived people of the institutions that lie at the roots of broad-based economic growth. By contrast, the early adoption of universal public education in the United States was an important factor in its long-run economic success.

That institutions tailored to the elite are inimical to economic growth is also the thesis of the MIT economists Daron Acemoglu and Simon Johnson, writing with the Harvard political scientist James Robinson.[41] Colonial powers who could set up colonies of their own citizens brought their institutions with them (think the United States, Australia, Canada, and New Zealand), while in places where it was too difficult to settle (for example, because of high disease prevalence), they set up "extractive" states that essentially plundered resources (think Bolivia, India, or Zambia), with institutions that were designed to serve the ruling elite but that could not support economic growth. Extractive regimes usually have no interest in protecting private property or promoting the rule of law, and without these institutions entrepreneurship and innovation are unlikely to flourish. Countries that were relatively wealthy and populous places in colonial times were particularly attractive targets for conquest, so much so that there has been a historical reversal of fortune. Among the countries that were conquered by European powers, the countries that were rich are now poor, and those that were poor are now rich.

Such reversals of fortune should warn us against taking modern prosperity and modern economic growth for granted, as something that we have always known and that can never go away. Rent seeking can lead to economic growth being replaced by internecine warfare in which each group fights ever more viciously for shares of a declining total. Interest groups can feather the nests of a few at the expense of the many, each of whom loses so little that it is not worth organizing to prevent the plunder; the cumulative effects of many such groups can eat away an economy from within and stifle growth.[42] Powerful and wealthy elites have choked off economic growth before, and they can do so again if they are allowed to undermine the institutions on which broad-based growth depends.

SIX

Globalization and the Greatest Escape

IN THE YEARS SINCE World War II, the modern world has seen the greatest escape of all. Rapid economic growth in many countries has delivered hundreds of millions of people from destitution. Material wellbeing has risen as death rates have fallen, and people are living longer and richer lives. As always, progress has not been even; some of the most rapidly growing countries have narrowed the gap with the rich countries, but their progress has opened up new gaps between them and the countries left behind. Once-poor countries in Asia have moved into the middle, leaving chasms between them and many countries in Africa.

The fall in mortality, especially among children, caused world population to increase at a rate that has no precedent in human history, a true explosion of population. That global poverty should have fallen in the face of such an increase in numbers would have astonished most commentators of the 1960s, for whom the looming "population bomb" threatened living standards everywhere in the world. The great economist and Nobel laureate James Meade used to complain that the three great disasters of the twentieth century were the "infernal" combustion engine, the population explosion, and the

Nobel Prize in economics. On the population explosion, most of his contemporaries would have agreed, and even today many continue to see population growth as a serious threat (along with the infernal combustion engine). Yet not only has the world added four billion people over the past half-century, but the seven billion who are alive today have also, on average, much better lives than their parents and grandparents.

Averages are no consolation to those who have been left behind. We have already seen that the average growth in the United States was far from equally shared. The United States is not the only country where inequality has been rising, and although there are important exceptions, rising income inequality is a common recent experience in many countries. What about inequality *between* countries? Many once-poor countries have seized the "advantage of backwardness": the opportunity to adopt (and even improve) the knowledge and technologies that have long been known in the now-rich countries. The catch-up countries can bypass the long process of trial and error that limited growth in the past. Countries such as the Asian tigers—Hong Kong, Singapore, South Korea, and Taiwan—and more recently China and India, have experienced rates of economic growth that are multiples of anything seen previously. But growth has been unequally distributed, and most of the countries that were poor fifty years ago have not been able to emulate China, India, or the tigers.

Perhaps surprisingly, and in spite of the achievements of the fast growers, there has been little or no narrowing of income inequality between countries; for every country with a catch-up story there has been a country with a left-behind story. The spread of average incomes between poor countries and rich countries is as large as it has ever been. If we arrange countries by their average incomes, from the poorest to the richest, we can compare the country that is a quarter of the way up from the bottom—a moderately poor country—with the country that is a quarter of the way down from the top—a moderately well off country. In 1960, the moderately well-off country had an average income that was seven times that of the moderately poor country; by 2009, that ratio had risen to eight and a half times.

This chapter looks at this postwar miracle—the greatest of great escapes: how it came about and how it closed old inequalities and opened new ones. We shall also look closely at the numbers and ask whether it is safe to believe them. Global measures of poverty and inequality are fraught with difficulties. We know less than we should and certainly less than one might think from reading and listening to the torrent of popular pronouncements.

Measuring the World

Measuring material wellbeing is no easy matter, and even *income,* an everyday term, is hard to nail down precisely. Our measures of poverty and inequality are only as good as our measures of income. Life gets even tougher when we want to make comparisons across countries. People have a pretty good idea what sort of income is needed to avoid being poor in the community in which they live. Even if national poverty lines do not capture what it costs to live in your community, let alone differences of opinion about needs, we can still hope that most citizens and policymakers will see the national poverty lines as reasonable figures that divide those who are getting by from those who are not. But if we are to count the poor of the whole world, we need a single poverty line that makes sense in Nairobi and Quito, Karachi and Timbuktu, and perhaps even in London and Canberra. For this, as for any international comparison of incomes, we need to be able to convert one currency into another, and it turns out that, for this purpose, foreign exchange rates are useless.

A good place to start, then, is by asking how to convert one currency into another, for example, dollars into rupees. There is an exchange rate, varying from day to day, which is the number of rupees that you can buy in the market for a dollar; as I write this, in April 2013, that rate is 54.33. So if I take a flight from New York to Delhi and go to the foreign exchange counter, I will get around 50 rupees for each dollar, or perhaps less depending on the bank's commission. Yet when I get into the city, I will find that, even in the most expensive hotel, I can buy a lot more for 50 rupees than I can buy for a dollar in New York; if I go to the canteen at the Delhi School of Economics, or buy street food, the difference is enormous.

One simple way of saying this is that the price level is lower in India than in New York; if money is converted at the market exchange rate, most things in India are cheap compared with their prices in the United States. In fact, according to the latest estimate, the price level in India is only about 40 percent of the price level in the United States, so that, if we take a typical bundle of things people buy, the bundle in India costs only 40 percent of what it costs in the United States. Put another way, prices would be the same in both places if the exchange rate were 20 rupees to the dollar, not 50 rupees. This "correct" exchange rate, the one that would make a dollar worth the same in both places, is called, appropriately enough, the purchasing power parity exchange rate or, for short, the PPP exchange rate. The PPP rate is the exchange rate from dollars into rupees that would give the same purchasing power in both places. If the price level is lower in Delhi than in New York, as it is in most poor countries, the PPP rate will be lower than the foreign exchange rate.

How do we know these numbers? There is no market in which currencies are converted at PPP rates, so there is no alternative but to go and find out what the prices are. Teams of international researchers and statisticians collect millions of prices in countries all around the world and average them to get a price level for each country. The first such calculations were carried out for six countries in the mid-1970s by a team of economists at the University of Pennsylvania led by Irving Kravis, Robert Summers, and Alan Heston, the last of whom continues to work in the area and is one of those responsible for many of the numbers in this book. These pioneers changed the way that economists see and think about the world; without their work, we would have no idea how to compare living standards across countries.[1]

One of the first things learned from these international comparisons is that my Indian example was and is quite common; price levels are lower in poorer countries, and the poorer the country, the lower is its price level. Many people find this conclusion both unlikely and surprising. How can we have a world in which things are cheaper in one place than in another? If something like steel or gasoline were much cheaper in Delhi than in New York, why would a trader not buy it in Delhi and get rich by selling it in New York? In fact, the prices of steel and gasoline are not very different once we take into account the costs of shipping and of local taxes and subsidies. But these arguments do not apply to everything. The fact that a haircut in Delhi or a dinner in Bangkok would be a splendid bargain in New York holds no attraction for a trader because these services are in Delhi and Bangkok, not New York, and it is not possible to get them from one place to the other. Because people are poor in poor countries, services are cheap there, but many of those services are immobile.

If everyone were free to migrate from one country to another, wages in rich countries would fall and wages in poor countries would rise, and the world would be a much more equal place. Of course, opposition to lower wages in rich countries is precisely why people are *not* permitted to migrate at will, and it is why meals and haircuts are so cheap in poor countries. The price of land, like the price of labor, cannot be arbitraged between rich countries and poor countries. Cheap housing in India or Africa cannot be brought up to American prices by simply moving the land across the ocean. The presence of cheap land and cheap labor in poor countries explains why price levels in poor countries are so much lower than in rich countries. The market sets the exchange rate to equalize the prices of steel, gasoline, automobiles, and computers—everything that can be and is part of international trade—but the price level depends on goods and services that cannot be traded. Because those are cheaper in poor places, the poorer the country, the lower are the average prices.

Because of lower prices in poorer countries, we get the wrong answer if we use market exchange rates to make conversions of the costs of living. Newspaper reports almost always get this wrong, and even economists sometimes forget it. In the spring of 2011, the Government of India (unwisely and ungenerously) argued before the Indian Supreme Court that 26 rupees a day was enough to avoid poverty, at least for those living outside the cities. In the uproar that followed, the Indian (and international) media noted that even the World Bank—not seen by most Indians as a benevolent institution—used a poverty line of $1.25, which, at the exchange rate of 53 rupees to the dollar, was more than twice as generous as the government's line. But at a PPP rate of 20 rupees to the dollar, the World Bank line is 25 rupees, close to the line that the government had suggested. Even the *Financial Times* used the market exchange rate to make the conversion from rupees into dollars and noted that the government's line was only $0.52 as opposed to the Bank's $1.25. A more accurate number would have been $1.30—a miserable pittance indeed, but almost three times the wrong number.

The United Nations Development Programme made this mistake for many years, opening itself to charges of deliberately exaggerating the poverty in poor countries. Any time we read about living standards in poor countries—whether a wage rate, what it costs to visit a doctor, or the price of food or transportation—and make the obvious conversion using a market exchange rate, the results will be too small by a factor of two to three. Wages are certainly low in poor countries—just another way of saying these countries are poor—but nothing is served by exaggerating just how poor they are relative to the rich countries of the world.

When we compare living standards across the world, or calculate global poverty or inequality, PPP exchange rates are always the right ones to use. The phrase "across the world" is important here; when we look across people in the same country to calculate inequality—as for the United States in Chapter 5—we might reasonably choose *not* to adjust for differences in prices across places. While it is certainly cheaper to live in Kansas or Mississippi than it is to live in New York City, there are more amenities in the city. Indeed, if people are free to choose where to live, the higher prices in the big city are likely to be a reasonable guide to the value of those amenities. If this is so, we can compare incomes across space without adjusting for prices; people with higher incomes in Manhattan, New York, really are better off than people with lower incomes in Manhattan, Kansas. Things are different when we compare the United States with India, or France with Senegal, where free movement of people is not possible. Even if living in America brings more amenities than living in India—and I do not know whether that is so—there is no reason to suppose that the difference between American and Indian price levels reflects those differences in amenities. So when we compare Indian and American incomes to assess world inequality, we must adjust for prices using PPP exchange rates.

PPP comparisons are better than comparisons at market exchange rates, but they are far from perfect. Price levels are calculated by collecting the prices of comparable items in different countries, like a kilo of rice or a haircut in Hanoi, London, or São Paulo. Not all items are easily priced, however. How do we price the dwelling that a poor family built for itself in a village, or a shack in an urban slum? There are often no rental markets for these properties, just as there are no rental markets for many kinds of housing in richer countries. As in the United States, it is hard to know how to value the services that are provided by governments to their people—items like Medicare—and it is even harder to do this in a consistent way for all countries, making sure that we are comparing like with like. For a substantial share of what people spend, there are no market prices and we have to make do with guesses that, while always sensible, may be wide of the mark. This does not mean that it is better to use regular exchange rates, which we know are wrong—only that the PPPs, which are the right numbers, are subject to unavoidable uncertainty.

Think for a moment about collecting prices of comparable items in different countries. Say we are pricing men's shirts. In the United States, a standard item might be a dress shirt from a well-known manufacturer, say a Brooks Brothers oxford cotton button-down shirt. If we are to compare this with a man's shirt in Bolivia, the Democratic Republic of the Congo, or the Philippines, we are faced with a choice between two equally unsatisfactory alternatives. The standard shirt in those countries is likely to be something much cheaper and of lower quality than the Brooks Brothers shirt, so that, if we price it, we are not comparing like with like, and we will be *understating* prices in the poor country relative to the rich country. The alternative is to hunt really hard for the Brooks Brothers shirt— perhaps in the fanciest store in the capital city—but this carries the opposite risk: that we find the shirt, but only in a very specialized and very expensive store that is used by a handful of wealthy patrons. If we follow this route, we *overstate* prices in the poor country, at least for ordinary people. There is a constant tug-of-war between two conflicting aims: collecting prices only on items that are internationally comparable and collecting prices only on items that are representative of what people buy. In extreme cases, comparisons are effectively impossible if something that is important and widely used in one country does not exist in another. Teff is the basic grain staple in Ethiopia and is rarely used anywhere else; tofu is important in Indonesia but not in India; alcohol is not available in many Muslim countries.

Even when all the prices are available, people spend their money on different things and in different proportions in different countries. One example will be familiar to anyone—like me—who was brought up in Britain and who now lives elsewhere. One of the basic necessities of existence for Brits is a product called Marmite. This is a (very) salty yeast extract that is a by-product of brewing, originally discovered by Louis Pasteur, who in turn licensed it to a British beer manufacturer. In Britain, Marmite is cheap and widely consumed; it comes in large black pots. In the United States, where I now live, Marmite is available, but it is expensive and comes in very small black pots. Marmite is a well-defined and precisely comparable item that is easily priced in both the United States and Britain. But if we compare prices in the United States and Britain by calculating the relative costs in the two countries of the goods that the British buy, including lots of Marmite, we will find that the United States is a very expensive place. If we look at relative prices using the goods that Americans buy—which include items like graham crackers or bourbon that are rare and pricey in Britain—we will find that Britain is the expensive place.

Comparisons between rich countries like Britain and the United States are not in fact very sensitive to whether we use American goods or British goods as the basis for the comparison, but the Marmite example illustrates a basic issue that affects all international price comparisons. Countries tend to buy a lot of things that are relatively cheap at home and fewer things that are relatively expensive at home, so that comparing the cost of living abroad using the home country's basket will tend to overstate the costs of living abroad. If we use the foreign country's basket, we tend to understate the relative costs. In practice, the statisticians tend to split the difference and take an average.

Splitting the difference is a sensible solution, but it doesn't make the problem go away, as we can see from thinking about what happened recently when the price statisticians compared prices in Britain with prices in the West African country of Cameroon. In Cameroon, as in much of Africa, air travel is very expensive, and there is very little of it; ordinary people do not fly. In Britain, air travel is cheap, and even relatively poor people fly abroad on vacation. Pricing what the British do at Cameroon's prices makes Cameroon seem like a very expensive place. Averaging helps, but whatever we do, the price of air travel has a substantial effect on Cameroon's PPP—the price level in Cameroon would be 2–3 percent cheaper if air travel were ignored— even though there is close to no air travel in Cameroon. It is one of the unfortunate facts of life that international comparisons depend on things like this that—at least in some contexts, such as measuring poverty—make little sense. Once again, the trouble here is that Cameroon and Britain, unlike the United States and Britain, are very different from one another.

The comparison of Cameroon and Britain is not a big deal; what is definitely a big deal is the comparison of the United States and China. According to the latest estimates from the World Bank, per capita GDP in China in 2011 was $5,445 compared with $48,112 for the United States, so that per capita income in the United States is nearly nine times that in China. But those calculations are at market exchange rates, and they take no account of the fact that the price level in China is about two-thirds of that in the United States. If we convert at PPP exchange rates, per capita income in China is \$8,400, so that the ratio of per capita incomes at PPP, a much better indicator of relative living standards, is only 5.7 times, not 8.8 times. For those worried about the absolute size of the two economies—the military or the diplomatic corps, for whom a country's influence in the world depends on *total* resources—we have to multiply by 4.31, which is the ratio of the Chinese to the American population. In total then, the Chinese economy is three-quarters the size of the American economy. Given that China is growing much more rapidly than the United States—on which more below—we might expect China to overtake the United States in the not-too-distant future—in only six years if China's growth rate is 5 percentage points higher than the U.S. growth rate.

The numbers in the previous paragraph treat the PPP exchange rate as if we really knew it in the way that we know the market exchange rate. But once we recognize the "Marmite" or "air travel in Cameroon" problems, as well as the uncertainties about making comparisons that are both representative and comparable, we should ask whether the true PPP exchange rate might be rather higher or rather lower. In my work with Alan Heston, we calculated that once the Marmite problem is recognized—or more precisely once we recognize that we can average the two sets of prices using either the Chinese or the American bundle of goods—there is about a 25 percent margin of error on either side of the PPP.[2] So we can say only that Chinese per capita income in international dollars in 2011 was somewhere between 13 and 22 percent of per capita income in the United States. The aggregate Chinese economy is somewhere between 56 percent and 94 percent of the aggregate American economy. While it is convenient to split the difference—if only because we do not want to work with a vast range of possibilities—the fact remains that splitting the difference is an arbitrary way of resolving a conceptual problem to which there is no fully satisfactory solution.

In the very special case of China, there are many other issues to which I cannot do justice here. Perhaps the most important is the long-running and still unsettled debate over whether the official Chinese growth rate is too high to be credible, as many scholars think, and if so, by how much it should be adjusted down.

I do not want to leave the impression that international comparisons are impossible, or always subject to very large margins of error. In 1949 my mentor at Cambridge University, Richard Stone, asked, "Why do we want to compare the United States with, say, India or China? What possible interest is there in it? Everybody knows that one country is, in economic terms, very rich, and another country very poor; does it matter whether the factor is thirty or fifty or what?"[3] Both China and India are much better off now than in 1949, and the media, not to mention the Pentagon and the State Department, are perennially interested in whether or not the Chinese economy has passed the American economy. We have also made a great deal of progress in data collection and in ways of thinking since Stone wrote, so that we really do have some idea of what the "factors" are. But the uncertainty is still there, especially when we are comparing rich countries with poor countries such as China or India or (even more so) anywhere in Africa. Among the rich countries, whose economic structures are similar to one another, the uncertainty is much smaller and comparisons can be made with some confidence. Market exchange rates are quite close to PPP exchange rates for countries like Canada, the United States, or the nations of Western Europe, and we are on firm ground when making comparisons between them.

Global Growth

Since the end of World War II, which left much of Europe in economic and social disarray, the richer countries of the world have grown rapidly—first repairing the damage and then surging ahead to new levels of prosperity. The rich countries have also grown closer together, and the differences between them are currently small compared with the differences between the group and the rest of the world. Figure 1 shows what has happened to (price-level-adjusted) national incomes for twenty-one rich countries. While measurement is always less than perfect, the data are good and the PPP exchange rates generally reliable for this group of rich countries. The box-and-whisker (or organ pipe) plot is interpreted in the same way as Figure 4 of Chapter 4; the tops and bottoms of the shaded boxes show the

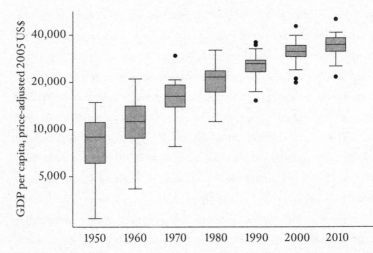

FIGURE 1 GDP per capita in twenty-four rich countries (Australia, Austria, Belgium, Britain, Canada, Denmark, Finland, France, Germany, Greece, Iceland, Ireland, Italy, Japan, Luxembourg, Netherlands, New Zealand, Norway, Portugal, Spain, Sweden, Switzerland, Turkey, and United States).

positions of the top and bottom quarters of countries, so that half the countries are in the shaded areas, with the line in the middle indicating the median. The whiskers give an idea of the dispersion of the data, and the dots indicate extreme cases.

The figure shows that other rich countries have shared the slow-down in growth that we have already seen for the United States. The decade of the 1960s was the postwar golden age, with an average growth rate of more than 4 percent a year, a rate that is high enough to increase incomes by a half in ten years. Growth fell to 2.5 percent a year in the 1970s, to 2.2 percent in the 1980s and 1990s, and to less than 1 percent in the decade up to 2010. The extent of the broad decline is exaggerated by, at one end, the catch-up growth after the war—which we would not expect to continue once repairs had been made—and at the other, by the financial crisis. Fixing devastation and destruction, though hard enough, is easier than striking out to levels of income that have not previously been achieved; people remember how things used to be done, and the technology needs to be recreated rather than created from scratch. Once the rebuilding is done, new growth relies on inventing new ways of doing things and putting them into practice, and this turning over of virgin soil is harder than re-plowing an old furrow. Of course, in an interconnected world, innovation can often spread from one country to another—especially to similar countries—so that the burden of invention is spread among many. This interconnectedness, by itself, will tend to speed up growth.

Globalization reduces the costs of moving goods and information from one place to another. It allows goods to be made and, increasingly, services to be performed where it is most efficient and cheapest to do so, and it allows discoveries that are made in one place to be quickly adopted elsewhere. As with new health knowledge or treatments—like knowing the health effects of smoking, or the life-saving drugs that reduce cholesterol and high blood pressure—discoveries that raised material living standards were quickly internationalized, bringing both health and incomes closer together in the rich countries. For them—where the right political, medical, and economic institutions enabled the changes to be adopted, albeit at different speeds in different countries—we see a remarkable convergence of average incomes, even if the rate of material progress has recently slowed. For these countries, new technology is *reducing* income inequality, just as it reduced health inequality.

The convergence of *average* incomes across these countries tells us nothing about what was happening *within* these countries. Indeed, we have already seen that, in one country, the United States, the growth in average incomes was not widely shared. That countries are drawing closer together does not imply that all of the citizens of the rich world as a whole are drawing closer together. Think of two large crowds that were once apart but are now merging and mixing. If the members of each group are flying apart from one another within their group, the internal divergence can offset and even overcome the merging of the crowds. Seen as a whole, ignoring who is in which country, dispersion might be increasing. I shall come back to this issue when I consider inequality among all the people of the world.

A world of economic growth and narrowing differences between countries is a world to which we have become accustomed, at least if we live in the rich world and if we were born after 1945. High living standards are normal and further growth is confidently expected. Income and health differences between countries have shrunk; travel has become faster, cheaper, and easier; and information is everywhere and instantly available.

The rest of the world doesn't look anything like this. Figure 2 is the same as Figure 1 but includes *all* the countries of the world, both rich and poor. Naturally enough, when we include the poor countries, the

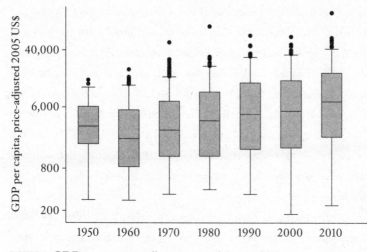

FIGURE 2 GDP per capita in all countries of the world.

range of average incomes is much larger; the boxes are taller, and the whiskers and dots extend farther out. The data are not as reliable, and errors of measurement likely make the spread of incomes appear wider than it really is. More interesting, and less obvious, is that when we look across all countries the spread of average incomes—international country-by-country income inequality—is *not* falling over time. The boxes for 1950 should be ignored for the moment; there are many countries for which there are no data, and many of the omitted countries were very poor, so that the box is too high and too short. After 1950, the difference between the country a quarter of the way up from the bottom and the country a quarter of the way down from the top— the distance between the top and bottom of each box—has remained more or less the same, and if we look at the bottom whiskers we see that the dispersion has actually increased, especially among the poorest countries of the world.

The convergence of average incomes among the rich countries is just what we would expect when growth is driven by new ideas and new ways of doing things and if new ideas spread rapidly across the world. What is more puzzling is the failure of the poor countries to catch up, which makes Figure 2 look so different from Figure 1. After all, the techniques and knowledge that are the basis for the high living standards in the rich countries are available to the poor countries too. Of course, possession of common knowledge does not imply that all countries should have the same living standards. To be able to use rich-country methods of production requires rich-country infrastructure—roads, railways, telecommunications, factories, and machines—not to mention rich-country educational levels, all of which take time and money to achieve. Yet the gaps between rich and poor provide plenty of incentives to make the investment in that infrastructure and equipment, and, as Robert Solow showed in one of the most famous papers in all of economics, average living standards should draw closer over time.[4] Why this has not happened is a central question in economics. Perhaps the best answer is that poor countries lack the *institutions*—government capacity, a functioning legal and tax system, security of property rights, and traditions of trust—that are a necessary background for growth to take place.

Growth rates in poor countries have been no lower than, and sometimes higher than, those in the wealthy countries. But while some countries have grown rapidly and are well on the way to catching up, others have fallen further and further behind. The *diversity* of growth experience has been much larger in the poorer countries. Some countries have been able to take advantage of the opportunities for catch-up. A group of Asian countries—China, Hong Kong, Malaysia, Singapore, South Korea, Taiwan, and Thailand—as well as one African country, Botswana, grew at more than 4 percent a year from 1960 to 2010—a more than *sevenfold* increase in average income over five decades. At the same time, the Central Africa Republic, the Democratic Republic of the Congo (DRC), Guinea, Haiti, Madagascar, Nicaragua, and Niger are actually *poorer* in 2010 than they were half a century ago, and there are other countries that almost certainly belong in the group, but for which the data are missing. (Afghanistan, Djibouti, Liberia, Sierra Leone, and Somalia are likely candidates, as are several of the countries that, in 1960, were part of what was then called the Eastern Bloc.) The rapid growth of the successful countries would, by itself, have narrowed the income gaps between countries, but there were enough failures to keep income inequality between countries from falling.

Two of the rapidly growing countries are China and Singapore, but the former has more than three hundred times the population of the latter. India, the other giant, did not pick up speed as early as China, nor has it grown as rapidly, but it has grown at more than twice the world average since 1990. Although China and India are only two countries, their rapid growth at the end of the century meant that around 40 percent of the world's population lived in countries that were growing very rapidly. In contrast, at the "bad" end of the growth distribution, the countries that have been going backwards are in many cases small (though there are exceptions, such as the DRC, which is both large and spectacularly unsuccessful).

Looking at growth rates—not in terms of how many *countries* had high growth, but in terms of how many *people* experienced high growth—global growth takes on a rosier hue. The average *country* grew at 1.5 percent a year in the half-century after 1960, but the average *person* lived in a country that was growing at 3 percent a year. China and India, where so many people live, have grown much faster than the typical country.

One way to think of what has been happening is to imagine a huge crowd of people, the whole population of the world, each carrying the flag of his or her country, like a giant opening ceremony at the Olympic Games. Think of the crowd as marching forward at speeds that are proportional to the rate at which their incomes are growing—the Indians and Chinese at a run, and some, including the Congolese and Haitians, walking backwards. As we watch the crowd, the two-fifths of all flags that belong to China and India move steadily forward through the crowd, starting near the back (both countries were very poor in 1960) and not yet reaching the front (they are still a long way behind the flags of Europe and North America) but edging closer to the middle. Of course, not everyone in those two countries is moving at the same pace, and, as we shall see, Indians are moving away from other Indians, and Chinese from other Chinese. Yet the rapid average growth of both countries has pulled hundreds of millions out of poverty. And even though all of the countries together are not getting any closer together, the rapid progress of the Indians and Chinese toward the middle has at least made it possible for the entire crowd—the population of the world—to move closer together.

When it comes to a big issue like income inequality among all the people of the world, the word *possible* is a gigantic cop-out. Surely we can do better? The trouble, once again, is the uncertainty in a few key measures. China's rate of growth is one big question; there is a large specialist literature that tries to solve the impenetrable mysteries of Chinese national accounting. Most writers agree that the official rates are too high, but we do not know by exactly how much.[5] We also don't have very good estimates of China's PPP exchange rate; Chinese (and other) PPPs are subject to a good deal of uncertainty, and the government of China has not participated in all of the price-gathering exercises. If world inequality were expanding or contracting really quickly, measurement uncertainty might not matter. As it is, the truth is that we do not know.

The two largest countries in the world have been among the most successful, at least over the past quarter of a century. Is this *because* they are large, or is it simply that the two countries that did so well happened to be the largest? Other large countries have also out-performed the world average, at least over some periods, though none have equaled China's staying power. Examples are Brazil, Indonesia, Japan, Russia, and the United States. The "BRIC" countries (Brazil, Russia, India, and China) certainly reap some advantages from their size. A diplomatic corps, a competent bureaucracy, a few well-trained leaders, and the faculty of a world-class university cannot *all* be filled with only a handful of good people, and larger countries have larger pools from which to choose. If scientific discovery—or, more relevant for poorer countries, figuring out how to adapt old knowledge to new conditions—depends on the absolute numbers of scientists or researchers and not on the fraction of the population who are scientists or researchers, then this too gives larger countries an advantage.

In response to a distinguished physicist who once asked me what I was working on, I said the measurement of global poverty. Interesting, he replied: which countries? India, I said, at which point he told me I was talking nonsense: India was one of the most advanced countries of the world. If you count the total number of scientists, and not per capita income or the number of poor people, he was correct, and if scientific work has spillovers that benefit everyone in the country, large countries are blessed. Whether these advantages to scale are enough to elevate growth rates, or whether larger countries tend to grow faster for other reasons, are open questions.

There is much that remains mysterious about why some countries grow rapidly and some grow slowly. In fact, it is not even true that there are perennial fast- and slow-growing countries. At least over the past half-century, the fast-growing countries in one decade have tended not to repeat their performance in the next or subsequent decades. Japan used to be the place that had perpetually high growth, until it didn't any more. India, now one of the most rapidly growing countries, seemed capable of only slow growth for much of its existence, not to speak of the half-century that preceded its independence, when there was no growth at all.[6] China is the current long-run superstar, but by historical standards the longevity of its growth spurt is extremely unusual. Economists, international organizations, and other commentators are fond of taking a few high-growth countries and looking for some common feature or policy, which is then held up as the "key to growth"—at least until it fails to open the door to growth somewhere else.[7] The same goes for attempts to look at countries that have done badly (the "bottom billion") and divine the causes of their failure.[8] These attempts are much like trying to figure out the common characteristics of people who bet on the zero just before it came up on a roulette wheel; they do little but disguise our fundamental ignorance.

The foolishness of these schemes reminds me of the search for the keys to success in the Scotland of my youth. Scotland is often cold, wet, and windy, and when I was a child, we knew little about economic growth, and cared less, but we worried all the time about the weather. The long, warm summers of 1955 and 1959 were endless, with golden days spent outdoors in the woods and on the rivers. What were the keys to those successes? I have often thought about it, and for a while had come to the conclusion that those were summers when I was in primary school, and that primary education was perhaps the magic key. But my cousin David, who is a few years older than I am, reminds me that he was in high school in those years, so we gave up on the primary education story. But we remembered that those were both years in which the Conservative party was in power. So perhaps it was not primary education that was the key to success, but politics. All of this is nonsense, but so are all attempts to look at a few successes and a few failures and make fatuous generalizations based on coincidence. Etruscan and Roman haruspices did the same with the entrails of chickens.

Growth, Health, and the Population Explosion

In the six decades since the end of World War II, there have been unprecedented reductions in mortality rates and unprecedented increases in life expectancy (described in Chapter 4), together with the rapid growth in average incomes described earlier. Yet this miracle was far from universally predicted at the time—in fact quite the reverse.

When knowledge of the germ theory of disease brought pest control, clean water, vaccinations, and antibiotics to the poor world, it saved millions of lives, especially the lives of children. Sparing those children brought rapid increases in life expectancy and pulled life chances in poor countries closer to life chances in rich countries. Millions of children lived who would otherwise have died. Alongside the universally welcomed increases in life expectancy came millions of additional people—an increase in global population that was far from universally welcomed. It took most of human history, until the early nineteenth century, for world population to reach a billion people. The two billion mark was reached around 1935, only a century and a quarter later, and three billion by 1960, only thirty-five years later. Instead of slowing down at that point, world population in 1960 was growing at 2.2 percent a year, the highest rate in history and enough to make population double every thirty-two years. The claim that population was exploding was no exaggeration.

The population explosion caused general alarm in the 1960s, among the general public—at least in the rich countries—and also among policymakers, academics, foundations, and international organizations. Much of the concern was humanitarian; many poor countries already appeared to find it hard to feed their populations, so that adding millions more would surely make things even worse. It was as if a poor family, having scraped and scavenged just enough for a meager meal, found a dozen hungry relatives at the door. Mass starvation loomed. Visitors to India in particular were horrified by the obvious—to them—overpopulation and were appalled at the prospect of adding hundreds of millions more. And indeed, it is easy for first-time Western visitors to be horrified by the poverty and disease in the slums of Delhi or Kolkata; by the beggars, the lepers, the crippled children; by people defecating in the street, and simply by the sheer mass of humanity. How could it be that the addition of yet more people would not make all this even worse?

National security was also a concern. Rising poverty would surely provide a fertile ground for communists—as had already happened in China—and the United States and its allies needed to do what it could to stop the dominoes from falling. Less attractive motives surely also played some role. Concerns about the "quality" of the population had long been a focus of the eugenics movement. Even if eugenic ideas were less popular and respectable after the defeat of Nazi Germany, the possibility that poor, uneducated people should multiply so much more rapidly than rich, educated people seemed to pose a threat to the future of mankind. At the extreme, the enthusiasm for controlling the population of Africa and Asia owed much to the skin color of those whose population was to be brought under control. So it became an object of policy—by countries in their foreign policy, by international organizations in their lending, and by foundations in their giving—to "help" the world's poor to control their populations by having fewer children. What the world's poor—the people who were actually having all these babies—thought about all this was not given much consideration.

Why should it have been so universally thought that more people meant poorer people? It may seem obvious that if the world's food and other goods are shared among more people there will be less for each person. Economists like to call this the lump fallacy: the notion that there is a fixed "lump" of "stuff," so that the impoverishment that comes from adding numbers is simply a matter of arithmetic, just as it is for the poor family who have unexpected visitors for dinner. Of course, even this analogy breaks down if the unexpected visitors bring food with them, so that the communal meal may well be better (both nutritionally and socially) than the one that was originally envisaged. The question of impoverishment by numbers is not a question of arithmetic; it is a question of what the new people add, not just what they cost. Perhaps the simplest narrative is that each mouth comes with a pair of hands—too simple for sure, but a better approximation to the truth than the lump story, in which each new person comes with nothing.

We also need to recognize that the African and Asian children who were causing the population explosion were, in the vast majority of cases, children who were wanted by their parents. At the time, even this conclusion was sometimes disputed; people were seen as slaves to their sexual passions, and children were the unfortunate but unavoidable consequence. Certainly, not everyone everywhere has access to convenient modern contraception at low cost, but there is overwhelming evidence—if indeed evidence is required—that on average, if not family by family, people want the children they have, with their own good reasons for having them. The story of unbridled passion provided a convenient rationale for what "we" wanted to do, which was to "help" poor people have fewer children that "they" wanted but "we" did not. No one presented evidence that people wanted such help or that having fewer children would improve their lives. Quite the contrary.

That parents want more children does not necessarily mean that more children are good for society; there may be consequences that parents do not know about, or that they know about but choose to ignore. Children might impose costs on other families. When the costs are borne by the family itself, we can likely trust the parents to weigh costs and benefits and have children when it makes sense for them to do so. Those children might reduce the resources available to other family members—and indeed, few babies are *born* ready to pull their economic weight. But taking everything into account, including the future economic prospects of the parents and their children as well as the joys of parenthood, we can safely suppose that the additional children add to the family's wellbeing. We might worry that a few parents have children only to exploit or otherwise abuse them, but even this does not makes the case that other people will make better choices on their behalf. The more serious argument comes when costs fall on others—more crowded schools or clinics; less common land, firewood, or clean water; or global warming. This argument, often described as the tragedy of the commons, implies that people will have too many children, and it has long been a key plank of the argument for population control.

There are various ways around the tragedy of the commons. Economists like to use prices to solve such problems, and it will sometimes be possible to use a tax to make people pay attention to a social cost that they would otherwise ignore. A classic example is a global tax on carbon, which would do much to combat global warming. But that strategy also illustrates the problem, which is that setting such a tax would require a degree of political agreement that is hard to achieve. Local problems—access to firewood, the use of the commons, who gets water rights—can be dealt with by local political agreement. Although there is never a guarantee that the need for political action will actually be met by the creation of suitable institutions, local political discussions often do solve these disagreements and stop people from doing things that inflict costs on others. The provision of clinics and schools can also be dealt with through local or national politics. The appropriate political institutions may include some sort of economic or social incentives to limit family size, and this sort of population control—if arrived at in a democratic way—is an appropriate solution to the tragedy of the commons and related difficulties. What such arguments do *not* support is population control by outsiders such as foreign governments, international institutions, or foundations, especially when those organizations have their own interests and an often too limited understanding of the lives of the people they are nominally trying to help.

In the event, much mischief—and worse—was done in the name of international population control. Some of the worst abuses were in India, where voluntary sterilization was often far from voluntary. Although it was Indian politicians and officials who did the abusing, institutions such as the United States Agency for International Development and the World Bank bear much responsibility for encouragement and for intellectual and financial support.[9] The one-child policy in China, imposed by a nondemocratic government inspired by Western concerns about overpopulation, remains in place today, and it is one of the most serious crimes perpetrated by a modern government against its people. It is not even clear that the policy has been effective: fertility has fallen much further in Taiwan, by exactly the same amount in Thailand, and almost as fast in southern India, and in none of those countries did governments coerce people or violate their deepest and most personal life choices.

In spite of the prophecies of doom, the population explosion failed to plunge the world into famine and destitution. On the contrary, the past half-century has seen not only the decrease in mortality that caused the explosion but also a mass escape from the poverty and deprivation that the population explosion was supposed to cause. What happened, and how could we all have been so wrong?

Not everyone *was* wrong. The economist and demographer Julian Simon consistently challenged the doomsayers, making uncannily correct predictions about future plenty using arguments that are much more widely accepted today than they were at the time. In his *The Ultimate Resource,* Simon argued that the real source of prosperity is neither land, nor natural resources that might one day be exhausted, but people.[10] Not only does each new mouth bring with it a future worker—which in the long run would make average incomes independent of population size—but it comes with a creative brain. The new ideas that come from some of these new brains are good not only for their owners but also for all of mankind. If having twice as many mouths and twice as many pairs of hands leaves everyone with the same as before, the extra minds can figure out new ways to enable *all* of the hands to do more. Of course, not every newborn is going to be an Einstein, an Edison, or a Henry Ford, nor is every new idea useful for everyone. But because ideas can be shared, not everyone has to be a genius, and any idea that can be applied elsewhere benefits all those who use it, not just the inventor. More children may bring new costs to others—all those schools and clinics—but they also bring benefits in terms of the new ideas and new ways of doing things that are the ultimate basis for economic growth, the tools for the Great Escape. And those benefits might easily outweigh the costs. If so, the world was twice blessed by the health improvements in the 1950s and 1960s—once because of the increase in life expectancy and once because of the explosion of global knowledge and creativity that came with the explosion in numbers.

The economist and demographer David Lam, in his magisterial 2011 presidential address to the Population Association of America, identified the keys to global prosperity in the face of record rates of population growth.[11] One key was a fall in fertility: In the face of unprecedented declines in the mortality of their children, families reduced their numbers of children. Parents cared not about the number of children who were *born* but about the number who *survived.*

The children who would have died in previous times no longer "needed" to be born, sparing their mothers the drudgery and dangers of bearing children and sparing their parents the agony of their deaths. We tend to think of the prime beneficiaries of declining child mortality as the millions of children who would otherwise have died but now get the chance to live good lives. True enough, but the parents —particularly mothers—also have their lives transformed; they are free to pursue other activities, such as education and work outside the home. They are also able to devote more resources and time to the nurturing and development of each surviving child.

When fewer children die, parents can reduce the number of children who are born while continuing to have just as many grown-up children to continue the family, to inherit its assets, and to continue its traditions, but at lower costs to themselves in terms of risk and effort. The reduction in fertility did not come immediately—or there would have been no population explosion—but it is visible in the data within a decade or so. As a result, the population explosion was a temporary—albeit a long-lived—event. The world went from a situation in which births and deaths were more or less in balance to one in which births greatly exceeded deaths; and then, after a while, it returned to a balance, but with both births and deaths lower than in 1950. The annual rate of growth of the world's population, which reached 2.2 percent in 1960, was only half of that in 2011. The people born between the drop in mortality and the drop in fertility made an enormous addition to the world's population, first as children, when their needs were greater than what they themselves could provide, then as adults, when they were productive and creative, and finally as elderly people, many of whom are retired.

Lam also emphasizes the success of the world economy in responding to the challenge of population growth. This is one of our running themes: that society tends to adapt to new problems, in part by coming up with new ways of doing things—in the case of the population explosion, helped along by all those additional brains—and in part by creating incentives to do things differently. The Green Revolution and other innovations increased the productivity of agriculture and food production grew faster than population. Globalization also helped speed global growth because it allowed production to be carried out in those countries and places where it could be done most efficiently. Limited resources were conserved or substituted for. The price system plays a central role in creating incentives; if nonrenewable resources are becoming uncomfortably scarce, their prices will rise, and people will either make do with less, make substitutions, or direct technical change to find ways of doing without the particular resources altogether.

Economists are often accused of trusting the price system altogether too blindly, and that is sometimes true. Yet both economists and their critics agree that there are great dangers when important resources have no prices, so that, in spite of their value, they are available to users at no cost. Without prices, there is no incentive to economize on such goods. The most important example today is global warming, which, if not addressed somehow, will pose one of the greatest threats to the continuation of the growth of global prosperity.

The misdiagnosis of the population explosion by the vast majority of social scientists and policymakers, and the grave harm that the resultant mistaken policy did to many millions, were among the most serious intellectual and ethical failures of a century in which there were many.

Contraception itself was not the problem. Contraceptives have allowed couples to tailor their fertility to benefit themselves and their children, and the ability to cheaply and effectively regulate fertility has brought better lives to women around the world. As with most innovations, the first beneficiaries were in the rich countries, and this situation opened up a global inequality. Closing the gap by making the new methods available around the world was rightly seen as a priority and held the potential to do great good in the same way that antibiotics and vaccinations do great good. What *was* deeply wrong was the coercion and the loss of freedom for millions. Rich countries, in the name of helping the poor, were complicit in the coercion. Instead of helping to eliminate a global inequality they added to it, creating greater global injustice. Some harm was done by mistake, and many policymakers and scientists believed that their diagnoses and prescriptions could help poor people. Yet the mistakes were made more likely by the interests of the rich countries themselves—their fear of what life would be like for them in a world with more poor people, and that the population explosion would bolster global communism.

Global Poverty

We have already seen that the growth in national prosperity did little to reduce poverty in the United States, at least after 1975. The world as a whole was more fortunate, and the rapid growth of average incomes, particularly in China and India, and *particularly after 1975*, did much to reduce extreme poverty in the world. In China most of all, but also in India, the escape of hundreds of millions from a traditional and long-established poverty qualifies as the greatest escape of all.

Although the story is clear in broad outline, and its conclusion not under serious challenge, I want to tell it with some care, if only because it is far from obvious how to measure global poverty and what it is we mean when we talk about the number of people living below $1.00 or $1.25 a day.

Deciding who is or is not poor is something that is easy for local communities. Development practitioners often conduct "participatory rural assessments," in which villagers gather around in a central meeting place—under the banyan tree, perhaps—and tell the data collectors about the village, its crops, its main occupations and activities, its water supply, its means of transport, and its people. Those who are seen as poor are often the disabled, or those who are old and have no family to support them. In rich countries too, people are happy to give sensible answers to questions about how much a family needs to "just get by" in their community. Setting a national poverty line is harder, if only because it often comes with an entitlement to special treatment, such as subsidies that are not available to others. Yet, as we saw for the United States, national lines get worked out somehow, and they can be revised or updated in later political debate. Very much the same happened in India, where the original lines, first proposed by academics measuring living standards, were later adopted by the government—in India, the Planning Commission is the guardian of the poverty line—and then revised from time to time—using a favorite device in India, the "expert committee"—whenever the existing lines appeared to be outdated or had stopped attracting widespread support.

The national poverty lines of India and the United States have been produced and discussed within a democratic system, with debate in the press and among interested parties. This gives them the great virtue of domestic legitimacy. Yet many national poverty lines, perhaps even most, cannot be so regarded. For the many governments for whom poverty reduction is of purely rhetorical significance, poverty measurement is done at the instigation of the World Bank, another international agency, or a nongovernmental organization (NGO). Their poverty lines often come, not from domestic debate, but from the guidelines that the World Bank helpfully provides.

Poverty lines constructed by the Bank or using its methods are usually sensible enough, at least as perceived by outside experts.

Indeed, they are most frequently calculated as the amount of income at which a typical family at that income level actually buys a minimally acceptable diet. The fault in these lines is not their lack of *plausibility*, but their lack of *legitimacy;* there is no guarantee that anyone in the country, let alone a poor person in the country, sees the line as a reasonable cut-off point that separates the poor from the nonpoor. In effect, these lines are essentially administrative conveniences for the international agencies that need to measure poverty for their own purposes.

The World Bank's original dollar-a-day global poverty line, and its recent update to $1.25, came from averaging the national poverty lines of a selection of the poorest countries of the world. These local poverty lines are expressed in local currency, so they have to be converted to a common unit before they can be averaged, and this is done using the PPP exchange rates that I have already discussed. When the Bank first made this calculation twenty years ago, the average was close to a (1985) dollar per person per day, or $1,460 a year for a family of four; the most recent average—over a different group of countries—is $1.25 (2005 dollars), or $1,825 a year for a family of four. At the last stage, this global poverty line, converted back into local currencies, is used in each of the poor countries in the world—the rich countries are excluded from the calculation—to count the number of people living on the local equivalent of the global line. The calculation gives the number of "globally" poor in each country of the world, and these numbers are added up to give totals by region and for the world as a whole.

This calculation has been done on a more or less consistent basis since 1990, and the World Bank now publishes data on global poverty from 1980 to 2008. These are the numbers that I introduced in Chapter 1; Figure 6 of Chapter 1 shows that the number people in the world living on less than a (2005) dollar a day fell from about 1.5 billion in 1981 to 805 million in 2008. This occurred in spite of an increase in the population in covered countries of nearly two billion people, so that the fraction of the population in poverty fell much faster than the total numbers, from 42 to 14 percent. The decline in numbers is driven almost entirely by the Chinese growth miracle; if China is excluded, 785 million people lived on less than a dollar a day in 1981 compared with 708 million in 2008. This is somewhat less impressive, yet as a fraction of the world's non-Chinese population those that are poor fell from 29 percent to 16 percent.

In India, the other giant modern growth miracle, the number living on less than a dollar a day fell from 296 million to 247 million, and the fraction of the population in poverty from 42 to 21 percent. China and India are the success stories; rapid growth in large countries is an engine that can make a colossal dent in world poverty. The great failure of poverty reduction has been in sub-Saharan Africa. The fraction of the population living on less than a dollar a day in 2008 was 37 percent compared with 43 percent in 1981 and, because Africa's fertility rate has not fallen like Asia's, the number of poor people has almost doubled, from 169 to 303 million.

Africa has a huge land area and looms large on any map, but it is much less densely populated than is either South Asia or East Asia, so that relative failure of poverty reduction in Africa has had less effect on the global poverty count than did the successes in Asia. Even so, we must not make the frequent mistake of somehow discounting the Chinese success. Poverty pessimists, perhaps especially in the aid industry, often make statements to the effect that, with the solitary exception of China, globalization and economic growth have done little to reduce global poverty. But this is exactly the wrong way to think about global poverty. China is not a solitaire, but a country of 1.3 billion people, and to discount their escape from poverty is to argue that Chinese people count for less than Ethiopians, Kenyans, or Senegalese. Each country is worth study and measurement in its own right, but when we are looking at and trying to measure the well-being of the world, one person has to count the same no matter where he or she lives. There is no premium for living in a small country nor is there a penalty for living in a large one. Global poverty is a cosmopolitan idea and its measurement must be performed on a cosmopolitan basis.

How credible are the poverty numbers? The World Bank measurement scheme that I have outlined is a sensible one—at least apart from its lack of local democratic input—but there are many difficulties along the way; those of us who have been involved in constructing and critiquing these numbers, like many data producers, are much more skeptical and hesitant in their use than most. Even so, I think that we can be confident about the general patterns of global poverty reduction. Rapid growth in China and India is real enough, and the directions of the poverty trends are not affected by possible overstatement of the growth of national income in either country, especially not in China. The African data are often of poor quality, and here there is a good deal more uncertainty, but the stagnation of poverty fits with other things that we know about Africa, such as its relatively slow growth in national income and slow fertility decline. Beyond those broad trends, the rest of the global poverty picture is a good deal murkier.

A weakness of global poverty estimates is their dependence on the PPP exchange rates, so that they are vulnerable to criticism of and uncertainties in those rates—the Marmite problem and more. Another weakness lies in the counts of the numbers of people in each country who are below the line. And there is the question of whether the lines themselves make any sense.

The PPP exchange rates are not calculated every year, but only irregularly; the last three calculations were in 1985, 1993, and 2005, and the results of a 2011 round are in preparation as I write. Not all countries participate in every year; China, whose size guarantees that it has a big effect on any results, did not participate before 2005, so that the earlier estimates were based on partial information—better than guesses, but far from solidly based. For these reasons, or just because of the difficulty of measurement (we do not know for sure), the global poverty numbers have an alarming tendency to change whenever the PPP rates are revised. These changes have affected the poverty numbers—not just for individual countries, which would be bad enough, but also for whole continents. The 1993 revision suddenly made Africa look much poorer and Latin America much less poor. These were not inconsequential revisions; in sub-Saharan Africa, poverty went from 39 percent to 49 percent.

In 2005, with new data once again, the World Bank upped its estimate of poverty by about a third; of those classified as poor, many more were in Asia than in Africa. Most of this increase came from the Bank changing its poverty line, but the change illustrates the general unreliability of the numbers, not to mention the undesirability of allowing the Bank to be the only source of the numbers on which its own antipoverty efforts are judged. Of course, all of these changes are *statistical* and not real; no one in the world is poorer or richer because the calculations have changed. But those changes can have real effects if international organizations or NGOs shift their efforts (and their rhetoric) to the places where they "see" the highest poverty rates. This is one of many reasons why measurement matters. Much of the recent focus on African poverty postdates the 1993 revision and was arguably influenced by it. Directing aid or attention to the poorest places in the world may be chasing after a chimera, because—to consider a different metaphorical animal—the map of global poverty changes colors like a chameleon.

Trends in global poverty tend not to change very much when the underlying data are revised. Even so, it is possible that the rate of decline of Chinese and Indian poverty may have been understated and that poverty rates are falling faster than the official numbers show. This issue, which is still unsettled, is both technical and deeply political.

It is surprisingly difficult to find out how many people are poor in each country, even once the poverty line is set. The calculations use a *household* survey to ask a random sample of families how much they earn or spend, and then to count the number of people who live in families below the line. There is a cross-check on the surveys from the national income accounts, which provide independent estimates of total spending and total income for the country as a whole. But in many countries, the cross-check fails; the total from the families is often much less than the statisticians think ought to be there, and, worse still, the two totals are drifting further and further apart. Put another way, if we go to households and ask them, they say that their living standards are not improving nearly as rapidly as we would expect from the national growth rate. In one sense, this is similar to what has been happening in the United States; national income is growing, but we see little or no growth for the typical family. The main reason in the United States—that inequality is increasing—is almost certainly *part* of the reason in India and elsewhere. But in India—and to a lesser extent in the United States—the family data are simply *inconsistent* with the aggregate data. This unfortunate gap in the statistics is not unique to India but appears in many countries.[12]

In India, the statistical inconsistency has given rise to a debate that is often vitriolic. On one side—broadly the political right—are those who choose to believe the aggregate data and argue that the poverty measures from the surveys—which are used both by the World Bank and by the Indian government—understate the decline in poverty. They tell stories of surveyors cheating, sitting under trees or in tea-shops and making up the data, instead of going to the trouble of asking people. The other—more leftist—side prefers the data from the sample surveys, claiming that if we do not see the poverty reduction when we ask people, then we have no basis for claiming it is there. On their side are the many deficiencies in India's national accounts, as well as the lack of evidence of surveyors sitting in teashops. No doubt both sides have some truth in their claims, yet the debate reminds us that discussions of poverty are sometimes based on facts that are far from solid—fertile ground for people to choose their own preferred version of the truth according to their politics. Underlying all of this is the fact that India's government has become much more pro-business and much less pro-poor in its rhetoric.[13] Much thus depends on the demonstration that Indian growth is benefiting everyone, and not just the burgeoning and prospering middle class that lives in a few areas of a few cities. Denying the validity of the survey statistics allows those who are doing well not to "see" the poor.

One of my favorite Indian examples illustrates how tiny changes can have huge effects. The great economist and statistician P. C. Mahalanobis, at the Indian Statistical Institute in Kolkata, made many important contributions to the theory and practice of survey design, particularly in household surveys that asked people about their consumer spending. After some experimentation, he decided to ask people how much they had consumed—for example, of rice or wheat—over the past thirty days. In the 1990s, the Indian National Sample Surveys continued to use Mahalanobis's thirty-day rule, although many other countries then used a shorter period of seven days because it was thought that respondents could not remember earlier events with any accuracy. This, it was argued by some, was why so much was being missed, and why poverty was being overstated. The argument won the day, the switch to a seven-day reporting period was made, and, as expected, average daily expenditures went up. This obscure and technical statistical change *cut the Indian national poverty rate by half:* 175 million people were no longer poor. The length of the reporting period is surely something that only statisticians can get excited about; in current parlance, it is about as deep into the weeds as it is possible to get. Yet a tiny technical issue like this can completely change the measurement and perception of poverty. Poverty reduction is much easier to achieve by statistical means than by actually making people better off!

As a postscript: The Indian change did not stand. After Mahalanobis's experiments were redone, it seemed that the thirty-day period was not terribly inaccurate, and often better than the seven-day period; the thirty-day period was reinstituted in the surveys, much to the delight of the leftists. A more general and more important point is that in India, as in any country where a substantial fraction of the population is poor, there are millions of people who are close to poverty, either just above or just below the line. There are millions who are poor, but who would not be poor if the line were just a little lower, and millions more who are not poor, but who would fall into poverty if the line were just a little higher. As a result, very small changes in the line, or in the way resources are measured, can have very large effects on the number of people classified as poor. Such super-sensitivity undermines the whole business of poverty measurement. We don't really know where the line should be, yet its precise position makes a huge difference. To put it more brutally, the truth is that we have little idea what we are doing, and it is certainly a mistake to let anything important depend on such numbers.

In Charles Dickens's novel *David Copperfield,* the character of Mr. Micawber has his own take on the poverty line. He observes, "Annual income twenty pounds, annual expenditures nineteen pounds nineteen and six, result happiness. Annual income twenty pounds, annual expenditures twenty pounds ought and six, result misery." One reason that this quote is so memorable is that it is so silly. Why should so much depend on such a tiny difference? And why is someone who is just below the poverty line classified as poor, and worthy of special assistance or the attention of the World Bank, while someone just above the line needs no help and can be left to his or her own devices? When we don't have much idea what the poverty line should be and have great difficulty in measuring income, making such Micawberish judgments is doubly absurd. It makes sense to worry more about people the poorer they are, but not to make sharp distinctions at any critical cut-off.

A final note about the global line. To most people, it is obviously impossible to live in the United States or in Europe on a dollar per person per day. Although no one is expected to do so, and although the United States and Europe are not included in the global counts, this impossibility undermines the validity of the line, even in other countries. After all, millions of people in India live on less than a dollar a day, converted at the PPP exchange rate of about 22 rupees per dollar, and the whole point of these exchange rates is to equalize purchasing power across countries. So if people can live in India on 22 rupees a day—and be far from the worst off—why can't people in the United States live on a dollar a day?

I am not sure that there is a totally convincing answer to this question. The poverty line in India excludes (most of) three things that are important and expensive in the United States: housing, health care, and education. Beyond that, in a warm country like India, there is little need for heating, and much less has to be spent on clothing. People who work near where they live need to spend almost nothing on transportation. If these items are excluded, perhaps an "off-thegrid" American family of four could buy enough cheap foods—like bulk rice, oatmeal, beans, and a few vegetables—to survive on $1,460 a year; one recent paper has priced out a "bare-bones" bundle for the United States at around $1.25 a person a day, or $1,825 a year for a family of four.[14] Advocates of the validity of the line can also note, correctly, that 22 rupees a day buys a miserable life in India too, and that poor people and their children in India, if not hungry on a daily basis, are among the most malnourished in the world.

Global Income Inequality

It is often claimed that globalization has made the world more unequal, that while the rich have been presented with new opportunities for getting richer, the poor of the world have gained little. These claims have a ring of plausibility. Those of us who are fortunate enough to live in Europe or North America have all of the benefits of the new, interconnected world. At the same time, it is hard to see what good globalization does to the citizens of a poor landlocked country with a poorly educated and unhealthy population.

There are arguments that go the other way. Globalization gives workers in Asia better access to rich-country markets than ever before, and they can do many of the jobs that used to be done in the rich countries, even without being able to migrate. If this happens on a large scale, Asian wages will rise, and American and European wages will fall, narrowing earnings inequality in the world as a whole. The owners of capital also have new investment opportunities with globalization. If capital is relatively plentiful in rich countries and relatively scarce in poor countries, opening up the world allows rich-country capitalists to get richer while poor-country capitalists get poorer. With capitalists getting richer and workers getting poorer, income inequality will expand in rich countries and contract in poor countries. (Of course, income inequality is not just about the division between workers and capitalists.)

At the beginning of this chapter, I produced data that showed that countries' average incomes are drifting apart, or at the best have shown no tendency to come closer together. Yet some of the world's giant countries are growing very rapidly, so that billions of people now live in countries whose average incomes are closer to middle-class than to impoverishment, and this has been an important force for equalizing incomes across the world. Yet we cannot assess the extent of inequality among all the citizens of the world—what we might call cosmopolitan inequality—using only the averages while ignoring what has been happening to inequality within countries. Just because the Chinese and Indian *averages* are growing very rapidly does not guarantee that the rising tide of prosperity is lifting all boats in China and India. Or, to switch back to my metaphor of the flags at the Olympic Games, the fact that the Chinese and Indian "average" flags are marching from the back of the parade to the middle does not imply that all of the *individual* Chinese and Indian flags are doing the same. The rich Indian tycoons of the high-tech cities might have long reached the front of the parade, leaving poor agricultural laborers right at the back where they have always been. Expanding inequality within countries, if it is severe enough, could offset the giant countries' march to the middle, and cosmopolitan income inequality could be widening..

Chapter 5 documented the recent growth in American inequality. Although the United States is only one country, some of the factors that were important there—new technologies and globalization— must show up elsewhere, or at least in other rich countries. Among the poor countries, there is also evidence that not everyone has benefited from the new opportunities that globalization has brought.

While I do not believe that there is any statement about income inequality that is true in every country of the world—except that it is difficult to measure—it is clear that the general trend has been toward higher income inequality, especially in recent years. The United States is exceptional, both in its level of inequality and in the size of the recent explosion, particularly at the top, but it is certainly not the only country where income inequality is currently increasing. In several of the rich countries, income inequality as measured by the share of the top 1 percent went on falling well into the 1980s, as it had fallen for most of the century, so that the recent uptick was not only smaller than that in the United States but also later.

Chinese economic growth has been geographically uneven, and the cities have done better than the countryside. Such inequalities between rural and urban people create incentives for people to migrate, which would work against huge income differentials, but migration is severely limited in China, and more than a hundred million migrant workers can access good jobs only by being separated from their families. In India, the evidence on expanding inequality is less clear, though again some areas, especially in the south and west of the country, have done better than others. Studies of income-tax records in China and India, part of a multinational research project on top incomes, have found that the share of the top 1 percent has been expanding quite quickly in both countries, though it is only a half (India) or a third (China) the size of the share going to the top 1 percent in the United States.[15] Just to complicate the picture, there is some evidence that inequality is declining in some other large countries, including two traditionally high-inequality countries, Argentina and Brazil.

Many rich countries have also seen increases in income inequality in recent years. Most countries saw a reduction in top incomes in the first half of the twentieth century as wars, inflation, and taxes eroded the largest fortunes. Over the past few decades, the English-speaking rich countries, like the United States, saw a substantial run-up in the share of the top 1 percent, but this did not happen in the rest of Europe (except for Norway) or in Japan. When the top 1 percent pulls away from everyone else, the bottom 99 percent does less well than the national average. The success of the 1 percent has been different from country to country, which means that the rankings of how well countries have done are sometimes different for the 99 percent than for the whole country.

One interesting comparison is between France and the United States. France has grown somewhat less rapidly than the United States in recent years, but the bottom 99 percent of the population in France saw more rapid growth in average incomes than did the bottom 99 percent of the population in the United States.[16] Or, put the other way around, all but the top 1 percent of the French population did better than all but the top 1 percent of the American population.

The split between English and non-English speakers is what might be expected if top English-speaking managers can sell their services in a world market that is driven by the explosion of top salaries in the United States, but is not open to French, German, or Japanese managers in the same way. A more benign interpretation is that globalization has generated a huge, rich market for top English-speaking managers who, like opera singers or sports stars, now live in an integrated cosmopolitan club of CEOs. In this version of the story, super-sized salaries in the United States and other English-speaking countries are the returns to super-sized talent in the new global market, not the result of American CEOs overpaying themselves and forcing the rest of the English-speaking world to do likewise.

All rich countries face changes in technology as well as competition from lower-wage countries. Not all have shown the same increase in earnings inequality that has occurred in the United States, and some that seemed originally resistant to the trend are most recently showing an expansion in inequality—a fanning out of earnings—especially above the median. The polarization of jobs and of earnings—with many middle-income jobs being replaced by machines or outsourcing while lower-paid service jobs are doing relatively well—appears to be widespread in rich countries.[17] Polarization, which is new, is limiting the expansion of inequality at the bottom of the income distribution. Other trends—including an increasing prevalence of single-parent families at the bottom and of power couples at the top—are also widespread. Tax and redistribution systems—more comprehensive in Europe than in the United States, and more focused on limiting inequality—seem not to have been able to prevent the recent increase in inequality.

What do these country experiences tell us about inequality in the world as a whole? Are the country expansions in inequality enough to offset the movement of the giants up the world distribution? If the average incomes of countries are moving apart from one another, and if the average country is becoming more unequal, does not that *imply* that the world is becoming more unequal?

Only the last question has a clear answer, which is no. Countries are vastly different in size, and in recent years at least, the giants have grown very rapidly, much more rapidly than average. When we look country by country, we count tiny countries—Guinea-Bissau with one and a half million people—as if they were the same as the giants—India with more than a billion. The fact that Guinea-Bissau and many other small African countries are not doing very well is why *countries* are moving apart, but it tells us nothing about what is happening when we look at whether *people* are moving apart.

What about the contribution of within-country inequality to world inequality? It is important—particularly at the very top of the world income distribution—but not decisive for the vast majority of people, if only because most inequality in the world comes from differences between countries, not from differences within them. So we are back to the giants—particularly China and India—and how fast they are growing relative to the rest of the world. Growth that is fast enough—even with expanding internal inequality, particularly in China—should sweep everything before it, and the world as a whole should become more equal, at least as long as China remains poorer than the average. Careful estimates, putting all the evidence together, suggest that this is in fact the case and that, in spite of countries pulling apart, and in spite of the growth in internal inequality, global inequality is stable or slowly falling.[18] That may well be correct, though I am not convinced that we know for sure. The big uncertainty is the true growth rates of China and India—whether they are as large as officially stated—and that uncertainty is amplified by the difficulties of making international comparisons between them and other countries.

Finally, we need to ask whether we should care about world inequality and, if so, why. Within a country, inequality tells us something about justice: whether all citizens of a country—who, whether they like it or not, have to pay taxes and conform to the laws and policies of the country—are getting reasonable rewards in line with their obligations. The philosopher Ronald Dworkin has written that "A political community that exercises dominion over its citizens, and demands from them allegiance and obedience to its laws, must take an impartial, objective attitude towards them all."[19] Admittedly, different people take different views about what justice requires of income distribution, and on whether the high and expanding inequality in the United States is itself unjust, but this is a key part of national discussions about income inequality, whether something ought to be done about it, and if so, just what.

The international situation is different. There is no world government to which people owe allegiance or that has the capability to address international inequalities that might arguably be unjust. The measurement of international inequality is not part of the statistical support for international policy in the way that it is for national policy. Indeed, there are no official statistics on global income inequality among individuals, and perhaps the topic is one that should be left to the curiosity of individual scholars. There is much truth in this, but there are counterarguments too. There may not be a world government, but there are global institutions—for example, the World Trade Organization or the World Bank—whose policies affect the incomes of people in many countries and whose activities are perhaps sufficiently state-like to support justice-based claims by those who are affected. None of these organizations has the authority or the ability to implement a global tax and redistribution system, yet their potential to do good and harm surely makes a case for their at least monitoring income distribution. The world may not be unified but neither is it a set of isolated states that do not interact with one another.

PART III **HELP**

SEVEN

How to Help Those Left Behind

ALMOST A BILLION PEOPLE still live in material destitution, millions of children still die through the accident of where they are born, and wasting and stunting still disfigure the bodies of nearly half of India's children. Those people are among the many that the Great Escape has left behind. As in the past, the very enormity of the inequality points to ways to eliminate it. The scientific and technological advances that supported the escape are available to all, and I need hardly restate the benefits of escaping or the horrors of being left behind. Some countries in South and East Asia have seized the opportunity to begin to catch up, and they have lifted millions of their people from poverty and saved millions from early death. Yet stark inequalities remain.

Since World War II, rich countries have tried to help close these gaps using foreign aid. Foreign aid is the flow of resources from rich countries to poor countries that is aimed at improving the lives of poor people. In earlier times, resources flowed in the opposite direction, from poor countries to rich countries—the spoils of military conquest and colonial exploitation. In later periods, rich-country investors sent funds to poor countries to seek profits, not to seek better lives for the locals. Trade brought raw materials to the rich countries in exchange for manufactured goods, but few poor countries have succeeded in becoming rich by exporting raw materials. Many have been left with a legacy of foreign ownership and internal inequality. Against this history, foreign aid, which is explicitly designed to benefit the recipients, is something completely different.

In the past, the best that those left behind could expect was to learn from previous escapees, but they were fortunate enough if those who had gone before did not fill in the tunnels behind them. That the newly fortunate should return to help is new. This chapter tries to figure out whether foreign aid did indeed hasten the Great Escape or whether—through mixed motives, politics, or the law of unintended consequences—it did the opposite.

Material Aid and Global Poverty

One of the stunning facts about global poverty is how little it would take to fix it, at least if we could magically transfer money into the bank accounts of the world's poor. In 2008, there were about 800 million people in the world living on less than $1.00 a day. On average, each of these people is "short" about $0.28 a day; their average daily expenditure is $0.72 instead of the $1.00 it would take to lift them out of poverty.[1] We could make up the shortfall with less than a quarter of a billion dollars a day; $0.28 times 800 million is $0.22 billion. If the United States were to try to do this on its own, each American man, woman, and child would have to pay $0.75 each day, or $1.00 a day each if children were exempted. We could cut this to $0.50 a person per day if the adults of Britain, France, Germany, and Japan joined in. Even this is more than we would really need. Almost all the poor of the world live in countries where food, housing, and other essentials are cheaper than in the rich countries; a dollar spent in India buys about $2.50 worth of purchasing power for the things that poor people buy.[2] Taking this into account, we have the remarkable conclusion that world poverty could be eliminated if every American adult donated $0.30 a day; or, if we could build a coalition of the willing from all the adults of Britain, France, Germany, and Japan, each would need to give only $0.15 a day.

It is hard to believe that global poverty can exist simply because of the failure to give such tiny sums. Understanding why this calculation tells us *nothing* about eliminating poverty is one of the main themes of this chapter. As we shall see, the problem is *not* that the $0.15 is too little. Ramping it up to $0.30 or even $1.50 would not make poverty history.

My calculation covers only the cost of bringing people up to a bare minimum of $1.00 a day. It does not address the even more important questions of improving health or saving lives. A number of websites make recommendations about which charities are particularly effective on this front. The website givingwhatwecan.org, run by the philosopher Toby Ord, says that if a person earning £15,000 a year tithes £1,500, "this means saving 1.5 lives per year, or treating nearly 5,000 children per year for neglected tropical diseases."[3] I shall challenge the basis for these numbers later, but they are serious estimates that are carefully calculated and are small relative to the benefits. More careless advocates often come up with much smaller numbers: the actor Richard Attenborough, whom we met in the Introduction, claimed in a 2000 newspaper article that UNICEF could save the life of a child in Mozambique for 17 pence, about $0.27.[4]

These calculations, including the one with which I began, are examples of what I call the *aid illusion,* the erroneous belief that global poverty could be eliminated if only rich people or rich countries were to give more money to poor people or to poor countries. I shall argue that, far from being a prescription for eliminating poverty, the aid illusion is actually an obstacle to improving the lives of the poor.

What do we make of the calculation that we can eliminate world poverty for $0.15 a day? How can world poverty still exist when it costs so little to eliminate? Here are four possible reasons:

- Moral indifference: rich people do not care.
- Lack of understanding: people do care, but they do not realize how easy it is to do something about poverty.
- Aid could be effective, but it is being misdirected and is currently ineffective.
- Aid is generally ineffective and may even do harm, at least in some circumstances.

I shall follow up all of these arguments below, but a good place to start is with the questions of moral indifference and whether poverty is easy to fix.

Might it be true that the rich are so callous that they refuse to make tiny sacrifices to remove a billion people from utter destitution? People may not be callous when it comes to their friends and families, but perhaps they feel little responsibility to help people who are very different from them and live thousands of miles away.

Adam Smith thought not. In a famous passage in which he imagines an enormous earthquake in China, he asks whether someone not living in China would refuse to lose his little finger to save the lives of a hundred million Chinese, none of whom he has ever met. He concludes: "the world, in its greatest depravity and corruption, never produced such a villain as would be capable of entertaining it."[5] Smith's contemporary David Hume argued that (eighteenth-century) globalization should make people more sympathetic and more willing to help those who were geographically distant, an argument that surely applies with even greater force to today's globalization.[6]

The philosopher Peter Singer has long argued against the idea that distance should make a difference, comparing the refusal of someone to help a child in Africa to the refusal of a passerby to help a child who is drowning in a shallow pond, even when the cost is trivial, such as minor damage to the rescuer's clothes. The fact that the child in Africa is far away makes no difference to the moral imperative to give assistance, because there are international charities, like Oxfam, that can conquer the distance on our behalf.

If we accept that Oxfam and other aid agencies are effective, the refusal to donate is morally equivalent to the refusal to help the drowning child. In 1971, during the war that eventually severed Bangladesh from Pakistan, Singer wrote about the suffering there and concluded, "Nor, I think, is it seriously disputed that we can do something about it, either through orthodox measures of famine relief or through population control, or both."[7] Singer's more recent writings maintain the effectiveness claims,[8] and a number of websites, such as giving-whatwecan.org and givewell.org, aim to help potential (but perhaps skeptical or cautious) donors by vetting international charitable organizations and recommending those that are particularly effective in reducing poverty and improving health. The ethical arguments for the duty to assist are surely overwhelming; the issue is not the moral but the practical one: whether "we" (meaning the world's non-poor) have the ability to assist "them" (the global poor).

It is perhaps obvious that the claim in the opening paragraph of this section—that for $0.15 a day each we can eliminate dollar-a-day poverty—is at best incomplete: things are not so simple. Indeed, many people's first reaction to the calculation is that they recognize that $0.15 may not be enough—that there are no doubt losses and administrative costs along the way—so that maybe it takes $0.50 a day, or even a dollar or two. The moral imperative depends, not on the cost being as low as $0.15, but on the cost being low relative to what "we" have. However, there is an even stronger moral imperative to do no harm, especially to people who are already in such great difficulty. All of the arguments about giving money—whatever the amount—depend on the proposition that more money will make things better. Paradoxical as it may at first appear, I shall argue that giving *more* aid than we currently give—at least if it were given as it is given now—would make things worse, not better.

The United States gives a smaller share of its national income in foreign aid than do many rich countries, but it still donates substantially more than $0.15 per person. The total amount of official foreign aid from all rich countries in 2011 was $133.5 billion,[9] which is $0.37 a day for each poor person in the world, or a bit less than a dollar a day of poor-country purchasing power. This takes no account of the very large sums ($30 billion or so) raised by private charities and international NGOs. Aid flows are more than enough to eliminate global dollar-a-day poverty, at least if the money were transferred from the people and governments in rich countries directly to those who are living on less than the global poverty line. We cannot say anything sensible about aid unless we understand why this does not happen.

The opening calculation is an example of the "hydraulic" approach to foreign aid: if water is pumped in at one end, water must pour out of the other end.[10] Fixing world poverty and saving the lives of dying children is seen as an engineering problem, like fixing the plumbing or repairing a broken car. We need a new transmission, at so much, and two new tires, at so much each, plus labor costs. Children's lives are saved by providing insecticide-treated bed nets (which protect against malaria) at a few dollars each, or by oral rehydration therapy at $0.25 a dose, or by administering vaccinations at a few dollars each.

Investing in projects, programs, and machinery can fire up economic growth, and growth is the best cure for poverty. Statistical analysis shows a robust correlation between economic growth and the share of national income that is invested, so it is straightforward to calculate how much additional capital a country "needs" in order to grow faster and eliminate poverty more quickly.

That such calculations are wrong has been argued for a long time, though it does not remove their seductiveness to many even today. Peter Bauer, writing in 1971, made a crucial point: "If all conditions for development other than capital are present, capital will soon be generated locally, or will be available to the government or to private businesses on commercial terms from abroad, the capital to be serviced out of higher tax revenues or from the profits of enterprise. If, however, the conditions for development are not present, then aid— which in these circumstances will be the only source of external capital—will be necessarily unproductive and therefore ineffective."[11] The availability and size of international private capital flows today dwarfs anything that Bauer could have dreamt of; if the argument was correct in 1971, it is stronger still today.

This is one central dilemma of foreign aid. When the "conditions for development" are present, aid is not required. When local conditions are hostile to development, aid is not useful, and it will do harm if it perpetuates those conditions. We shall see many examples of what happens when this dilemma is ignored. Development agencies again and again find themselves impaled on its horns; aid is effective only when it is least needed, but the ultimate donors are insistent on effective aid for those who need it most. While Bauer's formulation is about capital for investment and growth, it applies more widely. If poverty is not a result of lack of resources or opportunities, but of poor institutions, poor government, and toxic politics, giving money to poor countries—particularly giving money to the *governments* of

poor countries—is likely to perpetuate and prolong poverty, not eliminate it. The hydraulic approach to aid is wrong, and fixing poverty is
nothing like fixing a broken car or pulling a drowning child out of a
shallow pond.

Facts about Aid

One reason why today's aid does not eliminate global poverty is that
it rarely tries to do so. The World Bank flies under the flag of eliminating poverty, but most aid flows come not through multilateral
organizations like the Bank but as "bilateral" aid, from one country to
another, and different countries use aid for different purposes. In
recent years, some donor countries have emphasized aid for poverty
relief, with Britain's Department for International Development
(DFID) one of the leaders. But in most cases, aid is guided less by
the needs of the recipients than by the donor country's domestic
and international interests. This is hardly surprising given that donor
governments are democratic and are spending taxpayers' money.
Although there is a strong domestic constituency for global poverty
reduction in many countries—Britain being a good example—donors
must balance a number of considerations, including political alliances
and maintaining good relationships with ex-colonies where donors
often have important interests. Domestic donor interests include not
only citizens with humanitarian concerns but also commercial interests that see both opportunities (sales of their goods) and threats
(competition from developing countries) from foreign aid. Even so,
several countries, including Japan and the United States, cite general
objectives like creating a prosperous and democratic world, and these
are clearly consistent with global poverty reduction.[12]

The *stated* purpose of aid may be less important than it might seem.
Aid is typically fungible across uses, so that even military aid can con-

ceivably free up funds for schools or clinics, if the government would otherwise have bought tanks and planes. Diversion in the other direction is typically more of a concern. One of the pioneers of economic development, Paul Rosenstein-Rodan, noted in the 1940s that you might think you are building a power station when you have actually financed a brothel.[13] If the United States gives to an ally to cement its political support, there is nothing to prevent that ally from spending the funds on poverty reduction, health, or education. So classifying aid by its purpose may not make much sense.

The largest component of foreign aid is what is known as official development assistance (ODA); the term covers funds donated by the governments of rich donor countries for the welfare and development of poor recipient countries. According to the Development Assistance Committee (DAC) of the OECD, which is the scorekeeper, total ODA in 2011 was $133.5 billion. There are twenty-three DAC countries, who contributed between 0.1 percent of national income (Greece and Korea) and 1 percent of national income (Norway and Sweden); the 2011 average was just under 0.5 percent of national income. ODA rose rapidly through the 1960s and 1970s and doubled in real value from 1960 to 1980. The end of the Cold War brought substantial reductions—in itself an indication of donor intent—and the 1997 total was below the 1980 value. Since then, ODA has increased by more than 50 percent. The cumulative amount of aid since 1960 is approximately $5 trillion (at 2009 prices).

The United States is currently the largest provider of ODA, followed by Germany, Britain, and France, with Japan not far behind. In terms of share of national income—a measure of donor commitment, but obviously not of the satisfaction of poor people's needs— the United States, with less than 0.2 percent of national income, is one of the lowest, while the Scandinavian countries, the Netherlands, and Luxembourg are at the top of the table.

The focus on aid as a share of donor income is puzzling. Why should the UN have repeatedly urged countries to give 0.7 percent of donor income? If we are really rescuing a child from a pond, the income of the rescuer is irrelevant. There is a hydraulic explanation: that reaching targets, such as the Millennium Development Goals, will cost 0.7 percent of rich country GDP—a calculation akin to the one with which I began this chapter, and similarly nonsensical. It is also possible that the UN thinks the more aid the better—true for many of its member governments if not their people—and that 0.7 percent is the most that is likely to be forthcoming. A more important explanation is that governments that accept the target are those with strong domestic constituencies for helping the poor, and those constituencies can only monitor the amount spent, not the results. In such cases, aid is more about satisfying our own need to help, and less about improving the lot of the poor.

There is more to foreign assistance than *official* aid. Many thousands of charities and NGOs are involved in global humanitarian and development work, and the biggest of these are very large, with annual budgets in excess of half a billion dollars. They act independently but also as agents for the national and international agencies. Between them they are thought to add a further 25–30 percent to the total transfer from rich to poor countries. They vary greatly in their transparency and effectiveness. There are also nontraditional donors, such as Brazil, China, and Saudi Arabia, who do not report to the DAC and who are not included in DAC statistics.

About 80 percent of ODA is bilateral; the remainder is given via multilateral organizations such as the World Bank, the United Nations Development Programme (UNDP), or the Global Fund to Fight AIDS, Tuberculosis and Malaria, to name just three. It is sometimes argued that multilateral aid is less subject to domestic political considerations, and is more transparent and efficient than bilateral aid; however, the World Bank cannot easily go against the wishes of its largest donors, and UNDP has been rated as one of the least transparent and most inefficient donors.[14] The multiplicity of donors and agencies—even within one country, official aid is sometimes routed through many different government agencies that work independently (fifty in the United States)—not only makes it difficult to track totals but also poses enormous problems for any kind of coordination, or even for preventing agencies from undercutting each other's policies.

Aid is spread over many countries, with some donors providing funds to more than 150 different recipient countries. Donors seem to want to give aid to *countries,* rather than to *people,* and would prefer to give to as many countries as possible, paying little attention to where poor people live. As a result, small countries receive more aid than large countries, whether measured per person or as a proportion of their incomes. However, most of the world's poor live in *large* countries, so that "aid fragmentation" by donors is another reason why aid is not effectively targeted to the poor of the world.

According to World Bank data, the top aid recipients in per capita terms in 2010 were Samoa ($802), Tonga ($677), and Cape Verde ($664), while for the two giants, the *highest* amounts ever received per person were $3.10 for India (in 1991) and $2.90 for China (in 1995). As we have already seen, about half (48 percent in 2008) of the world's poor live in either India or China, yet China and India together in 2010 received only $3.5 billion in ODA, or only 2.6 percent of total aid. That half of the world's poor people received only a fortieth of the world's official development aid is surely one of the odder inequality measures in the world.

Of course, it may be that China and India, which have been growing very rapidly, are seen as capable of eliminating poverty on their own and have little need of ODA; certainly both receive inflows of private investment that are six times ODA for India, and fifty-seven times ODA for China. So one might hope that aid is simply being directed where it can do the most good. Yet it is not clear why Samoa and Tonga need *quite* so much. Nor have their growth rates been particularly impressive. These facts are hard to reconcile with the hydraulic view of a world of donors directing funds to pull people out of poverty at so much per person, or one in which aid reduces poverty by stimulating economic growth.

The distribution of aid reflects the different policies of different donor countries. Aid from France is heavily focused on French ex-colonies. U.S. aid has always reflected American foreign policy, supporting allies against communism during the Cold War, supporting Egypt and Israel after the Camp David accords, or focusing on funds for reconstruction in Iraq and Afghanistan. Some countries "tie" their aid, requiring that the funds be spent on donor goods (including food aid) or that donor goods be transported in donor-owned ships. By some estimates, 70 percent of aid from the United States never reaches the recipient countries, at least not in cash. Tying helps build a constituency for aid in the donor country, but it almost certainly reduces the usefulness of the aid to the recipient. In recent years, tying has been much reduced—for example, it is now illegal in Britain—but it is still widespread. A recent estimate finds that between 1987 and 2007, the fraction of ODA that was tied, together with the fraction that was food aid or technical assistance (both of which are typically of low value to the recipient), fell from 80 percent to 25 percent.[15]

In direct contradiction to any supposed poverty mandate, much ODA does not even go to low-income countries, let alone to those countries where the poor live. Once again, there has been a marked increase in targeting, but from an extraordinarily low base. The share of ODA going to what the OECD calls the least-developed countries has increased from a little more than 10 percent in 1960 to about a third today. Even today, more than half of ODA goes to middle-income countries. This is not necessarily as bad as it sounds. Because of their recent growth, the World Bank now classes China as an upper-middle-income and India as a lower-middle-income country; both may be able to tackle their own poverty. In today's world, targeting poor people is a very different thing from targeting poor countries.

Aid, including both official aid and humanitarian aid from NGOs, is often given to regimes that have little interest in or track record of helping their own populations. The donors may do this to meet political aims, as in the United States' long support for Mobutu Sese Seko in Zaire, its more recent support for Egypt and Ethiopia, and France's support of its ex-colonies, several of which have autocratic and corrupt governments. Almost half of ODA goes to autocratic regimes (though there is evidence that countries that become democratic receive an upsurge in aid).[16]

To take just one example, in 2010 Robert Mugabe's Zimbabwe received ODA worth more than 10 percent of its national income, or nearly $60 per person. In such cases, donors face an acute version of Bauer's dilemma. If aid were targeted to places where people are in great need, countries like Togo or Zimbabwe would be good candidates. But because of the way these countries are run, aid is unlikely to do much good, and it may actually help the autocrats remain in power, or enrich them, or both. Aid can be directed through NGOs that are independent of the government, but this is at best an imperfect remedy. Aid is fungible—so that schools and clinics operated by NGOs may free up funds for the government—and governments find ways of taxing (or simply diverting) the NGOs' resources. They can (and do) levy taxes on goods and equipment imported by the NGOs, or require expensive operating licenses. The same thing happens in humanitarian emergencies, especially in time of war, when warlords have to be bought off in order to allow humanitarian access to their own people. In extreme cases, this has led to international NGOs flying in weapons along with food, to pictures of starving children being used to raise funds that were used in part to prolong war, or to NGO-funded camps being used as bases to train militias bent on genocide.[17] There is always a tension between directing aid to well-run countries, where the aid can do some good but where it is less urgently needed, and directing aid to countries where there is great distress but where it can do little good and even risks doing harm.

This brief portrait of aid flows takes no account of the many other ways in which rich countries affect poor countries for good or ill; indeed aid is one of the *least* important of these links. Rich countries provide capital in the form of private investment, often more readily and with less bureaucratic fuss than does the World Bank. As a result, there is less demand for World Bank aid than once was the case, especially among middle-income countries. Private remittances from rich to poor countries, for example from immigrants to their families at home, are twice as large as ODA. Basic science—discoveries of new classes of drugs, of vaccines, or of the mechanisms underlying disease —has almost always come from rich countries but has also brought benefits to poor countries. So have inventions like cell phones or the Internet. At the same time, trade restrictions or patent enforcement can restrict poor countries' access to wealthy markets or important treatments. These non-aid links are often much more important—for good or ill—than is foreign aid, and I will return to this issue at the end of the chapter. Of course, this is not to deny that aid is important in those individual countries where it is the biggest game in town.

How Effective Is Aid?

When I first started studying aid and economic development, it seemed straightforward to find out how well it worked. Like most people, I started from the assumption that aid must work. After all, if I am poor and you are rich, and you give me money—or better still a steady year-by-year flow of money—I will be less poor. The belief that this intuition should apply to aid—what I now think of as the aid illusion—is so powerful that many people refuse to even consider the possibility that it might be wrong. The intuition is essentially the hydraulic account of aid, which, as we have seen, is just false.

Aid is not given person to person; most of it is government to government, and much of it is not designed to lift people out of poverty. My brief sketch of the actual aid system tells us that, but it does not tell us whether aid has helped or hindered economic growth and poverty reduction over the past fifty years. There are plentiful data on aid, from the DAC and other sources, as well as information on economic growth and poverty. Different countries are treated differently; some get more aid than others; and the amount of aid has changed from year to year. Surely we can use those data to find out what aid does? Or more precisely, do countries that receive more aid —per person or in relation to their national incomes—grow more rapidly? Of course, poverty reduction and growth are different things, but both theory and experience suggest that economic growth is the surest and most lasting solution to poverty.

The description in the previous section should make it clear that there is no easy answer, or at least no easy *positive* answer. China and India, which got very little aid relative to the sizes of their economies, are the two great success stories, while the much smaller countries of Africa, which have received a great deal of aid relative to their sizes, have much less impressive records of economic growth. Because agencies tend to spread out their aid, with something for everyone, smaller countries get more aid than larger countries, so that if aid is important for growth, smaller countries should grow more rapidly. By this test alone, aid has been a resounding failure. Of course, this is too quick a conclusion. There may be other reasons—having nothing to do with aid—why larger economies can grow faster; we saw some of these in Chapter 6. Even so, this is hardly a positive finding for the idea that aid helps countries grow more rapidly.

Another way to study aid effectiveness is to look at countries that were particularly favored in the aid process: those that had strong colonial ties (particularly ex-colonies of France), or countries that got extra aid for political reasons (places like Egypt, because of the Camp David accords), or even those that were seen as bulwarks against communism during the Cold War (countries like Zaire under Mobutu). Needless to say, those countries had some of the worst records of poverty reduction, and it is clear enough why. In Egypt, Togo, and Zaire, aid was used not for economic development but to help keep an externally favored regime in power, even when doing so *harmed* the population.

One might argue that aid to corrupt and oppressive regimes is not what we are talking about, and that it should never have been counted as development aid. But the excuse is too easy. Most of this aid took the form of unrestricted flows to regimes that could have used it for development had they chosen to do so; much of it also went to countries where there were many people in need. So, while these examples do not prove that better-designed aid, or aid to a different selection of countries, might not have done better, they show clearly enough that it is not generally a good idea to give unconditional aid to countries whose populations are in need. I shall also argue that the forces at work in these egregiously bad cases are a problem even under more favorable conditions.

Looking at what has happened to aid in sub-Saharan Africa is particularly instructive. Although a few of the world's poorest countries are not in Africa, most are. Afghanistan, Bangladesh, Cambodia, Haiti, Nepal, and Timor-Leste are (the only) non-African countries among the poorest forty countries in the world. Africa is the home of the poor country, even if it is not the home of the poor person. African countries have received lots of aid—enough to make a difference to their rates of growth had the aid been used for that purpose.

Figure 1 shows how African countries have grown since 1960, by five-year intervals, with 2010 incorporated into the most recent period. The World Bank lists forty-nine countries in sub-Saharan Africa. They are very different in size and importance—from the

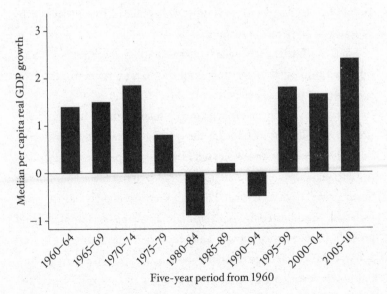

FIGURE 1 Median growth of per capita GDP (real PPP) in Africa.

Comoros Islands and Mayotte to Ethiopia, Nigeria, and South Africa
—so it is not a good idea to take a simple average. Instead, I work with
the *median* growth rate in each period, the rate around which half the
countries do worse and half do better.

In the 1960s and early 1970s, the typical growth rate of per capita
income was between 1 and 2 percent a year; these are not spectacular
growth rates by any standard, but Africans were generally getting better off. In the 1980s and early 1990s, the typical African growth rate
was *negative*. Africans lost ground, not just relative to the more successful Asian countries, but also absolutely, relative to what they
themselves had had before. By the dire standards of the 1980s and
1990s, the slow-growth years after independence were a golden age. It
was during the 1980s and 1990s that Africa gained the reputation of
being the basket case of the world. In 1960, Korea was three times
richer than Ghana; by 1995 it was nineteen times richer. In 1960,
India's per capita income was only 40 percent of that of Kenya; by
1995, it was 40 percent greater than Kenya's.

Since 1995, there has been a turnaround. Growth rates have rebounded into positive territory, and the sixteen years to 2010 have
seen Africa's best growth performance.

How much of this up, down, and up-again pattern can be attributed to fluctuations in aid from abroad? Figure 2 shows the aid numbers, again medians and expressed as dollars per person; these dollars
need to be multiplied by a factor of about two to take account of the
lower price levels in Africa. These figures are unadjusted for price
inflation; the adjusted figures have a similar shape but show less rapid
growth. In recent years, an inhabitant of the median country in sub-
Saharan Africa has been receiving about $100 a year in aid in purchas-
ing power terms, a sum equivalent to about 20 percent of national
income in the median country.

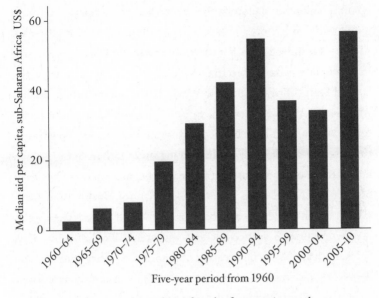

FIGURE 2 Median per capita aid to Africa by five-year intervals.

What do these two figures tell us about aid and growth in Africa? Obviously, other things are going on, but there is much to be said for starting with a simpleminded view, and once again, things look bad for aid. Growth *decreased* steadily while aid *increased* steadily. When aid fell off, after the end of the Cold War, growth picked up; the end of the Cold War took away one of the main rationales for aid to Africa, and African growth rebounded. There is a bitter joke to the effect that "the Cold War is over, and Africa lost." But the graph suggests that a more accurate punchline would be "the Cold War is over, and Africa won," because the West reduced aid. While this makes sense for Mobutu and Zaire, it is clearly too strong as a general proposition.

Those who are optimistic about aid look to the end of the period and emphasize that recent aid has been for development, not to prop up anticommunist dictators; they note that, in this period of more enlightened aid, more aid has brought more growth. Perhaps so. Mobutu has indeed gone, but the government of Meles Zenawi Asres in Ethiopia received more than $3 billion of aid in 2010, from the United States, Britain, and the World Bank, among others. Meles, who died in 2012, was one of the most repressive and autocratic dictators in Africa.[18] Ethiopia has nearly forty million people living on less than $1.25 a day (twenty million living on less than $1.00), which makes the country a favorite of those who believe in aid as a means of poverty relief; Meles was a staunch opponent of Muslim fundamentalism, which made him a favorite of the United States. The United States, of course, is entitled to choose its international allies. But if its aid is motivated by a combination of domestic security concerns and domestic constituencies that see the act of giving as more important than what giving accomplishes, we are giving aid for "us," not for "them."

One key to African growth is what happens to commodity prices. Many African countries have long been and are still dependent on exports of "primary" commodities, mostly unprocessed minerals or agricultural crops. Botswana exports diamonds; South Africa, gold and diamonds; Nigeria and Angola, oil; Niger, uranium; Kenya, coffee; Côte d'Ivoire and Ghana, cocoa; Senegal, groundnuts; and so on. The world prices of primary commodities are notoriously volatile, with huge price increases in response to crop failures or increases in world demand and equally dramatic price collapses, none of which are easily predictable. Many African governments own the mines, wells, and plantations, while others tax the export of commodities like cocoa and coffee, so that booms and busts in commodity prices cause dramatic and hard-to-handle swings in government revenues. Later in this chapter, I shall draw a comparison between revenue from commodity sales and foreign aid, but for the moment, I need only note that commodity prices were generally rising in the 1960s and early 1970s, fell steadily from 1975, and have, for some commodities, like oil and copper, revived in the past decade. The revenue from those high prices is a part of national income, so that it is almost impossible for an economy whose commodity exports are booming not to grow, at least for a while. More formal evidence confirms that African incomes grow in response to commodity price booms.[19]

Those who live high on the hog have a tendency to fall off, and so it was with the commodity crash after 1975. Private foreign lenders abetted the mismanagement of African governments—as did poor advice from the World Bank—so that when the collapse came, it was much worse than it need have been.[20] This is one of the most important causes of the growth patterns in Figure 1. Another factor, more contentious but still plausible, is that African countries now have much better fiscal and monetary policies than had previously been the case. This is in part the legacy of the structural adjustment policies of the 1980s, but there are also now many better-trained African finance ministers and central bankers. If we are going to assess the effects of aid, we need to allow for these other factors, including commodity booms and busts.

Aid increased very rapidly during the "bad" years after the commodity busts. This might tell us that aid did not do very much good, but it might also tell us something more positive—that aid to Africa came in response to distress. Indeed, at least some of the new aid was lent in order to enable countries to "repay" old debts on which they would otherwise have defaulted. When aid follows poor economic outcomes—humanitarian aid being the obvious example—a negative relation between growth and aid is exactly what we would hope to see! That aid goes to low-growth countries is a mark not of aid's failure, but of its success—it is being sent where it is needed. When the lifeboat crew rescues drowning sailors, and the sailors are still wet and distressed from their near-fatal experience, we would hardly blame the rescuers for the fact that the sailors are worse off than they were before the storm.

Aid researchers have expended an enormous amount of ingenuity —and even more foolishness—on trying to disentangle the effects of aid on growth, making allowance for other things that are going on at the same time and trying to take into account the feedback from distress to assistance. Taking account of other things is relatively straightforward. The correlation between aid (as a share of national income) and growth remains *negative* even when other important causes of growth have been taken into account. This fact is not decisive, because it ignores the feedback from distress to aid, but it is important nevertheless. When similar studies look at the effect of investment—expenditures on machines, factories, computers, and infrastructure, the things that underpin future prosperity—the effect on growth is very easy to see.[21] Aid, evidently, does not work like investment. Yet the old hydraulic theory of aid assumed exactly this—that poor countries, because they were poor, could not afford to invest for the future, and that aid would fill the gap. Once again, whatever aid does, this is not it.

What about the feedback from distress to aid? Perhaps there really is an effect of aid on growth, but it is offset by episodes in which aid responds to disaster. Disentangling this is a classic chicken-and-egg problem, and about as difficult to solve. Although many studies have tried, none is really convincing. Indeed, we have already seen how the question is typically studied. If we can find countries where aid is *not* given in response to poor performance, we can study its effects uncontaminated by the effects of distress, and get a clean reading of how aid affects growth. What examples do we have? The fact that large countries get less aid than small countries is one. And that politically favored allies or ex-colonies get more aid is another. As we have seen, neither of these thought experiments yields a positive reading for aid, but both approaches can readily be challenged.

Where does this leave us? Different scholars draw the balance in different ways. One position is that the statistical analysis is so murky that no answer can be found; looking at aid and performance over time and across countries simply cannot answer the question. My own view is a little more positive on the literature, and a good deal more negative on aid. Many donors still cling to the hydraulic idea that aid provides capital to poor countries that cannot otherwise afford it and thus gives them a better future. But this is contradicted by the data, because aid does not work like investment, and indeed the whole idea makes no sense given the access that many poor countries have to private international capital markets. The fact that neither smaller countries nor politically favored countries grow faster is also evidence against aid, certainly not decisive—there may be other reasons why large countries grow quickly, or why politically favored countries do badly—but still quite suggestive. That the governments of many politically favored countries are corrupt is not an excuse, unless we can show that giving unrestricted aid to "better" governments is different, a topic to which I shall return.

The Effectiveness of Development Projects

Many people—laypeople and development professionals alike—do not care to assess aid by looking for its effects on economic growth. For them, aid is about *projects:* the funding of a school or of a clinic, or giving aid to an organization that provides insecticide-treated bed nets, that offers information about how to avoid HIV/AIDS, or that sets up microfinance groups. It is about the road that changed life in a village or the dam that created livelihoods for thousands. Every organization that works in international development—the NGOs,

UNDP, and the World Bank—has its success stories. Those who are involved often have firsthand experience, and they have no doubt about the effectiveness of what they have done. They will admit to failures, but they count them as the cost of doing business—a business that overall is a great success. How can we reconcile this knowledge with the ambiguous or even negative assessments from the statistical evidence?

One possibility is that the evaluations, by the NGOs or by the World Bank, are overly rosy. Critics point to the fact that NGOs have strong incentives not to report failure and to exaggerate success—after all, they are in the fund-raising business as much as in the fund-dispersing business. They also point to methodological failings in the assessments, especially the fact that it is difficult to know what would have happened to the recipients of aid had they not received the aid. The World Bank and UN agencies have similar incentives to evaluate their work in positive terms. World Bank evaluations are often done before the project has had time to work out in full, and there is constant pressure to provide evaluations quickly. With the membership of its board changing regularly, and with staff rotating through positions, the incentives for Bank staff are to get the money out the door, not to show that their long-completed projects did well. Career success is independent of whether or not projects have been successful, so there is no pressure for convincing evaluation.

These arguments have led to a movement toward more careful evaluation, often with an emphasis on randomized controlled trials as the best way of finding out whether a given project worked and, beyond that, of finding out "what works" in general. (In randomized controlled trials, some "units"—people or schools or villages—get treated, and some—the controls —do not, with units assigned to one of the two groups at random.) According to this view, aid has been much less effective than it would have been had past projects been seriously evaluated. If the World Bank had subjected all of its projects to rigorous evaluation, the argument goes, we would by now know what works and what does not work, and global poverty would have vanished long ago. Those who favor randomized controlled trials—the *randomistas*—tend to be very skeptical of typical self-evaluations by NGOs, and they have worked with cooperative NGOs to help strengthen their evaluation procedures. They have also persuaded the World Bank to use randomized controlled trials in some of its work.

Finding out whether a *given* project was or was not successful is important in itself but unlikely to reveal anything very useful about what works or does not work *in general*. Often, the experimental and control groups are very small (experiments can be expensive), which makes the results unreliable. More seriously, there is no reason to suppose that what works in one place will work somewhere else. Even if an aid-financed project is the cause of people doing well—and even if we were to be absolutely sure of that fact—causes usually do not operate alone; they need various other factors that help them to work. Flour "causes" cakes, in the sense that cakes made without flour do worse than cakes made with flour—and we can do any number of experiments to demonstrate it—but flour will not work without a rising agent, eggs, and butter—the helping factors that are needed for the flour to "cause" the cake.[22]

Similarly, teaching innovations may work in an experiment in one place and fail, or at least not work so well, in another village or in another country. The success of a microfinance scheme may depend on how women are organized and what men allow them to do. Agricultural education services may work well where the farmers live near one another and regularly talk and be a failure in an area of isolated farms. Without understanding these mechanisms—what it takes to bake a cake—it is not possible to get to "what works" from "this project worked"; indeed the whole idea of an unqualified "what works" is unhelpful. Replication that is not guided by an explicit search for these mechanisms does not solve the problem; there are just too many possible configurations of helping factors. So while the world might well be a better place if aid agencies demonstrated that the projects they undertook were successful on their own terms, such demonstrations are not in and of themselves going to give us the secrets to global poverty eradication.

It is also possible for aid-funded *projects* to work very well and for *aid* to fail. Even if an "ideal" aid agency were to fund only those projects that have passed a rigorous set of evaluations, its aid could still fail. For one thing, there is the irritating but frequently encountered problem that projects do much better as experiments than when rolled out for real. Prototypes are not the same as production. This could happen because policies implemented by real-life bureaucrats are not carried out as well as policies implemented by academics or World Bankers. There can also be spillovers that are not accounted for in the evaluation. An important example is the situation in which private provision of a service—funded by aid—undercuts government provision of that same service. Even if the government's system of antenatal clinics is not very good, and even if nurses and doctors are frequently absent, NGO-run clinics have to get nurses and doctors from somewhere, and the higher wages that they pay can hollow out the public system. The net benefit of the aid is then lower than it appears from any evaluation that does not take the diversion into account. The evaluation of dams is another example that has been much contested, if only because it is difficult to identify all of the people who are directly and indirectly affected.

Using pilot projects to evaluate new ideas will often be informative, but the results will typically be different when the project is scaled up. An education project might help people graduate from high school or college and get good jobs with the government, which in many poor countries are among the most desirable of all jobs. Yet if the scheme is extended to everyone, and the government does not expand, there will be no net benefit, at least in terms of government jobs. Agricultural projects can have a similar problem. One farmer can increase his productivity, but if all do so, the prices of the crops will fall, and what is profitable for one may not be profitable for all. Almost all projects that involve production by farmers, firms, or traders will affect the prices of goods and services when they are scaled up, but not when they are tested in isolation. So once again, a project may be successful on its own terms, but scaling up to the national level may be a failure. Perfect project evaluation can coexist with aid failure for the country as a whole.

Aid agencies often place a heavy administrative burden on overstretched local governments. Government agencies have to approve projects; they have to monitor the activities of NGOs; and they have to come to meetings with the dozens if not hundreds of foreign agencies that are working in their countries. State capacity and regulatory ability are scarce in many poor countries, and this, by itself, limits development and poverty reduction. It is ironic when aid, in an attempt to help, distracts government officials from more important tasks and undermines the state capacity that is central for successful development. As we shall see, this is only one example of aid diverting government away from its own citizens and toward the aid agencies themselves. Such diversions have more serious consequences the smaller is the country, the less competent is its government, and the greater is the volume of aid.

There is much to be said for careful project evaluation, for finding out whether or not a project met its goals, and for trying to learn lessons that are useful elsewhere. A successful and convincing evaluation can identify places where money can help make lives better, even if the examples are local and not readily generalizable. But project evaluation cannot, by itself, tell us what works and what does not in general. Nor can successful project evaluation guarantee the effectiveness of aid, which is ultimately a question about the economy as a whole, not about specific projects or about distinguishing good projects from bad. There is no escape through project evaluation from thinking about aid as a whole and its *national* consequences.

Aid and Politics

To understand how aid works we need to study the relationship between aid and politics. Political and legal institutions play a central role in setting the environment that can nurture prosperity and economic growth. Foreign aid, especially when there is a lot of it, affects how institutions function and how they change. Politics has often choked off economic growth, and even in the world before aid, there were good and bad political systems. But large inflows of foreign aid change local politics for the worse and undercut the institutions needed to foster long-run growth. Aid also undermines democracy and civic participation, a direct loss over and above the losses that come from undermining economic development. These harms of aid need to be balanced against the good that aid does, whether educating children who would not otherwise have gone to school or saving the lives of those who would otherwise have died.

From its beginnings after World War II, development economics saw growth and poverty reduction as *technical* problems. Economists would provide the knowledge that would tell the newly independent rulers how to bring prosperity to their people. If development economists thought about politics at all, they saw politicians as the guardians of their people, motivated by the promotion of social welfare. Politics as an end in itself, as a means of civic participation, or as a way of managing conflict was not part of their operations manual. Nor would development experts much concern themselves with the fact that, in many cases, the governments through which they were working had interests of their own that made them improbable partners in a broad-based development effort. There have been dissenting voices over the years, but it is only relatively recently that mainstream development economics has focused on the importance of institutions, including political institutions, and on politics itself.

Economic development cannot take place without some sort of contract between those who govern and those who are governed. The government needs resources to carry out its functions—preserving territorial integrity and maintaining its monopoly of violence, at the very least, and beyond that providing a legal system, public safety, national defense, and other public goods—and the resources that these functions require must be raised in taxes from the governed. It is this need to raise taxes, and the difficulty of doing so without the participation of those who are taxed, that places constraints on the government and to some extent protects the interests of taxpayers. In a democracy, direct feedback from the electorate evaluates the government's performance, in effect a sort of project evaluation on the programs that are carried out using taxpayers' money. While this sort of feedback works best in a democracy, the need to raise funds exists everywhere, and it will often constrain the ruler to pay attention to the demands of at least some of the population. One of the strongest arguments against large aid flows is that they undermine these constraints, removing the need to raise money with consent and in the limit turning what should be beneficial political institutions into toxic ones.[23]

Without an adequate capacity to tax, a state denies its citizens many of the protections that are taken for granted in the rich world. They may lack the protection of the law, because the courts do not work or are corrupt, and the police may harass or exploit poor people instead of protecting them. People may be unable to start businesses, because debts are not paid and contracts are not enforced or because civil "servants" extort bribes. They may face threats of violence from gangs or warlords. They may lack clean water or minimal sanitation facilities. There may be local endemic pests that threaten them and especially their children with medically preventable but potentially fatal diseases. They may lack access to electricity, to functioning schools, or to a decent health service. All of these risks are part of what it means to be poor in much of the world, all are causes of poverty, and all are attributable to the lack of state capacity. Anything that threatens that capacity is inconsistent with improving the lives of poor people.

The argument that aid threatens institutions depends on the amount of aid being large. In China, India, or South Africa, where ODA in recent years has been less than 0.5 percent of national income, and only occasionally more than 1 percent of total government expenditures, aid is not important in affecting government behavior or the development of institutions. The situation is quite different in much of Africa. Thirty-six (out of forty-nine) countries in sub-Saharan Africa have received at least 10 percent of their national income as ODA for three decades or more.[24]

Given that ODA comes to governments, the ratio of aid to government expenditure is larger still. Benin, Burkina Faso, the DRC, Ethiopia, Madagascar, Mali, Niger, Sierra Leone, Togo, and Uganda are among the countries where aid has exceeded 75 percent of government expenditure for a run of recent years. In Kenya and Zambia, ODA is a quarter and a half of government expenditure, respectively. Given that much of government expenditure is pre-committed and almost impossible to change in the short run, for these countries (and others for which the data are not available) discretionary expenditures by governments are almost entirely dependent on funds from foreign donors. As we shall see, this does not mean that the donors are dictating what governments spend—far from it. Yet the behavior of both donors and recipients is fundamentally affected by the existence and magnitude of these aid flows.

Aid is not the only way in which rulers can rule without consent. A commodity price boom is another. One famous example comes from Egypt in the mid-nineteenth century. Then, at the height of the Industrial Revolution, with its insatiable demand for cotton, the two main sources were the American South and Egypt, and Egypt's sales of cotton accounted for most of its trade with the outside world. Egypt's ruler, Muhammad Ali Pasha, often described as the founder of modern Egypt, paid only a fraction of the world price to the *fellaheen* who produced the cotton, and he and his court became fabulously wealthy on the proceeds. The American Civil War tripled the world price in only three years, and under Ali's successor Isma'il Pasha, this led to what a British report later described as "fantastic extravagance," while "immense sums were expended on public works in the manner of the East, and on productive works carried out in the wrong way or too soon," including the Suez Canal.[25] The scale of the spending was so great that it could not be supported even by the wartime cotton price, and Isma'il borrowed on the international capital market. When the price of cotton collapsed after the war, there were riots, armed intervention, and ultimately foreign occupation by Britain.

Cotton prices rose from $9.00 for 112 pounds in 1853 to $14.00 in 1860, to a peak of $33.25 in 1865, and they fell to $15.75 in 1870. One might have thought that the foreign lenders—if not Isma'il—would have understood the trouble that lay ahead, but then, as now, the lenders could rely on another government—Britain—to protect and recover their investments. Yet this story of catastrophe is not without its bright side; the Suez Canal, after all, was a useful investment whose benefits need to be counted.

There are many parallels between commodity price booms and foreign aid.[26] One is that cash flows come and go in a way that is divorced from domestic needs or domestic politics. In the cotton boom, the cause was the Civil War in America; with aid, it is the economic and political conditions in the donor countries, or international events such as the Cold War, or the war on terror. That aid stimulates government expenditure has been repeatedly documented, and, as in the Egyptian case, the government is freed of the need to consult or to gain the approval of its people. With state-owned mines, a high world price, an unlimited supply of poor workers, or a well-funded army, a ruler can stay in power without the consent of his people. With sufficient foreign aid, the ruler can even do without the mines, as eventually happened in Zaire under Mobutu. Aid from abroad kept the regime in business, and most of the aid went to doing so, so that when the regime eventually fell, there was little left, in Swiss bank accounts or elsewhere.[27] Of course, with aid the government has a responsibility to the donors, and, unlike in the Mobutu case, which was driven by Cold War geopolitics, one might hope that the donors have the interests of the people in mind. But as we shall see, there are good reasons why this does not work in practice; the motivation of the donors helps much less than one might think.

Aid, like commodity price booms, can have other unhappy effects on local institutions. Without unrestricted inflows, governments not only need taxes, but also need to be able to collect them. The huge oil revenues in the Middle East are partly responsible for poor democratic institutions in the oil-producing countries. In Africa, presidential systems are common, and an externally funded president can govern through patronage or military repression. Parliaments have limited power; they are rarely consulted by the president; and neither parliaments nor judiciaries have power to rein in the presidency.[28] There are no checks and balances. In extreme cases, large external flows, from aid or commodity sales, can increase the risk of civil war, because rulers have the means to avoid sharing power, and because the value of the inflows gives both sides a prize that is worth fighting over.[29]

Why does accountability to the donors not replace accountability to the local population? Why can't the donors withhold aid if the president refuses to consult parliament, declines to reform a corrupt police force, or uses aid flows to bolster his own political position? One problem is that the donor governments and their constituents— the ultimate donors—can't make the right calls because they do not experience the effects of aid on the ground. Even when the crunch comes, and the donors see what is happening, it is rarely in the interests of the donor countries to withhold aid, even in the face of egregious violations of agreements, however much they may have wished to do so in advance.

It is the local people, not the donors, who have direct experience of the projects on which aid is spent and who are in a position to form a judgment. Such judgments will not always be well informed, and there will always be domestic debate on cause and effect and on the value of specific government activities; but the political process can mediate these normal divergences of views. For foreign donors or their constituents—who do not live in the recipient countries—there is no such feedback. They have no direct information on outcomes; they must rely on the reports of the agencies disbursing the aid, and so tend to focus on the *volume* of aid, not its *effectiveness*. The aid agencies, in turn, are accountable to their ultimate donors, and there is no mechanism that holds them responsible if things go wrong for the recipients. I once asked an official of one of the most prominent nongovernmental aid agencies in which part of the world she spent most of her time. "The West Coast"—which turned out not to be Africa, but the United States, where several of the agency's largest donors lived. As we have already seen, World Bank officials have long moved on to other things by the time the effects of their handiwork become visible. There is no responsibility of donors to the recipients of their aid.[30]

Sometimes the agencies *know* that aid is going wrong and are alarmed by what they see, but can do nothing about it. The director of one national aid agency gave me a bloodcurdling account of how aid funds had gone to gangs of murderers—people who had already carried out one massacre and were training and arming themselves to return to finish the job. I asked him why he continued to supply aid. Because, he replied, the citizens of this country believe that it is their duty to give and will accept no argument that aid is hurting people. The best that he could do was to try to limit the harm.

Even when donors *know* what conditions ought to be imposed, they will often be reluctant to penalize recipient governments who flout them. Donors may threaten punishment to induce good behavior, but when the good behavior is not forthcoming they may be reluctant to take action if the penalties harm themselves or their constituents. This would hardly apply to the arming of murderers, but it can be a problem in lesser cases. In effect, aid conditionality is "time-inconsistent," a favorite term of economists: what you want to do in advance is no longer in your interests after the fact. The governments who are receiving aid understand this very well; they can call the donor's bluff and ignore the conditions with impunity.

Why the reluctance to enforce conditionality?

The economist Ravi Kanbur was the World Bank representative in Ghana in 1992. He was called upon to enforce conditionality by withholding a tranche of a previously agreed loan in response to the government having violated the agreement by awarding an 80 percent pay increase to public-sector workers. The tranche was large, almost an eighth of Ghana's annual import bill. Opposition to the cut-off came from many sources, not just the government of Ghana. Many innocent bystanders would be hurt, both Ghanaians and foreign contractors, who would likely not be paid. More fundamentally, the normal, good relations between the donors and the government would be disrupted, threatening not only the government but also the operations of the aid industry itself; "the donors control so much in the way of funds that to stop these, at any rate to stop them sharply, would cause major chaos in the economy." In effect, it is the aid industry's job to disburse funds, and its operatives are paid to do so and to maintain good relations with its client countries. A face-saving compromise was eventually reached, and the loan went ahead.[31]

Kenya provides another example of the dance among donors, the president, and parliament. The donors periodically become exasperated by the corruption of the president and his cronies, and they turn off the flow of aid. Parliament meets and starts discussing how to raise the revenue required for the government to meet its obligations. The donors heave a huge sigh of relief—they too are under threat if the aid ceases to flow—and turn the taps back on; parliament is shuttered until the next time.[32] Government ministers also sigh with relief and order up the latest-model Mercedes from Germany; the locals refer to these wealthy beneficiaries as the "WaBenzi."

The award for sheer creativity might go to Maaouya Ould Sid'Ahmed Taya, president of Mauritania from 1984 to 2005. He adopted a pro-Western stance and in 1991 abandoned his previous support for the Saddam Hussein regime in Iraq. Even so, in the early 1990s, his domestic repression became too much for donors, and aid was withdrawn. Real political reforms were begun—at least until the president had the brilliant idea of becoming one of the few Arab countries to recognize Israel. The aid taps were reopened and the reforms rescinded.

Domestic policies in the *donor* countries can also make it difficult to turn off aid. Government aid agencies are under pressure from

their domestic constituencies to "do something" about global poverty
—a pressure that is stoked by a well-intentioned but necessarily poorly
informed domestic population—and this makes it hard for government agencies to cut back on aid even when their representatives on
the ground know that it is doing harm. Politicians in both donor and
recipient countries understand this process. Recipient governments
can use their own poor people as "hostages to extract aid from the
donors."[33] In one of the worst such cases, government officials in
Sierra Leone held a party to celebrate the fact that UNDP had, once
again, classed their country as the worst in the world and thus guaranteed another year's worth of aid.[34]

On the other side, donor politicians can give aid to buy political
credibility at home when they are deeply unpopular for unrelated reasons; they too will oppose the cessation of aid, even when it is clearly
being misused. When this happens—as it did with British aid during
the Kenyan elections in 2001, when aid was used to subvert the elections and preserve the power of a corrupt elite—Africans suffer to
burnish the tarnished reputations of Western politicians.[35] Lyndon
Johnson helped hype a largely nonexistent famine in India in order to
distract attention from the Vietnam War, not to mention to gather
support from American farmers by buying their crops.[36] The givers
and receivers of aid, the governments in both countries, are allied
against their own peoples. All that has changed from colonial times is
the nature of what is being extracted.

There are also practical reasons that restrict the ability of donors
to enforce conditionality. Aid is fungible; a recipient can promise to
spend aid on health care and do so with projects that would have been
undertaken in any case, freeing up funds for nonapproved purposes.
It is often difficult for donors to monitor such diversions. The aid
industry is competitive, and if one country refuses to fund another
will often step in, with a different set of priorities and conditions. The

donor who tries to enforce conditions is then shut out and may lose political influence or commercial opportunities, with no compensating gain.

Aid agencies have recently tried to move away from conditionality, and their language has moved toward an emphasis on partnership. The recipient proposes a plan according to its own needs, and the donor decides what to finance. Of course, none of this disposes of the reality that the donors are responsible to their constituents in the rich world, and that the recipients, knowing this, will design plans that mimic just what they think the donors would have proposed on their own—a process that has been aptly described as "ventriloquism."[37] It is not clear what sort of partnership is sustainable when one side has all the money.

Politics and politicians, doing what they regularly do, undermine aid effectiveness, but it works the other way too: aid flows undermine the effectiveness of politics. Donors decide matters that should be decided by recipients; even democratic politics in donor countries has no business deciding whether HIV/AIDS should be prioritized over antenatal care in Africa. Conditionality violates national sovereignty. Imagine a well-funded Swedish aid agency coming to Washington, D.C., and promising to pay off the national debt and fund Medicare for fifty years. The conditions are that the United States abolish capital punishment and fully legalize gay marriage. Perhaps some governments are so dysfunctional that such violations have little cost to their populations. But taking a country into foreign receivership is hardly a good start on building the kind of contract between government and governed that might support economic growth over the long haul. It is not possible to develop someone else's country from the outside.

We have already seen that it is difficult to give convincing evidence of the effects of aid on economic growth, and the same applies when we look at the effects of aid on democracy or on other institutions. Yet once again, we have the fact that small countries that get a lot of aid also tend to be less democratic; sub-Saharan Africa is the least democratic area of the world, and the one that receives the most aid. Countries that receive aid from their ex-colonists are not the most democratic. Perhaps most interesting is a counterpoint to Figures 1 and 2: there has been an upsurge not only in growth but also in democracy in Africa since the cut in aid that followed the end of the Cold War. As always, there are other possible explanations for these facts, but they are what we would expect if democracy were undermined by foreign aid.

The antidemocratic aspects of foreign aid have been exacerbated by the long-held donors' belief that aid—and economic development itself—is a technical issue, not a political one. In the hydraulic theory (recall, we are just fixing the plumbing), there can be no legitimate dispute over what needs to be done. This belief has led donors and advisers to ignore or be impatient with local politics. Worse still, the donors have often deeply misunderstood what people needed or wanted. Population control is the worst case; to the donors it was obvious that if there were fewer people each person would be better off, while to the recipients, the opposite was just as obviously (and correctly) true. Western-led population control, often with the assistance of nondemocratic or well-rewarded recipient governments, is the most egregious example of antidemocratic and oppressive aid. Effective democracy is the antidote to the tyranny of foreign good intentions.[38]

The anthropologist James Ferguson, in *The Anti-Politics Machine*, one of the greatest books about aid and economic development, describes a large Canadian-funded development project in Lesotho in the 1980s that was based on a profound misunderstanding of the way the economy functioned; what in reality was a reservoir of labor for the South African mines was reimagined as a textbook subsistence-farming economy. The agricultural investment projects designed for the imagined economy were about as likely to be successful as a project to grow flowers on the moon. The project administrators—busily fixing the plumbing—remained unaware of how the project was being manipulated by the ruling party for its own political purposes and against its political opponents. In the end, there was no development or poverty reduction, only an extension of the state's monopoly of political control, an anti-politics machine that made an extractive elite even less responsive to its people.[39]

The technical, anti-political view of development assistance has survived the inconvenient fact that the apparently clear technical solutions kept changing—from industrialization, planning, and the construction of infrastructure to macroeconomic structural adjustment, to health and education, and most recently back to infrastructure. That the ideas kept changing did nothing to imbue the developers with humility or uncertainty, nor did the sensitivity of the fashions to first-world politics appear to undercut the technical certainty of the aid industry. The antipoverty rhetoric of the World Bank when Lyndon Johnson was U.S. president was replaced by the "getting prices right" rhetoric when Ronald Reagan was president. "Our" politics seems to be a legitimate part of development thinking, while "their" politics is not.

Aid and aid-funded projects have undoubtedly done much good; the roads, dams, and clinics exist and would not have existed otherwise. But the negative forces are always present; even in good environments, aid compromises institutions, it contaminates local politics, and it undermines democracy. If poverty and underdevelopment are primarily consequences of poor institutions, then by weakening those institutions or stunting their development, large aid flows do exactly the opposite of what they are intended to do. It is hardly surprising then that, in spite of the direct effects of aid that are often positive, the record of aid shows no evidence of any overall beneficial effect.

The arguments about foreign aid and poverty reduction are quite different from the arguments about *domestic* aid to the poor. Those who oppose welfare benefits often argue that aid to the poor creates incentives for poor behavior that help to perpetuate poverty. These are not the arguments here. The concern with foreign aid is not about what it does to poor *people* around the world—indeed it touches them too rarely—but about what it does to *governments* in poor countries. The argument that foreign aid can make poverty worse is an argument that foreign aid makes governments less responsive to the needs of the poor, and thus does them harm.

The harm of aid—even in the presence of some good—poses difficult ethical problems. The philosopher Leif Wenar, criticizing Peter Singer's vision, with which I began this chapter, notes that "poverty is no pond"; Singer's analogy is not helpful.[40] Those who advocate more aid need to explain how it can be given in a way that deals with the political constraints. They should also think hard about the parallels with the colonialism that came before the era of aid. We now think of colonialism as bad, harming others to benefit ourselves, and aid as good, hurting us (albeit very mildly) to help others. But that view is too simple, too ignorant of history, and too self-congratulatory. The rhetoric of colonialism too was all about helping people, albeit about bringing civilization and enlightenment to people whose humanity was far from fully recognized.[41] This may have been little more than a cover for theft and exploitation. The preamble to the charter of the UN, with its ringing and inspiring rhetoric, was written by Jan Smuts, premier of South Africa, who saw the UN as the best hope of preserving the British Empire and the dominance of white "civilization."[42] Yet at its worst, decolonization installed leaders who differed little from those who preceded them, except for where they were born and the color of their skins.

Even today, when our humanitarian rhetoric acts as a cover for our politicians to buy themselves virtue, and when aid is our way of meeting our moral obligations to deal with global poverty, we need to be sure that we are *not* doing harm. If we are, we are doing it for "us," not for "them." [43]

Is Health Aid Different?

External aid has saved millions of lives in poor countries. UNICEF and other agencies brought antibiotics and vaccinations to millions of children, reducing infant and child mortality. The control and elimination of disease-bearing pests have made safe once-dangerous regions of the world. An international effort eliminated smallpox, and a current effort is close to doing the same for polio. Aid agencies have made oral rehydration therapy available to millions of children and are providing insecticide-treated bed nets to protect against malaria, a disease that still kills a million African children every year. Between 1974 and 2002, a joint effort by the World Bank, the World Health Organization, UNDP, and the UN Food and Agriculture Organization all but eliminated river blindness as a public health problem in Africa. [44]

Most recently, billions of dollars have been donated for the treatment of HIV/AIDS, again mostly in Africa. By the end of 2010, the number of people receiving antiretroviral treatment—which is not a cure but keeps people alive—had reached ten million from less than a million in 2003. [45] The most important donors are the Global Fund to Fight AIDS, Tuberculosis and Malaria, whose largest funder is the United States, and the President's Emergency Plan for AIDS Relief (PEPFAR); the former acts multilaterally to fund country-driven plans, while the latter acts bilaterally, funding those projects that the United States sees as the highest priority. These agencies have also helped drive research on prevention and cure—including using antiretroviral drugs to prevent transmission and even infection—as well as on the protective value of voluntary male circumcision. An effective vaccine is still a long way off, but it is being pursued. Cynics wonder whether the U.S. commitment to AIDS research and treatment would have been as strong if no Americans had suffered from the disease, but questioning the motivation hardly undercuts the achievements.

If this were all of it, the story of health and aid would be one of untarnished success. The moral imperative is particularly strong when people are dying and when we have the means to help them at no great cost to ourselves. That we are doing so is no more than should be expected of civilized people. We long ago escaped from this sort of mortality, and we are extending that escape to the rest of humanity.

Of course, we understand that many people, most of them children, are still dying of conditions—respiratory infections, diarrhea, inadequate nutrition—from which they would not die had they not been born in the "wrong" places. But this is presumably an argument for more aid. And perhaps health is the story of aid as a whole? Saving a life is a clearer target, and one more easily counted than the murkier benefits of roads, dams, or bridges, let alone of structural adjustment programs to "get prices right" or repair government finances. Yet perhaps aid for those things helps just as aid for health helps, only less transparently. And perhaps the problem discussed in the previous section—that aid corrupts politics—is either overstated or at least a reasonable price to pay for the benefits.

Yet all is not well in the garden of health. It is far from clear that aid can do much more than it is already doing. Nor did the successes to date come without costs—although it may still be true that those costs were worth paying.

Most of the successful initiatives—the ones that have been responsible for most of the increase in life expectancy around the world—are what are called vertical health programs. The term refers to programs run from above by an agency such as UNICEF, albeit with the cooperation of local health authorities and the recruitment of local health workers. The term applies clearly to some of the early vaccination programs, as well as to the programs to eliminate pests—for example, mosquito control for malaria—or a disease such as smallpox or polio. It applies less well to AIDS programs, in which the delivery of antiretroviral drugs calls for large-scale involvement of clinics and local health personnel—though, even here, special clinics have often been built for the AIDS drugs alone.

The expressions "single-disease program" and "disease-based program" overlap with "vertical program" and refer not only to programs to eliminate a disease but also to programs like PEPFAR or the Global Fund that are targeted at specific diseases such as AIDS, tuberculosis, or malaria. These vertical or disease-based programs are typically contrasted with "horizontal" or local health-care systems. The latter include not only physicians, clinics, and hospitals that provide routine health care but also public health measures, such as safe water and sanitation, essential drugs, nutrition adequate for health, and the control of local endemic diseases. The success of the vertical programs is often contrasted with the failure of horizontal programs, and particularly with the failures to construct adequate primary health-care systems. The famous 1978 Declaration of Alma Ata (now Almaty in Kazakhstan) emphasized the importance of "health for all" and of primary health care as the means of achieving it. Governments, international agencies, and aid groups were urged to increase financial and technical support for primary health care in poor countries. The declaration has remained a rallying cry for those who call for a different kind of aid for health.

The provision of primary health care requires state capacity in a way that vertical programs do not; "helicoptering in" is fine for the latter but does nothing for the former. Indeed, vertical programs sometimes even undermine the provision of local health care, for example by taking nurses and paramedics away from their routine tasks of antenatal care or vaccinations and sending them off to track down an outbreak of polio in a remote village. But routine health-care systems are complex to set up and to maintain, not only in poor countries but also in rich ones, and, as we saw in Chapter 3, they require a degree of state capacity that is in short supply in the poorest countries. This reminds us that aid and the development of local capacity are often at loggerheads. Yet it is clearly true that if aid is to help tackle the remaining health problems in poor countries, and stop the scandal of children dying because they were born in the wrong place, it will have to go beyond dealing with "named" diseases. The question, as always, is whether this can be achieved with outside funds.

Many governments around the world spend little on primary health care but instead, to quote the World Bank economists Deon Filmer, Jeffrey Hammer, and Lant Pritchett, "the public budget for health is principally absorbed by public hospitals staffed by doctors expensively trained at public expense who use costly medical technology to treat conditions of the urban elite, while in those same countries children die from diseases that could have been treated for a few cents or avoided altogether with basic hygiene practices." Corrupt officials often divert money designated for health, and there is rarely a public outcry. The same authors tell the story of a newspaper that accused the health ministry of misappropriating $50 million of outside funds; the health ministry protested vigorously that the newspaper had not made it clear that the misappropriation was over several years, not just one.[46] Helen Epstein writes that according to a local joke in Uganda, there are two kinds of AIDS, "fat AIDS" and "slim AIDS." "Those with 'slim AIDS' grow thinner and thinner and thinner until they finally disappear. 'Fat AIDS' afflicts development agency bureaucrats, foreign consultants, and medical experts who attend lavish conferences and workshops in exotic places, earn large salaries, and get fatter and fatter."[47] The lack of money for primary health care and corruption in health-care spending are commonplace in poor countries.

Public spending on health care in many countries is too little to meet the health-care needs of the population, often with the implication that aid from abroad is needed to fill the gap. That too little is spent is true more often than not, but nothing would be served by expanding the health-care systems as they are; there would simply be more clinics that open only irregularly, more officials diverting funds, and more health-care workers being paid not to do their jobs.

Even if it is true that vertical programs do little to promote "health for all," and even if the large inflows associated with them bring all sorts of negative unintended side effects—as with other aid—we may still want to undertake them if the lives saved are worth the costs. As for the provision of high-quality health care, either through the public sector or a well-regulated private sector, it must be recognized that doing so is difficult for states with a great deal more capacity than exists in most low-income countries. In any case, it cannot be provided from the outside through foreign aid. This does not mean that there are no health-care measures that can be usefully provided in low-capacity settings. Examples are the classic public goods of public health provision, such as safe water, basic sanitation, and pest control. None of these is easy, but there is a stronger case for trying them, at least on the grounds that the private sector cannot provide them, and because they are likely to be easier to accomplish than building a personal health-care system.

What Should We Do?

The aid endeavor is inspired by the question of what we should do, or by its imperative version that we must do *something*. Yet this may be precisely the wrong question, and asking it may be part of the problem, not the beginnings of a solution. Why is it *we* who must do something? Who put *us* in charge?[48] As I have argued throughout this chapter, *we* often have such a poor understanding of what *they* need or want, or of how *their* societies work, that our clumsy attempts to help on *our* terms do more harm than good. The stories of agricultural aid in Lesotho, of "helping" the world's poor control *their* population, and of the horrors of humanitarian aid in time of war are leading examples. Negative unintended consequences are pretty much guaranteed when *we* try. And when we fail, we continue on because *our* interests are now at stake—it is *our* aid industry, staffed largely by *our* professionals, and generating kudos and votes for *our* politicians—and because, after all, *we* must do something.

What surely ought to happen is what happened in the now-rich world, where countries developed in their own way, in their own time, under their own political and economic structures. No one gave them aid or tried to bribe them to adopt policies for their own good. What we need to do now is to make sure that we are not standing in the way of the now-poor countries doing what we have already done. We need to let poor people help themselves and get out of the way—or, more positively, stop doing things that are obstructing them. The previous generation of escapees has done its part by showing that escape is possible and developing the methods of escape, some (if not all) of which are still useful in different circumstances.

Aid, paradoxically enough, is one of several things that we are doing that gets in the way, especially in sub-Saharan Africa and a few other countries, where aid is so large that it undermines local institutions and blights long-term prosperity. Aid that maintains extractive politicians or political systems to create alliances against communism or terrorism is aid that impoverishes ordinary citizens of poor countries for *our* benefit. That we pretend it is helping them merely adds insult to injury. An ocean of aid from abroad can corrupt even potentially good leaders and good political systems.

So one thing that we need to do is to stop asking what it is we need to do. We also need to help citizens of the rich world understand that aid can be harmful as well as helpful, and that it is nonsense to set targets such as giving 1 percent or 0.75 percent of *our* GDP irrespective of whether the money is helping or harming *them*. Such blind targetry is what leads ambassadors and aid administrators to plead for a cease-fire, and to mourn that the careers they dedicated to helping others have turned into careers of mitigating harm.

Aid is far from being the only roadblock that rich countries have set to the escape from poverty. Poor and rich countries are economically and politically interdependent—through trade, through treaties, through institutions like the World Trade Organization, the International Monetary Fund and the World Bank, WHO, and the UN. These institutions and the rules of international engagement have profound effects on the opportunities for poor countries to become rich countries, and I will consider them later in this chapter.

Defenders of aid will often concede at least some of the arguments against it but then go on to argue that while past aid has not been effective, and has sometimes done harm, we can (and must) do better in the future. They believe that aid can be smarter and more effective, and that it can be given in a way that avoids the pitfalls. That we have heard such arguments many times in the past—my next drink will certainly be my last—does not by itself rule out the possibility that better rules exist—that there is a twelve-step program that will do the trick.

Another reason for thinking about smarter aid is that, even if we think the world would be a better place without a World Bank or a DFID, or if the only good aid is no aid, the fact is that aid is not going away any time soon. There is no global authority that, once persuaded, could call off the international and national aid agencies, nor the hundreds of thousands of NGOs. So how might aid be made better?

The economist and UN adviser Jeffrey Sachs has consistently and persistently argued that the problem with aid is not that there is too much of it, but that there is too little.[49] Sachs advocates what I have referred to as the hydraulic approach to aid, seeing a long list of problems that need to be fixed—in agriculture, in infrastructure, in education, and in health—and then costing each item and adding up the tab. The total comes to many times what is currently being given. If it is true, as he argues, that to make anything work, everything needs to be fixed at once, through what many decades ago was called a "Big Push," then aid should be increased. Yet history does not suggest that the now-rich countries needed any sort of Big Push, and certainly not a Big Push from someone else. And there is no evidence that the Millennium Development Villages—put in place by the UN to implement Sachs's ideas—are doing any better than other villages in the same countries. The hydraulic approach to aid ignores what I have argued is the central issue, that such amounts of aid corrupt local politics in a way that makes development more difficult. You cannot develop other people's countries from the outside with a shopping list for Home Depot, no matter how much you spend.

The principles of better aid were enshrined in a document called the Paris Declaration, signed in 2005 by 111 countries and 26 multilateral organizations.[50] The declaration is a list of New Year's resolutions calling for many good things, including partnership, recipient country ownership, high-quality evaluation, accountability, and predictability. The declaration appears to have been about as effective as most New Year's resolutions. Or, to switch metaphors, it is as if a sick patient made a list of what good health would look like, rather than diagnosing *why* she is ill and figuring out a course of treatment. As we have seen in this chapter, the failures of partnership, of accountability, of country ownership, and of evaluation all have reasons that are rooted in the reality of aid. It is impossible to have a real partnership when one "partner" has all of the money, and it is impossible to have recipient ownership when the accountability is owed to ill-informed (if well-meaning) foreigners. Declarations that virtue is good are easy to subscribe to, but good intentions that run counter to the political realities of aid will do little to improve its operation.

Aid could perhaps do better if it came with conditions to ensure its success. This is no easy matter. Kanbur's story of his time as World Bank representative in Ghana illustrates that it is difficult or impossible for donors to stop the cash when recipients go back on their promises. And if one donor turns off the aid, there is often another donor in the wings who takes a different view of what is good policy, or who doesn't think it is his business to interfere in domestic political arrangements. Even so, the aid industry is ultimately accountable to its donors in the rich countries, so they surely need *some* kind of conditionality. The question is whether there is some effective way of enforcing it.

One idea is to have recipient governments demonstrate a commitment to good policies that benefit their people *before* they become candidates for aid. This is referred to as *selectivity,* and it can be thought of as a form of conditionality; the U.S. Millennium Challenge Corporation works like this. Countries demonstrate their virtue first, and only then do donors offer a partnership to work toward their common goals. Selectivity stops aid from being used to maintain oppressive regimes in power, though if a regime strays from the path of righteousness—which aid itself might actually encourage—we are back again with the difficulties of disengagement.

The Achilles heel of selectivity is that it excludes from aid many of those who need it most—those who live in countries where the regime has no interest in the welfare of the people. These are also the people for whom the moral imperative to provide assistance is the most compelling. In rich countries whose citizens have a strong commitment to aid—which is not the case in the United States—pressure from concerned citizens makes it all but impossible for aid agencies to ignore those who live in countries that fail the "good policy" test. This is a fundamental problem of all aid in a world of nation-states. In "good" states, there is a reasonable chance that poverty can be tackled locally, and there is relatively little need for outside help. In "bad" states, outside aid is likely to make things worse. Giving through NGOs is not a solution, because the regime can prey on them just as well as on its people.

Another idea comes from the Center for Global Development (CGD), a Washington think tank that is a gold mine of information about economic development as well as a source of new ideas about improving aid. CGD President Nancy Birdsall and health economist William Savedoff have developed an aid proposal they call "cash on delivery."[51] Donors and countries work out a set of mutually desirable targets—vaccinating 80 percent of the country's children by a given date, reducing the infant mortality rate by twenty deaths per thousand over five years, or providing clean water—and the aid is paid only when the target is met. As the proponents are aware, cash-on-delivery aid would stress already weak measurement systems in poor countries and reward (and encourage) cheating on the numbers. Many of the targets are not entirely under the control of the recipient government—bad weather may disrupt delivery, or an epidemic may raise infant mortality. If payment is made nevertheless, incentives are weakened, while if the donors take an inflexible line, recipient governments may not be prepared to take the risk of undertaking an expensive program for which they do not have funds and might not be reimbursed.

Cash-on-delivery aid does not solve the now-familiar dilemma of good regimes and bad regimes. For basically decent countries, there is no need for *us* to incentivize *them* to undertake projects that they would not otherwise want to do. If our priorities are naturally aligned, the assistance is not necessary. If they are not, it is unethical for us to try to impose our priorities on them; recall again my reverse example of the Swedish aid agency paying the United States to abolish capital punishment and legalize gay marriage. For extractive and oppressive regimes, bribery might work; they are just as happy to extract resources from us as from their own people, and since they don't care about their own people, they are just as happy for people to be helped as hurt, as long as they get paid. I suppose that an argument could be made for this sort of dealing with the devil. But we are back in the world of aid agencies providing weapons as a quid pro quo for being allowed to deliver humanitarian assistance, or of arming gangs of past and future murderers in order to be allowed to help their families, as happened in Goma after the genocide in Rwanda.

Large-scale aid does not work because it cannot work, and attempts to reform it run aground on the same fundamental problems over and over again. Bridges get built, schools are opened, and drugs and vaccines save lives, but the pernicious effects are always there.

The most compelling case for reducing funding is seen in those (mostly African) countries in which foreign aid is a large share of national income and accounts for almost all of government expenditures. It is also important that people in the donor countries better understand the problems of aid, and that the "obvious" argument that giving money will reduce poverty is in fact obviously false. One of the reasons so much harm is being done is because of the "aid illusion" and the political pressure in the donor countries that makes reform so much harder than it ought to be. That dedicated and ethical people are doing harm to people who are already in such distress is not the least of the tragedies of aid.

There may also be cases in which aid is doing good, at least on balance. I have already made that case for aid directed toward health. Other cases are likely to be found among countries with decent governments, where aid is a relatively small share of the economy, and where, against the odds, effective local providers have not been captured or deformed by the donors and use the aid for legitimate local purposes.

I am often asked how much is too much, where should the cut-off be, and how do we know where to stop. This is not a useful question, because there is no "we," in the sense of a supranational authority that is capable of putting on the brakes. For now, the most urgent task is to undo the work that has been done by those who want more aid and to persuade the citizens of the rich world that much aid is harmful, that more aid would be more harmful still, and that they can best help the poor of the world by not giving them large-scale aid. If we were to succeed in this, and give less aid, what then could we do to discharge our obligation to assist?

Doing less harm would be a good start. Beyond cutting back on aid, there are several other bad things that we could stop doing, and several good things that we should think about doing.

Many of the difficulties with aid come from its unintended consequences within the recipient countries. If we can act at a distance, staying out of the countries, perhaps those consequences can be avoided. As the economist Jagdish Bhagwati has argued, "it is hard to think of substantial increases in aid being spent effectively *in* Africa. But it is not so hard to think of more aid being spent productively elsewhere *for* Africa."[52] We have already seen many examples. Basic knowledge—of the germ theory of disease, of high-yielding seed varietals, of vaccinations, of the fact that HIV/AIDS is sexually transmitted, and of antiretroviral therapies—has been of enormous value to the rest of the world and has had none of the baleful side effects of foreign aid spent in the recipient country.

We need not wait for such discoveries to come along spontaneously or in response to the needs of the rich world. Diseases that do not threaten rich countries—malaria is a leading example—could be invested in as a form of foreign aid. Right now, pharmaceutical companies recoup their investments in research and development by selling drugs, typically at high prices under temporary patent protection, to people—or their insurers, or their governments—in rich countries. Patients in poor countries may not be able to afford the new drugs while they are under patent, and the governments of rich countries— under pressure from commercial interests—have negotiated international rules that make it difficult or impossible for poor countries to work around the patents. These rules go under the name of TRIPS, for trade-related aspects of intellectual property rights, and while agreeing to them is not in the interests of poor countries, adherence to them comes with other things—including membership of the World Trade Organization—that poor countries *do* want. Pharmaceutical companies argue that they should have worldwide protection for their intellectual property and that they are less concerned with maintaining high prices in poor countries than with drugs being copied in poor countries by manufacturers who did not pay for the development of the drugs, and then exported back to the rich countries.

TRIPS and high prices for drugs have been much discussed in the context of antiretroviral drugs for HIV/AIDS, especially a decade or so ago, when these drugs were essentially unavailable outside the rich countries. But as we have seen, that problem, although not solved, is being seriously tackled, and the number of sufferers receiving therapy is more than ten million and rising. For diseases other than HIV/ AIDS, such as those responsible for the deaths listed in Table 1 of Chapter 3, the essential drugs are mostly off patent and are cheaply available. Apart from HIV/AIDS, expensive drugs are not the main problem.

The nonexistence of vaccines or drugs is another matter. For diseases like malaria or tuberculosis, which are rare or unknown in rich countries, there is no incentive for pharmaceutical companies to develop new drugs, because the potential purchasers are poor. There is a need for the drugs, and there is the possibility of developing them, but the link that will bring them together is missing. For lack of incentives, new technology does not get directed in the right way. If aid can provide the incentives, with donors filling in for the missing purchasing power of the poor, perhaps the new drugs will be developed.

The philosopher Thomas Pogge has argued for what he calls a Health Impact Fund, which would reward drug companies in proportion to the health benefits that they bring.[53] Such a fund would solve the problems of high drug prices and the lack of incentives to provide new drugs, while providing access to new and old drugs at low prices for those who need them throughout the world. The pharmaceutical companies would be paid out of the fund. This is an immensely ambitious scheme, and it would have the great advantage of allowing companies to choose the disease they target in a way that would maximize the global health benefits. The problem—which is one that we have seen many times in this book—is that it is impossible to attribute health improvements even to a class of innovations, let alone to a specific new medicine. Medical historians are still arguing over the role of vaccines and new drugs in reducing mortality over the past two centuries, long after all of the data are in. We do not have good data on mortality or morbidity for much of the world today, and even with better data we would not be able to tell what caused health to improve or decline. Without these data, there would be no acceptable way of deciding how much each company should be paid.

Advance market commitments—in which a consortium of governments and international agencies agree to buy a currently nonexistent drug with prespecified properties at a prespecified price—are less ambitious, but more specific and more practical.[54] The pre-commitment gives the drug companies the incentives that are currently missing. One such advance market commitment has already been successful, and children are now being immunized in ten countries against pneumococcal disease, which currently kills half a million children each year. The main donors were Canada, Italy, and Britain, with lesser amounts from Norway, Russia, and the Gates Foundation. The scheme is run by the Global Alliance for Vaccines and Immunisation (GAVI Alliance), whose website provides details on the manufacturers, as well as the rules of the scheme for both manufacturers and donors.[55]

Aid could also be used not to make loans but to provide advice. The current structure of the World Bank makes it difficult to provide substantial technical assistance except in association with loans—which effectively pay for the assistance. Yet there is more appetite for technical knowledge than the World Bank can satisfy. The idea that World Bank projects should provide a valuable fund of experience-based knowledge is a sensible one, though randomized controlled trials are not the way to generate the understanding of *why things worked* that would make such knowledge transferable from one place to another. A government undertaking a dam-building program or considering the privatization of a water supply wants to know what happened to other governments that went down similar paths—not just the average outcome, but the possible pitfalls, who benefited and who lost, and what to look out for. Of course, the knowledge from the World Bank and other donor agencies is not infallible, and there are many examples of ignorance and arrogance.

International organizations could also supplement country capacity in international negotiations, particularly in trade agreements. The United States and other rich countries negotiate bilateral trade treaties with other countries, and when those countries have few lawyers or experts representing them, these negotiations are not conducted on a level playing field. The World Bank could help provide the missing expertise. Of course, this is likely to be difficult. If the World Bank were to provide advice that effectively blocked an initiative favored by the American pharmaceutical industry, for example, the United States would almost certainly bring pressure to bear through its executive director on the World Bank's board. It would be easy to conclude that its largest shareholder only tolerates the World Bank as long as it does not do anything that would *really* help the poor. While that conclusion is too cynical, it points to the constraints that prevent removal of *some* of the practices that are maintaining global poverty.

Aid is not the only roadblock to development. The rich world is only too happy to provide arms to almost anyone who will pay for them. We are also quick to recognize, trade with, and lend money to regimes that are clearly not interested in furthering the wellbeing of their people. There are a number of proposals in this area too. The economists Michael Kremer and Seema Jayachandran have argued for the use of international loan sanctions against "odious" regimes; once a regime has been so declared, international lenders would not be able to use international courts to recover debts from successor regimes.[56] Such rules would cut off loans to odious regimes, or at least make them much more difficult and much more expensive. The international community might also be more reluctant to buy oil and other commodities from regimes, or at least to be more transparent about when it does so, and under what terms.[57] Recent financial reform in the United States has required that United States–listed oil, gas, and mining companies must publish all payments to governments.[58] Of course, we need complete coordination; countries that are not signatories to an agreement can still buy the commodities and use them or re-export them—what are euphemistically called "tourist" commodities.

Trade restrictions in rich countries often harm farmers in poor countries. Farming accounts for nearly three-quarters of employment in Africa, and rich countries spend hundreds of billions of dollars each year to support their own farmers. For sugar and cotton, for example, subsidies to producers in rich countries lower world prices and restrict opportunities for poor farmers. They also hurt consumers in rich countries, and their existence is a testimony to the political power of well-organized minorities against the majority. For agricultural goods for which poor countries are net importers, such as many foods, rich-country subsidies can actually help poor consumers by lowering world prices. American biofuel subsidies do the opposite. International collective action to limit or eliminate the harmful supports would help reduce poverty in the world.

The effects of migration on poverty reduction dwarf those of free trade. Migrants who succeed in moving from poor countries to rich countries become better off than they were at home, and their remittances help their families do better at home. Remittances have very different effects than aid, and they can empower recipients to demand more from their government, improving governance rather than undermining it. Of course, the politics of migration is even tougher than the politics of free trade, even in countries where the urge to help is most strongly developed. A helpful type of temporary migration is to provide undergraduate and graduate scholarships to the West, especially for Africans. With luck, these students will develop in a way that is independent of aid agencies or of their domestic regimes. Even if they do not return home, at least at once, the African diaspora is a fertile (and internal) source of development projects at home.

These are all strategies to reduce global poverty in a way that current aid arrangements do not, and in some cases to do so at modest or no cost to rich countries. Some are likely to be more politically feasible than others, and some—such as advance market commitments—are already working on a small scale. None involves aid delivery to poor countries with all of the attendant problems. When Princeton students come to talk with me, bringing their deep moral commitment to helping make the world a better, richer place, it is these ideas that I like to discuss, steering them away from plans to tithe from their future incomes, and from using their often formidable talents of persuasion to increase the amounts of foreign aid. I tell them to work on and within their own governments, persuading them to stop policies that hurt poor people, and to support international policies that make globalization work for poor people, not against them. These are our best opportunities to promote the Great Escape for those who have yet to break free.

What Comes Next?

MY STORY OF THE GREAT ESCAPE is a positive one, of millions saved from death and destitution, and of a world that, in spite of its inequalities and of the millions still left behind, is a better place than at any time in history. Yet the movie that I have used as a running metaphor did not have a happy ending. All but a handful of the escapees were recaptured, and fifty of them were executed. Can we be confident that our Great Escape will be different?

Probably not, but it is reasonable to hope.

Our children and grandchildren cannot possibly expect a unique exemption from the forces that brought down previous civilizations. In Europe and North America we have grown to believe that things will always get better. The past 250 years have seen unprecedented progress, but 250 years is no great span of time compared with the long-lived civilizations of the past who doubtless thought that *they* were destined to last forever.

Many threats could bring us down. Climate change is the most obvious, and there is no clear solution that is politically feasible. That private interest can triumph over public need is unforgettably captured in Jared Diamond's musing about what might have been going on in the head of the person who cut down the last tree on Easter Island.[1]

Wars have not ceased. Dangerous politics are everywhere. Imagine the convulsion that could consume the Chinese leadership when China's economic growth comes to a stop, as history suggests it will. An invasion of Taiwan is not a far-fetched response, and it could be a fatal misadventure. The world has changed much in the past fifty years, but the nature of the Chinese leadership has changed much less, and we should not rule out another disaster as bad as Mao Zedong's Great Famine. It is comforting to imagine that no such famine could happen today, given that the world would know about it. But what, exactly, could the world do?

The Scientific Revolution and the Enlightenment brought us sustained improvements in material wellbeing and in health. Yet science is under attack from religious fundamentalists in many places around the world, including the United States. Many of those fundamentalists are politically powerful and are supported by those whose interests are threatened by scientific knowledge.

Science cannot bring immunity from disease. New infectious diseases can appear at any time. The most terrifying will kill a few people, burn out, and slink back to their animal hosts. But the HIV/AIDS pandemic warns us of what can happen, and it is by no means the worst possibility. Although thirty-five million people have died—making it one of the greatest catastrophes of modern times—the virus was quickly identified and therapies were developed; another disease could be harder to decipher and to treat. More mundanely, global health systems rely on antibiotics whose efficacy is under threat, largely from uncontrolled agricultural use and the resultant evolution of resistance. Our victory against germs is not finally won; it is more like an ongoing battle in which the tides go one way and then the other. We may be in the ascendant now, but it could be just a phase in the battle, not a prelude to its end. Evolution is not independent of human activity; bugs fight back.

Economic growth is the engine of the escape from poverty and material deprivation. Yet growth is faltering in the rich world. Growth in each recent decade has been lower than in the previous one. Almost everywhere, the faltering of growth has come with expansions of inequality. In the case of the United States, current extremes of income and wealth have not been seen for more than a hundred years. Great concentrations of wealth can undermine democracy and growth, stifling the creative destruction that makes growth possible. Such inequality encourages the previous escapees to block the escape routes behind them.

Mancur Olson predicted that rich countries would decline like this, undermined by the rent seeking of an ever-growing number of focused interest groups pursuing their own self-interest at the expense of an uncoordinated majority.[2] Slower growth makes distributional conflict inevitable, because the only way forward for me is at your expense. It is easy to imagine a world with little growth but endless distributional conflict between rich and poor, between old and young, between Wall Street and Main Street, between medical providers and their patients, and between the political parties that represent them.

Even so, I am cautiously optimistic. The desire to escape is deeply ingrained and will not be easily frustrated. The means of escape are cumulative: future escapees can stand on the shoulders of giants. People may block the tunnels behind them, but they cannot block the knowledge of how the tunnels were dug.

The slowdown in growth is likely overstated, because the statisticians miss a lot of quality improvements, especially for services, which represent an increasing share of national output. The information revolution and its associated devices do more for wellbeing than we can measure. That these pleasures are barely captured in the growth statistics tells us about the inadequacies of the statistics, not the inadequacies of the technology or the joys that it brings.

Most of the world's population does not live in the rich countries, and for them there has been no slowdown in growth. Indeed, the more than 2.5 billion people who live in China and India have recently seen growth rates that are unparalleled in any country or period. Even if these growth rates slow down, the "advantages of backwardness" should afford them better-than-average catch-up growth for years to come.

There are endless possibilities for Africa, some of which are being seen now as improved economic management avoids some of the self-inflicted disasters of the past. And if the West can cure itself of its addiction to aid, and stop undermining African politics, there is real hope for locally driven development. We need to stop strangling the expression of the unbounded talents of Africans.

Although the rate of improvement of life expectancy is slowing down, that is a good thing, not a bad thing; death is aging, and saving lives at older ages has a smaller effect on life expectancy than saving the lives of children. Once again, the problem is the measure, not the substance. Life expectancy is not always the right measure of how well a society is doing, and there is nothing that says that saving the lives of the middle-aged and elderly is inherently less valuable than saving the lives of children.

If there are threats to health, there are also major improvements to come, with signs of real progress against cancer that, with luck, will parallel the improvements against cardiovascular disease over the past forty years.

The ultimate reason that health will continue to improve is that people want it to improve and are prepared to pay for the basic science, behavioral research, drugs, procedures, and devices that support it. Innovations cannot be bought off the shelf, nor do they always come along when they are needed. But there is no doubt that well-funded needs bring results.

Even the HIV/AIDS pandemic, in spite of its horrendous toll, contains a success story about how new basic knowledge and new treatments can respond to needs, and can do so on a time scale that, while too short for those who died, is fast by the standards of other historical epidemics. Science really works.

There are many other continuing improvements that I have not discussed in this book. Violence has fallen; people today have a much lower chance of being murdered than once was the case.[3] Democracy is more widespread in the world than was the case fifty years ago. Oppression of one social group by another is less usual, and becoming more unusual. People have greater opportunities to participate in society than has ever been the case.

People are growing taller throughout the world, and likely smarter too.

Education is on the rise in most of the world. Four-fifths of the people of the world are literate, compared with only half in 1950.[4] There are areas of rural India where almost no adult women ever went to school, and where almost all of their daughters now do so.

None of these things can be expected to improve everywhere, or to do so uninterruptedly. Bad things happen, and new escapes, like old ones, will bring new inequalities. Yet I expect those setbacks to be overcome in the future, as they have been in the past.

Notes

INTRODUCTION: WHAT THIS BOOK IS ABOUT

1. *The Great Escape,* directed by John Sturges, starring Steve McQueen, James Garner, and Richard Attenborough, the Mirisch Company, distributed by United Artists, 1963 (based on a book of the same title by Paul Brickhill).

2. Lant Pritchett, 1997, "Divergence, big time," *Journal of Economic Perspectives* 11(3): 3–11, and Kenneth Pomeranz, 2000, *The Great Divergence: China, Europe, and the making of the world economy,* Princeton University Press.

3. Jack Goldstone, 2009, *Why Europe? The rise of the West in world history, 1500–1850,* McGraw-Hill.

4. Ian Morris, 2010, *Why the West rules—for now: The patterns of history, and what they reveal about the future,* Farrar, Straus and Giroux.

5. Ibid.

6. Eric L. Jones, 2000, *Growth recurring: Economic change in world history,* University of Michigan Press.

7. Robert Allen, 2011, *Global economic history: A very short introduction,* Oxford University Press.

8. Daron Acemoglu and James Robinson, 2012, *Why nations fail: The origins of power, prosperity, and poverty,* Crown.

9. E. Janet Browne, 2002, *Charles Darwin,* Volume 2: *The power of place,* Jonathan Cape.

10. Allen, *Global economic history.*

11. Roy Porter, 2000, *The creation of the modern world: The untold story of the British Enlightenment,* Norton, and Joel Mokyr, 2009, *The enlightened economy: An economic history of Britain, 1700–1850,* Yale University Press.

12. Morris, *Why the West rules.*

13. Acemoglu and Robinson, *Why nations fail.*

14. Amartya Sen, 1992, *Inequality re-examined,* Harvard University Press, and 2009, *The idea of justice,* Harvard University Press.

15. Sen, *Idea of justice,* and Jonathan Haidt, 2012, *The righteous mind: Why good people are divided by politics and religion,* Pantheon.

16. Daniel Kahneman and Jason Riis, 2005, "Living, and thinking about it: Two perspectives on life," in Felicia Huppert, Nick Baylis, and Barry Keverne, eds., *The science of well-being,* Oxford University Press, 285–304.

17. Ronald Inglehart and Hans-Dieter Klingemann, 2000, "Genes, culture, democracy and happiness," in Ed Diener and Eunkook M. Suh, eds., *Culture and subjective well-being,* MIT Press, 165–83; Richard Layard, 2005, *Happiness: Lessons from a new science,* Penguin; and Richard Wilkinson and Kate Pickett, 2009, *The spirit level: Why greater equality makes societies stronger,* Bloomsbury.

CHAPTER ONE: THE WELLBEING OF THE WORLD

1. For a related calculation, see James Vaupel and John M. Owen, 1986, "Anna's life expectancy," *Journal of Policy Analysis and Management* 5(2): 383–89.

2. Robert C. Allen, Tommy E. Murphy, and Eric B. Schneider, 2012, "The colonial origins of the divergence in the Americas: A labor market approach," *Journal of Economic History* 72(4): 863–94.

3. Amartya Sen, 1999, *Development as freedom,* Knopf.

4. Layard, *Happiness.*

5. Samuel Preston, 1975, "The changing relation between mortality and level of economic development," *Population Studies* 29(2): 231–48.

6. Wilkinson and Pickett, *Spirit level,* p. 12, and Richard Wilkinson, 1994, "The epidemiological transition: From material scarcity to social disadvantage," *Daedalus* 123: 61–77.

7. Elizabeth Brainerd and David M Cutler, 2005, "Autopsy on an empire: The mortality crisis in Russia and the former Soviet Union," *Journal of Economic Perspectives* 19(1): 107–30, and Jay Bhattacharya, Christina Gathmann, and Grant Miller, 2013, "The Gorbachev anti-alcohol campaign and Russia's mortality crisis," *American Economic Journal: Applied* 5(2): 232–60.

8. Robert W. Fogel, 2004, *The escape from hunger and premature death, 1700 to 2100: Europe, America, and the Third World,* Cambridge University Press, and 1997, "New findings on secular trends in nutrition and mortality: Some implications for population theory," in Mark R. Rosenzweig and Oded Stark, eds., *Handbook of population and family economics,* Elsevier, 433–81.

9. Sen, *Development as freedom.*

10. Yang Jisheng, 2012, *Tombstone: The great Chinese famine, 1958–62,* Farrar, Straus and Giroux.

11. Ainsley J. Coale, 1984, *Rapid population change in China, 1952–1982,* National Academy Press, and Cormac Ó Gráda, 2009, *Famine: A short history,* Princeton University Press.

12. Preston, "The changing relation between mortality and level of economic development."

13. Stanley Fischer, 2003, "Globalization and its challenges," *American Economic Review* 93(2): 1–30.

14. Martin Ravallion and Shaohua Chen, 2010, "The developing world is poorer than we thought, but no less successful in the fight against poverty," *Quarterly Journal of Economics* 125(4): 1577–625. Update to 2008: "An update of the World Bank's estimates of consumption poverty in the developing world," http://siteresources.worldbank.org/INTPOVCALNET/Resources/Global_Poverty_Update_2012_02-29-12.pdf.

15. Charles Kenny, 2011, *Getting better,* Basic Books.

16. Joseph E. Stiglitz, Amartya K. Sen, and Jean-Paul Fitoussi, 2009, *Report of the commission on the measurement of economic performance and social progress,* http://www.stiglitz-sen-fitoussi.fr/en/index.htm.

17. Anna Wierzbicka, 1994, "'Happiness' in cross-linguistic and cross-cultural perspective," *Daedalus* 133(2): 34–43, and Ed Diener and Eunkook M. Suh, 2000, *Culture and subjective wellbeing,* MIT Press.

18. Amartya K. Sen, 1985, *Commodities and capabilities,* Elsevier; 1987, *On ethics and economics,* Blackwell; and 2009, *The idea of justice,* Belknap.

19. Martha C. Nussbaum, 2008, "Who is the happy warrior? Philosophy poses questions to psychology," *Journal of Legal Studies* 37(S2): S81–S113.

20. Richard A. Easterlin, 1974, "Does economic growth improve the human lot? Some empirical evidence," in R. David and M. Reder, eds., *Nations and households in economic growth: Essays in honor of Moses Abramowitz,* Academic Press, 89–125, and 1995, "Will raising the incomes of all increase the happiness of all?" *Journal of Economic Behavior and Organization* 27(1): 35–47.

21. Betsey Stevenson and Justin Wolfers, 2008, "Economic growth and subjective wellbeing: Reassessing the Easterlin paradox," *Brookings Papers on Economic Activity* (Spring), 1–86, and Daniel W. Sacks, Betsey Stevenson, and Justin Wolfers, 2012, "Subjective wellbeing, income, economic development and growth," in Philip Booth, ed., . . . *And the pursuit of happiness,* Institute for Economic Affairs, 59–97.

22. Angus Deaton, 2008, "Income, health, and wellbeing around the world: Evidence from the Gallup World Poll," *Journal of Economic Perspectives* 22(2): 53–72.

23. Daniel Kahneman and Angus Deaton, 2010, "High income improves evaluation of life but not emotional wellbeing," *Proceedings of the National Academy of Sciences* 107(38): 16489–93.

24. Keith Thomas, 2009, *The ends of life: Roads to fulfillment in early modern England,* Oxford University Press.

25. Adam Smith, 1767, *The theory of moral sentiments,* third edition, printed for A. Millar, A. Kincaid, and J. Bell in Edinburgh and sold by T. Cadell in the Strand, 272, 273, 273, and 271.

26. David E. Bloom, 2011, "7 billion and counting," *Science* 333 (July 29), 562–68.

CHAPTER TWO: FROM PREHISTORY TO 1945

1. See Massimo Livi-Bacci, 2001, *A concise history of world population,* third edition, Blackwell; James C. Riley, 2001, *Rising life expectancy: A global history,*

Cambridge University Press; and Mark Harrison, 2004, *Disease and the modern world*, Polity Press.

2. The data are taken from the Human Mortality Database, http://www.mortality.org/.

3. The following account relies on Graeme Barker, 2006, *The agricultural revolution in prehistory: Why did foragers become farmers?* Oxford University Press, and Mark Nathan Cohen, 1991, *Health and the rise of civilization,* Yale University Press. See also Morris, *Why the West rules.*

4. David Erdal and Andrew Whiten, 1996, "Egalitarianism and Machiavellian intelligence in human evolution," in Paul Mellars and Kathleen Gibson, eds., *Modelling the early human mind,* McDonald Institute Monographs, 139–50.

5. Marshall Sahlins, 1972, *Stone age economics*, Transaction.

6. Cohen, *Health and the rise of civilization,* p. 141.

7. Ibid., p. 30.

8. Esther Boserup, 2005 [1965], *The conditions of agricultural growth*, Transaction.

9. Morris, *Why the West rules,* p. 107.

10. Clark Spenser Larsen, 1995, "Biological changes in human populations with agriculture," *Annual Review of Anthropology* 24: 185–213.

11. John Broome, 2006, *Weighing lives*, Oxford University Press.

12. E. A. Wrigley and R. S. Schofield, 1981, *The population history of England, 1541–1871*, Harvard University Press, and E. A. Wrigley, R. S. Davies, J. E. Oeppen, and R. S. Schofield, 1997, *English population history from family reconstitution 1580–1837,* Cambridge University Press.

13. Thomas Hollingsworth, 1964, "The demography of the British peerage," *Population Studies* 18(2), Supplement, 52–70.

14. Bernard Harris, 2004, "Public health, nutrition, and the decline of mortality: The McKeown thesis revisited," *Social History of Medicine* 17(3): 379–407.

15. Massimo Livi-Bacci, 1991, *Population and nutrition: An essay on European demographic history,* Cambridge University Press.

16. Roy Porter, 2001, *The creation of the modern world: The untold history of the British Enlightenment,* Norton.

17. Thomas, *The ends of life*, p. 15.

18. Peter Razzell, 1997, *The conquest of smallpox*, Caliban.

19. http://www.nlm.nih.gov/exhibition/smallpox/sp_variolation.html.

20. Sheila Ryan Johansson, 2010, "Medics, monarchs, and mortality, 1600–1800: Origins of the knowledge-driven health transition in Europe," electronic copy available at http://ssrn.com/abstract=1661453.

21. Thomas McKeown, 1976, *The modern rise of population,* London, Arnold, and 1981, *The origins of human disease,* Wiley-Blackwell.

22. Thomas McKeown, 1980, *The role of medicine: Dream, mirage, or nemesis,* Princeton University Press.

23. Robert W. Fogel, 1994, "Economic growth, population theory, and physiology: The bearing of long-term processes on the making of economic policy," *American Economic Review* 84(3): 369–95, and Robert W. Fogel and Dora L. Costa, 1997, "A theory of technophysio evolution, with some implications for forecasting population, healthcare costs, and pension costs," *Demography* 34(1): 49–66.

24. Richard Easterlin, 1999, "How beneficent is the market? A look at the modern history of mortality," *European Review of Economic History* 3: 257–94.

25. Livi-Bacci, *Population and nutrition.*

26. Samuel J. Preston, 1996, "American longevity: Past, present, and future," Center for Policy Research, Maxwell School, Syracuse University, Paper 36, http://surface.syr.edu/cpr/36.

27. George Rosen, 1991, *A history of public health,* Johns Hopkins University Press.

28. John Snow, 1855, *On the mode of transmission of cholera,* London, John Churchill. See also Steven Johnson, 2007, *The ghost map: The story of London's most terrifying epidemic and how it changed science, cities, and the modern world,* Riverhead.

29. David A. Freedman, 1991, "Statistical analysis and shoe leather," *Sociological Methodology* 21: 291–313.

30. Nancy Tomes, 1999, *The gospel of germs: Men, women and the microbe in American life,* Harvard University Press.

31. Alfredo Morabia, 2007, "Epidemiologic interactions, complexity, and the lonesome death of Max von Pettenkofer," *American Journal of Epidemiology* 166(11): 1233–38.

32. Simon Szreter, 1988, "The importance of social intervention in Britain's mortality decline c. 1850–1914: A reinterpretation of the role of public health," *Social History of Medicine* 1(1): 1–36.

33. Tomes, *The gospel of germs,* and Joel Mokyr, *The gifts of Athena: Historical origins of the knowledge economy,* Princeton University Press.

34. Samuel J. Preston and Michael Haines, 1991, *Fatal years: Child mortality in late nineteenth century America,* Princeton University Press.

35. Howard Markel, 2005, *When germs travel: Six major epidemics that have invaded America and the fears they have unleashed,* Vintage.

36. Valerie Kozel and Barbara Parker, n.d., "Health situation assessment report: Chitrakot district," World Bank, unpublished.

CHAPTER THREE: ESCAPING DEATH IN THE TROPICS

1. Davidson R. Gwatkin, 1980, "Indications of change in developing country mortality trends: The end of an era?" *Population and Development Review* 6(4): 615–44.

2. "Water with sugar and salt," *The Lancet,* August 5, 1978, pp. 300–301; quote on p. 300.

3. Preston, "The changing relation between mortality and level of economic development."

4. Joshua H. Horn, 1970, *Away with all pests: An English surgeon in the People's Republic of China, 1954–1969,* Monthly Review Press.

5. Jean Drèze and Amartya Sen, 2002, *India: Development and participation,* Oxford.

6. Deaton, "Income, health, and wellbeing around the world."

7. Nazmul Chaudhury, Jeffrey Hammer, Michael Kremer, Karthik Muralidharan, and F. Halsey Rogers, 2006, "Missing in action: Teacher and health worker absence in developing countries," *Journal of Economic Perspectives* 20(1): 91–116.

CHAPTER FOUR: HEALTH IN THE MODERN WORLD

1. For many of the issues discussed in this section, see Eileen M. Crimmins, Samuel H. Preston, and Barry Cohen, 2011, *Explaining divergent levels of longevity in high-income countries,* National Academies Press.

2. These and other data about smoking are compiled by P. N. Lee Statistics and Computing Ltd. in their International Mortality and Smoking Statistics database, http://www.pnlee.co.uk/imass.htm.

3. Tomes, *The gospel of germs,* and Mokyr, *The gifts of Athena,* especially Chapter 5.

4. Graphs are from the author's calculations using data from the World Health Organization's mortality database, http://www.who.int/healthinfo/morttables/en/.

5. http://www.mskcc.org/cancer-care/adult/lung/prediction-tools.

6. Crimmins, Preston, and Cohen, *Explaining divergent levels of longevity.*

7. http://www.mayoclinic.com/health/diuretics/HI00030.

8. Veterans Administration Cooperative Study Group, 1970, "Effects of treatment on morbidity in hypertension. II. Results in patients with diastolic blood pressure averaging 90 through 114 mm Hg," *Journal of the American Medical Association* 213(7): 1143–52.

9. Earl S. Ford, Umed A. Ajani, Janet B. Croft, et al., 2007, "Explaining the decrease in U.S. deaths from coronary disease, 1980–2000," *New England Journal of Medicine* 356(23): 2388–98.

10. David Cutler, 2005, *Your money or your life: Strong medicine for America's health care system,* Oxford, and David Cutler, Angus Deaton, and Adriana Lleras-Muney, 2006, "The determinants of mortality," *Journal of Economic Perspectives* 20(3): 97–120.

11. John C. Bailar III and Elaine M. Smith, 1986, "Progress against cancer?" *New England Journal of Medicine* 314(19): 1226–32, and John C. Bailar III and Heather L. Gornik, 1997, "Cancer undefeated," *New England Journal of Medicine* 336(22): 1569–74.

12. David M. Cutler, 2008, "Are we finally winning the war on cancer?" *Journal of Economic Perspectives* 22(4): 3–26.

13. Archie Bleyer and H. Gilbert Welch, 2012, "Effects of three decades of screening mammography on breast-cancer incidence," *New England Journal of Medicine* 367(21): 1998–2005.

14. Siddhartha Mukherjee, 2010, *The emperor of all maladies,* Scribner.

15. H. Gilbert Welch, Lisa Schwartz, and Steve Woloshin, 2011, *Overdiagnosed,* Beacon Press.

16. Gabriele Doblhammer and James W. Vaupel, 2001, "Lifespan depends on month of birth," *Proceedings of the National Academy of Sciences* 98(5): 2934–39.

17. For my own experience with hip replacement, see http://www.princeton.edu/~deaton/downloads/letterfromamerica_apr2006_hip-op.pdf.

18. Henry Aaron and William B. Schwartz, 1984, *The painful prescription: Rationing hospital care*, Brookings.

19. Nicholas Timmins, 2009, "A NICE way of influencing health spending: A conversation with Sir Michael Rawlins," *Health Affairs* 28(5): 1360–65.

20. http://www.dartmouthatlas.org/. See also John E. Wennberg and Megan M. Cooper, 1999, *The quality of medical care in the United States: A report on the Medicare program. The Dartmouth atlas of healthcare 1999*, American Hospital Association Press; John E. Wennberg, Elliott Fisher, and Jonathan Skinner, 2002, "Geography and the debate over Medicare reform," *Health Affairs* 96–114, DOI: 10.1377/hlthaff.w2.96; and Katherine Baicker and Amitabh Chandra, 2004, "Medicare spending, the physician workforce, and beneficiaries' quality of care," *Health Affairs Web Exclusive* W4: 184–97, DOI: 10.1377/hlthaff.W4.184.

21. A brief and readable summary is Ezekiel J. Emanuel and Victor R. Fuchs, 2008, "Who really pays for health care?: The myth of 'shared responsibility,'" *Journal of the American Medical Association* 299(9): 1057-59. See also Jonathan Gruber, 2000, "Health insurance and the labor market," in A. J. Culyer and J. P. Newhouse, eds., *Handbook of health economics,* Volume 1, Elsevier, 645–706, and Kate Baicker and Amitabh Chandra, 2006, "The labor market effects of rising health insurance premiums," *Journal of Labor Economics* 24(3): 609–34.

22. Victor R. Fuchs, "The financial problems of the elderly: A holistic view," in Stuart H. Altman and David I. Shactman, eds., *Policies for an aging society,* Johns Hopkins University Press, 378–90.

23. Katherine M. Flegal, Barry I. Graubard, David F. Williamson, et al., 2003, "Excess deaths associated with underweight, overweight, and obesity," *Journal of the American Medical Association* 293(15): 1861–67; Edward W. Gregg, Yiling J. Chen, Betsy L. Caldwell, et al., 2005, "Secular trends in cardiovascular disease risk factors according to body mass index in US adults,"

Journal of the American Medical Association 293(15): 1868–74; S. Jay Olshansky, Douglas J. Passaro, Ronald C. Hershow, et al., 2005, "A potential decline in life expectancy in the United States in the 21st century," *New England Journal of Medicine* 352(12): 1138–45; and Neil K. Mehta and Virginia W. Chang, 2011, "Secular declines in the association between obesity and mortality in the United States," *Population and Development Review* 37(3): 435–51.

24. Jim Oeppen and James W. Vaupel, 2002, "Broken limits to life expectancy," *Science* 296 (May 10), 1029–31. See also Jennifer Couzin-Frankel, 2011, "A pitched battle over life span," *Science* 333 (July 29), 549–50.

25. Morris, *Why the West rules;* quote on p. 296.

26. Alfred W. Crosby, [1973] 2003, *The Columbian exchange: Biological and cultural consequences of 1492,* Greenwood; Jared Diamond, 2005, *Guns, germs, and steel: The fates of human societies,* Norton; and Charles C. Mann, 2011, *1493: Uncovering the new world that Columbus created,* Knopf.

27. Phyllis B. Eveleth and James M. Tanner, 1991, *Worldwide variation in human growth,* Cambridge University Press, and Roderick Floud, Kenneth Wachter, and Anabel Gregory, 2006, *Height, health, and history: Nutritional status in the United Kingdom, 1750–1980,* Cambridge University Press.

28. Anne C. Case and Christina H. Paxson, 2008, "Stature and status: Height, ability, and labor market outcomes," *Journal of Political Economy* 116(3): 499–532.

29. T. J. Cole, 2003, "The secular trend in human physical growth: A biological view," *Economics and Human Biology* 1(2): 161–68.

30. Timothy J. Hatton and Bernice E. Bray, 2010, "Long-run trends in the heights of European men, 19th–20th centuries," *Economics and Human Biology* 8(3): 405–13.

31. Timothy J. Hatton, 2011, "How have Europeans grown so tall?" CEPR Discussion Paper DP8490, available at SSRN: http://ssrn.com/abstract= 1897996.

32. Rosen, *History of public health,* p. 182.

33. Dean Spears, 2012, "How much international variation in child height can sanitation explain?" http://www.princeton.edu/rpds/papers/Spears_ Height_and_Sanitation.pdf.pdf.

34. Floud, Wachter, and Gregory, *Height, health, and history.*

35. Angus Deaton, 2008, "Height, health, and inequality: The distribution of adult heights in India," *American Economic Review* 98(2): 468–74.

36. S. V. Subramanian, Emre Özaltin, and Jocelyn E. Finlay, 2011, "Height of nations: A socioeconomic analysis of cohort differences and patterns among women in 54 low- to middle-income countries," *PLoS ONE* 6(4): e18962.

CHAPTER FIVE:
MATERIAL WELLBEING IN THE UNITED STATES

1. Lant Pritchett, 1997, "Divergence, big time," *Journal of Economic Perspectives* 11(3): 3–17.

2. François Bourguignon and Christian Morrisson, 2002, "Inequality among world citizens: 1820–1992," *American Economic Review* 92(4): 727–44.

3. These numbers and those in Figure 1 come from http://www.bea.gov/iTable/iTable.cfm?ReqID=9&step=1#reqid=9&step=3&isuri=1&903=264.

4. William Nordhaus and James Tobin, 1972, "Is growth obsolete?" in *Economic Research: Retrospect and prospect,* Volume 5: *Economic growth,* National Bureau of Economic Research, 1–80.

5. Gordon M. Fisher, 1992, "The development and history of the poverty thresholds," http://www.ssa.gov/history/fisheronpoverty.html.

6. Connie F. Citro and Robert T. Michael, 1995, *Measuring poverty: A new approach,* National Academies Press.

7. Amartya K. Sen, 1983, "Poor, relatively speaking," *Oxford Economic Papers,* New Series 35(2): 153–69.

8. The Census Bureau maintains a website covering the experimental measures, http://www.census.gov/hhes/povmeas/.

9. Bruce D. Meyer and James X. Sullivan, 2012, "Winning the war: Poverty from the Great Society to the Great Recession," *Brookings Papers on Economic Activity,* Fall, 133–200.

10. David S. Johnson and Timothy M. Smeeding, 2012, "A consumer's guide to interpreting various U.S. poverty measures," *Fast Focus* 14, Institute for Research on Poverty, University of Wisconsin at Madison.

11. James C. Scott, 1999, *Seeing like a state: How certain schemes to improve the human condition have failed,* Yale University Press.

12. Jan Tinbergen, 1974, "Substitution of graduate by other labor," *Kyklos* 27(2): 217–26.

13. Lawrence F. Katz and Claudia Goldin, 2010, *The race between education and technology,* Belknap.

14. Anthony B. Atkinson, 2008, *The changing distribution of earnings in OECD countries,* Oxford University Press.

15. Daron Acemoglu, 2002, "Technical change, inequality, and the labor market," *Journal of Economic Literature* 40(1): 7–72.

16. Jonathan Gruber, 2000, "Health insurance and the labor market," in Anthony J. Culyer and Joseph P. Newhouse, eds., *Handbook of health economics,* Volume 1, Part A, Elsevier, 645–706.

17. Emanuel and Fuchs, "Who really pays for health care?"

18. Robert Frank, 2007, *Richistan: A journey through the American wealth boom and the lives of the new rich,* Crown.

19. David H. Autor, Lawrence F. Katz, and Melissa S. Kearney, 2006, "The polarization of the U.S. labor market," *American Economic Review* 96(2): 189–94, and David Autor and David Dorn, "The growth of low-skill service jobs and the polarization of the US labor market," *American Economic Review,* forthcoming, available at http://economics.mit.edu/files/1474.

20. David Card and Alan B. Krueger, 1994, "Minimum wages and employment: A case study of the fast food industry in New Jersey and Pennsylvania," *American Economic Review* 84(4): 772–93, and David Card and Alan B. Krueger, 1995, *Myth and measurement: The new economics of the minimum wage,* Princeton University Press.

21. James Buchanan, 1996, "A commentary on the minimum wage," *Wall Street Journal,* April 25, p. A20.

22. David S. Lee, 1999, "Wage inequality in the United States during the 1980s: Rising dispersion or falling minimum wage," *Quarterly Journal of Economics* 114(3): 977–1023.

23. Congressional Budget Office, 2011, *Trends in the distribution of household income between 1979 and 2007,* Washington, DC.

24. Thomas Piketty and Emmanuel Saez, 2003, "Income inequality in the United States 1913–1998," *Quarterly Journal of Economics* 118(1): 1–41.

25. Simon Kuznets, 1953, *Shares of upper income groups in income and saving*, National Bureau of Economic Research.

26. Incomes in the Piketty-Saez analysis are taxable incomes and are incomes of tax units, not of families or of households, which would include unrelated individuals. The Congressional Budget Office income numbers quoted earlier include some of the items included in the national accounts, but not in the surveys. In some studies, family or household incomes are corrected for the number of people in the unit and for whether they are adults or children. I have tried to spare the reader these details, which I do not believe affect the broad story that I am telling, but it can be dangerous to compare the different definitions of income without correction or adjustment.

27. Congressional Budget Office, *Trends in the distribution of household income*.

28. Miles Corak, "Inequality from generation to generation: The United States in comparison," University of Ottawa, http://milescorak.files.wordpress .com/2012/01/inequality-from-generation-to-generation-the-united-states-in-comparison-v3.pdf.

29. Martin S. Feldstein, 1998, "Income inequality and poverty," National Bureau of Economic Research Working Paper 6770; quote from abstract.

30. Marianne Bertrand and Sendhil Mullainathan, 2001, "Are CEOs rewarded for luck? The ones without principals are," *Quarterly Journal of Economics* 116(3): 901–32.

31. Thomas Philippon and Ariell Reshef, 2012, "Wages and human capital in the U.S. financial industry: 1909–2006," *Quarterly Journal of Economics* 127(4): 1551–1609.

32. Jacob S. Hacker and Paul Pierson, 2011, *Winner-take-all politics: How Washington made the rich richer—and turned its back on the middle class*, Simon and Schuster.

33. Gretchen Morgenson and Joshua Rosner, 2011, *Reckless endangerment: How outsized ambition, greed, and corruption created the worst financial crisis of our time*, St. Martin's Griffin.

34. Thomas Piketty, Emmanuel Saez, and Stefanie Stantcheva, 2011, "Optimal taxation of top labor incomes: A tale of three elasticities," National

Bureau of Economic Research Working Paper 17616. Note that these authors interpret the relationship differently than I do in the text.

35. Larry Bartels, 2010, *Unequal democracy: The political economy of the new gilded age*, Princeton University Press, and Martin Gilens, 2012, *Affluence and influence: Economic inequality and political power in America*, Princeton University Press.

36. Anne O. Krueger, 1974, "The political economy of the rent-seeking society," *American Economic Review* 64(3): 291–303, and Jagdish N. Bhagwati, 1982, "Directly unproductive profit-seeking (DUP) activities," *Journal of Political Economy* 90(5): 988–1002.

37. Gilens, *Affluence and influence*.

38. Joseph E. Stiglitz, 2012, *The price of inequality: How today's divided society endangers our future*, Norton.

39. Eric Jones, 1981, *The European miracle: Environments, economies, and geopolitics in the history of Europe and Asia*, Cambridge University Press, and 1988, *Growth recurring: Economic change in world history*, Oxford University Press.

40. Stanley Engerman and Kenneth L. Sokoloff, 2011, *Economic development in the Americas since 1500: Endowments and institutions*, Cambridge University Press.

41. Daron Acemoglu, Simon Johnson, and James Robinson, 2002, "Reversal of fortune: Geography and institutions in the making of the modern world income distribution," *Quarterly Journal of Economics* 117(4): 1231–94, and Acemoglu and Robinson, *Why nations fail*.

42. Mancur Olson, 1982, *The rise and decline of nations: Economic growth, stagflation, and social rigidities*, Yale University Press.

CHAPTER SIX: GLOBALIZATION AND THE GREATEST ESCAPE

1. See https://pwt.sas.upenn.edu/icp.html for information on the International Comparison of Prices Program. The price collection program is housed at the World Bank; see http://siteresources.worldbank.org/ICPEXT/Resources/ICP_2011.html.

2. Angus Deaton and Alan Heston, 2010, "Understanding PPPs and PPP-national accounts," *American Economic Journal: Macroeconomics* 2(4): 1–35.

3. Milton Gilbert, Colin Clark, J.R.N. Stone, et al., 1949, "The measurement of national wealth: Discussion," *Econometrica* 17 (Supplement, Report of the Washington Meeting): 255–72; quote on p. 261.

4. Robert M. Solow, 1956, "A contribution to the theory of economic growth," *Quarterly Journal of Economics* 70(1): 65–74.

5. Angus Maddison and Harry X. Wu, 2008, "Measuring China's economic performance," *World Economics* 9(2): 13–44.

6. William Easterly, Michael Kremer, Lant Pritchett, and Lawrence H. Summers, 1993, "Good policy or good luck? Country growth performance and temporary shocks," *Journal of Monetary Economics* 32(3): 459–83.

7. Commission on Growth and Development, 2008, *The growth report: Strategies for sustained growth and inclusive development,* World Bank.

8. Paul Collier, 2008, *The bottom billion: Why the poorest countries are failing and what can be done about it,* Oxford University Press.

9. Matthew Connelly, 2008, *Fatal misconceptions: The struggle to control world population,* Harvard University Press.

10. Julian L Simon, 1983, *The ultimate resource,* Princeton University Press.

11. David Lam, 2011, "How the world survived the population bomb: Lessons from 50 years of extraordinary demographic history," *Demography* 48(4): 1231–62.

12. Angus Deaton, 2005, "Measuring poverty in a growing world, or measuring growth in a poor world," *Review of Economics and Statistics* 87(1): 1–19.

13. Atul Kohli, 2012, *Poverty amid plenty in the new India,* Cambridge University Press.

14. Robert C. Allen, Tommy E. Murphy, and Eric B. Schneider, 2012, "The colonial origins of the divergence in the Americas: A labor market approach," *Journal of Economic History* 72(4): 863–94.

15. Anthony B. Atkinson, Thomas Piketty, and Emmanuel Saez, 2011, "Top incomes in the long run of history," *Journal of Economic Literature* 49(1): 3–71.

16. Ibid.

17. Maarten Goos, Alan Manning, and Anna Salomons, 2009, "Job polarization in Europe," *American Economic Review* 99(2): 58–63.

18. Branko Milanovic, 2007, *Worlds apart: Measuring international and global inequality,* Princeton University Press. An important update is Branko Milanovic, 2010, "Global income inequality," http://siteresources.worldbank .org/INTPOVRES/Resources/477227-1173108574667/global_inequality_ presentation_milanovic_imf_2010.pdf.

19. Ronald Dworkin, 2000, *Sovereign virtue,* Harvard University Press, p. 6. Quoted in Thomas Nagel, 2005, "The problem of global justice," *Philosophy and Public Affairs* 33(2): 113–47, p. 120.

CHAPTER SEVEN: HOW TO HELP THOSE LEFT BEHIND

1. These numbers and calculations are from the World Bank's website for poverty calculations, http://iresearch.worldbank.org/PovcalNet/index.htm?3.

2. Angus Deaton and Olivier Dupriez, 2011, "Purchasing power parity exchange rates for the global poor," *American Economic Journal: Applied Economics* 3(2): 137–66.

3. http://www.givingwhatwecan.org/.

4. Richard Attenborough, "17p to save a child's life," *The Observer,* March 4, 2000, http://www.guardian.co.uk/world/2000/mar/05/mozambique .theobserver.

5. Smith, 1767, *Theory of moral sentiments,* p. 213.

6. David Hume, 1912 [1777], *An enquiry concerning the principles of morals,* Project Gutenberg edition, part I (originally published in 1751).

7. Peter Singer, 1972, "Famine, affluence, and mortality," *Philosophy and Public Affairs* 1(1): 229–43; quote on p. 242.

8. Peter Singer, 2009, *The life you can save: Acting now to end world poverty,* Random House.

9. The data on aid in this chapter, unless otherwise noted explicitly, come from Development Assistance Committee, OECD, http://www.oecd .org/dac/stats/, or from World Bank, World Development Indicators, http:// databank.worldbank.org/data/home.aspx.

10. The term comes from Jonathan Temple, 2010, "Aid and conditionality," *Handbook of development economics,* Elsevier, Chapter 67, p. 4420.

11. Peter Bauer, 1971, *Dissent on development,* Weidenfeld and Nicolson, quoted in Temple, "Aid and conditionality," p. 4436.

12. The source for many of the facts in this section is Roger Riddell, 2007, *Does foreign aid really work?* Oxford.

13. Quoted in Devesh Kapur, John P. Lewis, and Richard Webb, eds., 1997, *The World Bank: Its first half century*, Volume 1: *History*, Brookings Institution Press, p. 128.

14. William Easterly and Claudia R. Williamson, 2011, "Rhetoric v. reality: The best and worst of aid agency practices," *World Development* 39(11): 1930–49.

15. Ibid., and for the next two paragraphs.

16. Alberto Alesina and David Dollar, 2000, "Who gives foreign aid to whom and why," *Journal of Economic Growth* 5(1): 33–63.

17. Michael Maren, 2002, *The road to hell: The ravaging effects of foreign aid and international charity*, Free Press; Alex de Waal, 2009, *Famine crimes: Politics and the disaster relief industry in Africa*, Indiana University Press; and Linda Polman, 2011, *The crisis caravan: What's wrong with humanitarian aid*, Picador.

18. Helen Epstein, 2010, "Cruel Ethiopia," *New York Review of Books*, May 13.

19. Angus Deaton and Ronald I. Miller, 1995. *International commodity prices, macroeconomic performance, and politics in sub-Saharan Africa*, Princeton Studies in International Finance 79, Princeton University Press.

20. Angus Deaton, 1999, "Commodity prices and growth in Africa," *Journal of Economic Perspectives* 13(3): 23–40.

21. Arvind Subramanian and Raghuram Rajan, 2008, "Aid and growth: What does the cross-country evidence really show?" *Review of Economics and Statistics* 90(4): 643–65.

22. Nancy Cartwright and Jeremy Hardie, 2012, *Evidence-based policy: A practical guide to doing it better*, Oxford University Press.

23. Nicolas van de Walle, 2005, *Overcoming stagnation in aid-dependent countries*, Center for Global Development; Todd Moss, Gunilla Pettersson, and Nicolas van de Walle, 2007, "An aid-institutions paradox? A review essay on aid dependency and state building in sub-Saharan Africa," in William Easterly, ed., *Reinventing foreign aid*, MIT Press, 255–81; and Timothy Besley and Torsten Persson, 2011, *Pillars of prosperity: The political economics of development clusters*, Princeton University Press.

24. Moss, Pettersson, and van de Walle, "An aid-institutions paradox?"

25. Quoted in Deaton, "Commodity prices and growth in Africa," p. 23.

26. Arvind Subramanian and Raghuram Rajan, 2011, "Aid, Dutch disease, and manufacturing growth," *Journal of Development Economics* 94(1): 106–18.

27. Michela Wrong, 2001, *In the footsteps of Mr. Kurz: Living on the brink of disaster in Mobutu's Congo,* Harper.

28. Nicolas van de Walle, *Overcoming stagnation.*

29. Besley and Persson, *Pillars of prosperity;* see also Timothy Besley and Torsten Persson, 2011, "Fragile states and development policy," *Journal of the European Economic Association* 9(3): 371–98.

30. Jakob Svensson, 2003, "Why conditional aid does not work and what can be done about it," *Journal of Development Economics* 70(2): 381–402, and 2006, "The institutional economics of foreign aid," *Swedish Economic Policy Review* 13(2): 115–37.

31. Ravi Kanbur, 2000, "Aid, conditionality, and debt in Africa," in Finn Tarp, ed., *Foreign aid and development: Lessons learnt and directions for the future,* Routledge, 318–28; quote on p. 323.

32. Robert H. Bates, 2006, "Banerjee's approach might teach us more about impact but at the expense of larger matters," *Boston Review,* September, pp. 67–72.

33. William Easterly, 2002, *The elusive quest for growth: Economists' adventures and misadventures in the tropics,* MIT Press; quote on p. 116.

34. Polman, *The crisis caravan.*

35. Michela Wrong, 2009, *It's our turn to eat: The story of a Kenyan whistle-blower,* Harper.

36. Nick Cullather, 2010, *The hungry world: America's Cold War battle against poverty in Asia,* Harvard University Press.

37. Nicolas van de Walle, *Overcoming stagnation.*

38. Connelly, *Fatal misconceptions.*

39. James Ferguson, 1994, *The anti-politics machine: "Development," depoliticization, and bureaucratic power in Lesotho,* University of Minnesota Press.

40. Leif Wenar, 2010, "Poverty is no pond: Challenges for the affluent," in Patricia Illingworth, Thomas Pogge, and Leif Wenar, eds., *Giving well: The ethics of philanthropy,* Oxford University Press, pp. 104–32.

41. William Easterly, 2006, *The White Man's Burden: Why the West's efforts to aid the rest have done so much ill and so little good,* Penguin.

42. Mark Mazower, 2009, *No enchanted palace: The end of empire and the ideological origins of the United Nations,* Princeton University Press.

43. Michela Wrong, 2006, *I didn't do it for you: How the world betrayed a small African nation,* Harper.

44. Ruth Levine et al., 2004, *Millions saved: Proven successes in global health,* Center for Global Development.

45. Anthony S. Fauci and Gregory K. Folkers, 2012, "The world must build on three decades of scientific advances to enable a new generation to live free of HIV/AIDS," *Health Affairs* 31(7): 1529–36.

46. Deon Filmer, Jeffrey Hammer, and Lant Pritchett, 2000, "Weak links in the chain: A diagnosis of health policy in poor countries," *World Bank Research Observer* 15(2): 199–224; quote on p. 199.

47. Helen Epstein, 2005, "The lost children of AIDS," *New York Review of Books,* November 3.

48. A favorite (and effective) question put by William Easterly; see, for example, 2012, "How I would not lead the World Bank: Do not, under any circumstances, pick me," *Foreign Policy,* March 5.

49. World Health Organization, 2001, *Macroeconomics and health: Investing in health for economic development,* http://www.cid.harvard.edu/archive/cmh/cmhreport.pdf, and Jeffrey Sachs, 2006, *The end of poverty: Economic possibilities for our time,* Penguin.

50. http://www.oecd.org/dac/aideffectiveness/parisdeclarationandaccra agendaforaction.htm#Paris.

51. Nancy Birdsall and William Savedoff, 2010, *Cash on delivery: A new approach to foreign aid,* Center for Global Development.

52. Abhijit Vinayak Banerjee, 2007, *Making aid work,* MIT Press, pp. 91–97; quote on pp. 95–96.

53. Thomas Pogge, 2012, "The Health Impact Fund: Enhancing justice

and efficiency in global health," *Journal of Human Development and Capabilities,* DOI: 10.1080/19452829.2012.703172.

54. Michael Kremer, Ruth Levine, and Alice Albright, 2005, *Making markets for vaccines: Ideas to action,* Report of the Advance Market Commitment Working Group, Center for Global Development.

55. http://www.gavialliance.org/funding/pneumococcal-amc/about/.

56. Michael Kremer and Seema Jayachandran, 2006, "Odious debt," *American Economic Review* 96(1): 82–92.

57. The Extractive Industries Transparency Initiative, www.eitc.org.

58. Kofi Annan, 2012, "Momentum rises to lift Africa's resource curse," *New York Times,* September 14, http://www.nytimes.com/2012/09/14/opinion/kofi-annan-momentum-rises-to-lift-africas-resource-curse.html?_r=0.

POSTSCRIPT: WHAT COMES NEXT?

1. Jared Diamond, 2004, *Collapse: How societies choose to fail or succeed,* Viking.

2. Olson, *Rise and decline of nations.*

3. Steven Pinker, 2011, *The better angels of our nature: Why violence has declined,* Viking.

4. Kenny, *Getting better.*

Index

Page numbers for entries occurring in figures are followed by an *f* and those for entries in tables, by a *t*.

great escapes: from death, xi–xii, xiii, 23, 37;
in future, 325–29; obstacles to, 312–13;
from poverty, ix–xi, xiii, 23; those left
behind, xii–xiii, 2–3, 23–24, 215, 219, 267,
268. *See also* economic growth; health; life
expectancies; poverty reduction
Green Revolution, 246
gross domestic product (GDP): components
of, 30–31, 169f, 170–71, 175–78, 179;
criticism of, 172; of United States, 169–72,
169f. *See also* economic growth; incomes
gross national product (GNP), 30–31
growth. *See* economic growth
Gwatkin, Davidson R., 103

Hacker, Jacob S., 211
Haines, Michael, 98
Haiti: child mortality in, 118; incomes in,
234–35; women's heights in, 160
Hammer, Jeffrey, 310
happiness: pursuit of, 84; surveys of, 17–22,
29, 47–49, 51, 52–53, 174–75. *See also* life
evaluation measures
Harris, Bernard, 82
Hatton, Timothy, 158
health: effects of globalization, 149–52; in
future, 326–27, 328–29; improvements in,
6–7, 26, 37, 59, 91, 126–27; incomes and,
26–28, 32–33, 35, 113–14; morbidity, 143–45;
perceived, 122; public opinion on, 122. *See
also* diseases; life expectancies; mortality
health aid: "cash on delivery" approach,
316–17; corruption and, 310–11; disease-
based, 307–8, 309; effectiveness of, 121,
307–12, 318; horizontal programs, 309–10;
vertical programs, 104–5, 309, 310
health care: absenteeism in, 123, 125; access
to, 144–45; inoculations, 84–86; oral
rehydration therapy, 10, 104, 307; in poor
countries, 123–25, 152, 309–11; primary,
309–10; public confidence in, 122–23, 124;
rationing of, 144–45; unnecessary, 145–46,
147; value of, 145, 177; wages in, 123. *See also*
medicine
health care spending: in Africa, 120–21;
arguments for increasing, 145; in Britain,
121; in GDP, 177; in poor countries, 120–21,
311; trade-offs, 146–47; in United States,
35, 121, 144, 145–47, 195; variations in,
145–46
health inequalities: within countries, 140;
in Enlightenment, 87; examples of, 7;
medical innovations and, 87, 126–27;

140, 142; persistence of, 127; reductions
in, 154
health insurance, 146–47, 177, 195. *See also*
Medicare
heights: cognitive function and, 157; of
European men, 158, 162; factors affecting,
162; genetic differences in, 156–57; as
health measure, 127; incomes and, 157,
159–62, 160f, 164; increases in, 26, 158,
163, 164; nutrition and, 91–92, 156–58,
161, 162, 163; stunting, 91–92; of women,
159–64, 160f
Henry VIII, 83
Heston, Alan, 222, 228
Hispanics: mortality rates of, 67; poverty
rates of, 181
HIV/AIDS: in Africa, 25, 34, 40, 151, 154; aid
programs, 307–8, 309, 311; antiretroviral
drugs, 40, 108, 113, 307, 308, 309, 319–20;
mortality from, 101–2, 108, 113, 326;
research on, 10, 151, 308, 329; spread of, 151
Hollingsworth, T. H., 82
housing, imputed rent on, 176–77
humanitarian aid, 280, 287–88. *See also*
foreign aid; nongovernmental
organizations
Human Rights Watch, 198
Hume, David, 270–71
hunter-gatherers: activities of, 74–75; bands
of, 75–76; birth rates of, 75; child
mortality, 75; diets of, 74–75, 76, 77, 79;
evolution of, 73–74; health of, 75, 76–77;
wellbeing of, 74–78

immigrants. *See* migration
imperialism, 5, 216, 267, 282, 306
income inequalities: after taxes, 199–200,
206; cosmopolitan, 258; between countries,
168, 219–20, 232, 233–35, 257–58; within
countries, 5–6, 232, 258–61; factors in,
190–96, 202, 208; fairness of, 262–63; of
families, 200–202; Gini coefficient,
187–88; global, 257–59, 261–63; importance
of, 11, 168, 207–8, 213–14; increases in,
167–68, 189, 219–20, 259–61, 327; politics
and, 196–200, 202, 211–14, 215–16;
reductions in, 44, 232, 259, 262; in rich
countries, 259–61; top earners, 202–6,
204f, 208–14, 259, 260; in United States,
175, 187–89, 188f, 200–206, 204f, 207,
260–61, 327
incomes: education and, 191, 192, 193;
emotional wellbeing and, 52–56, 53f;